Material Feminisms

Material Feminisms: New Directions for Education provides a range of powerful theoretical and innovative methodological examples to illuminate how new material feminism can be put to work in education to open up new avenues of research design and practice. It poses challenging questions about the nature of knowledge production, the role of the researcher, and the critical endeavour arising from inter- and post-disciplinarity. Working with diffractive methodologies and new materialist ecological epistemologies, the book offers resources for hope which widen the scope for how educational problems are interrogated, and provides a political counter-movement to neo-positivist, outcomes-based approaches within education.

Inspired by writers such as Barad, Bennett, and Deleuze and Guattari, the book makes a radical break with cognitive, dualist, and universal conceptions of human subjectivity and intelligence in education. By taking its starting point as the co-consitutiveness of discourse, materiality, corporeality, and place, the book foregrounds educational practices as material enactments of multiple, non-linear, entangled, affective, and relational forces. It offers new insights into how gender, class, and ethnicity are constituted in, and by, material assemblages that are often submerged or 'unseen'.

This book is an essential starting place for those intrigued by what new theoretical accounts of materiality, posthumanism, and affect can offer educational research. Diffractive methodologies challenge readers to take a fuller range of actors into account than in 'objective' humanist methodologies, and in so doing to pay closer attention to what data is. It invites researchers to engage with long-standing feminist concerns about power and knowledge production in research processes. This book was originally published as a special issue of *Gender and Education*.

Carol Taylor is a Reader in the Sheffield Institute of Education at Sheffield Hallam University, UK, where she leads the Higher Education Research Group. Her research focuses on space, gender and bodies, mundane materialities, student engagement, and ethics. She has recently co-edited two journal special issues: one on New Material Feminisms for *Gender and Education* (with Gabrielle Ivinson) and one on student engagement and ethics for the *Journal of Applied Research in Higher Education* (with Carol Robinson). Her work has been published in *Cultural Studies ⇔ Critical Methodologies*, *Studies in Higher Education,* and *Gender and Education*. Her recent funded projects include the development of an ethical framework for student partnership (Higher Education Academy) and an installation on workplace objects for the 2015 ESRC Festival of Social Science.

Gabrielle Ivinson is Professor in Education at the School of Education, University of Aberdeen, UK. She is the author of *Rethinking Single-sex teaching: Gender, school subjects and learning* (with Murphy, 2007), co-editor *of Knowledge and Identity: concepts and applications in Bernstein's sociology of knowledge* (with Davies and Fitz, 2011), and co-editor of the journal special issue 'Material Feminisms: New Directions for Education' for *Gender and Education* (with Carol Taylor). As a social and developmental psychologist, she researches the intergenerational transmission of knowledge as a social resource in places of poverty. Her recent projects involve working with a range of artists to co-produce art forms and artefacts to enable young people to communicate with persons in authority by drawing on the affective power of art to move.

Material Feminisms

New directions for education

Edited by
Carol Taylor and Gabrielle Ivinson

Routledge
Taylor & Francis Group

LONDON AND NEW YORK

First published 2016 by Routledge

2 Park Square, Milton Park, Abingdon, Oxfordshire OX14 4RN
711 Third Avenue, New York, NY 10017

Routledge is an imprint of the Taylor & Francis Group, an informa business

First issued in paperback 2018

British Library Cataloguing in Publication Data
A catalogue record for this book is available from the British Library

ISBN 13: 978-1-138-19561-5 (hbk)
ISBN 13: 978-1-138-39152-9 (pbk)

Typeset in Times New Roman
by RefineCatch Limited, Bungay, Suffolk

Publisher's Note
The publisher accepts responsibility for any inconsistencies that may have
arisen during the conversion of this book from journal articles to book chapters,
namely the possible inclusion of journal terminology.

Disclaimer
Every effort has been made to contact copyright holders for their permission to
reprint material in this book. The publishers would be grateful to hear from any
copyright holder who is not here acknowledged and will undertake to rectify
any errors or omissions in future editions of this book.

Contents

Citation Information

The chapters in this book were originally published in *Gender and Education*, volume 25, issue 6 (October 2013). When citing this material, please use the original page numbering for each article, as follows:

Introduction

Chapter 1

Chapter 2

Chapter 3

Chapter 4

Chapter 5

Chapter 6

Gendered subjectivities of spacetimematter
Malou Juelskjaer
Gender and Education, volume 25, issue 6 (October 2013), pp. 754–768

Chapter 7

Making matter making us: thinking with Grosz to find freedom in new feminist materialisms
Alecia Youngblood Jackson
Gender and Education, volume 25, issue 6 (October 2013), pp. 769–775

Chapter 8

Materialist mappings of knowing in being: researchers constituted in the production of knowledge
Lisa A. Mazzei
Gender and Education, volume 25, issue 6 (October 2013), pp. 776–785

Chapter 9

Re-turning feminist methodologies: from a social to an ecological epistemology
Christina Hughes and Celia Lury
Gender and Education, volume 25, issue 6 (October 2013), pp. 786–799

For any permission-related enquiries please visit:
http://www.tandfonline.com/page/help/permissions

Notes on Contributors

Christina Hughes is Professor of Women and Gender and Pro-Vice-Chancellor at the University of Warwick, UK. Her work focuses on gender issues in family life, education, and employment. Christina is co-author of the books, *Feminism Counts*: *Quantitative Methods and Researching Gender (Routledge, 2011),* and *Women's Contemporary Lives*: *Within and Beyond the Mirror (Routledge, 2002).*

Gabrielle Ivinson is Professor of Education and Community at the Manchester Met University, UK. She is the author of *Rethinking Single-sex teaching*: *Gender, school subjects and learning* (with Murphy, 2007), co-editor *of Knowledge and Identity*: *concepts and applications in Bernstein's sociology of knowledge* (with Davies and Fitz, 2011), and co-editor of the journal special issue 'Material Feminisms: New Directions for Education' for *Gender and Education* (with Carol Taylor). As a social and developmental psychologist, she researches the intergenerational transmission of knowledge as a social resource in places of poverty. Her recent projects involve working with a range of artists to co-produce art forms and artefacts to enable young people to communicate with persons in authority by drawing on the affective power of art to move.

Alecia Youngblood Jackson holds a PhD from The University of Georgia, Athens, USA, and teaches educational research at Allpachian State University, Boone, USA. Alecia is co-author of the book, *Thinking with Theory in Qualitative Research*: *Viewing Data Across Multiple Perspectives* (Routledge, 2011), which was awarded the American Educational Studies Association's Critics Choice Award in 2013.

Malou Juelskjaer is Associate Professor at the University of Aahus, Copenhagen, Denmark. She specialises in education, teaching, and philosophy. Malou's articles have appeared in such journals as *Theory and Psychology* and *Gender & Education.*

Mindy Legard Larson is Associate Professor at Linfield College, McMinnville, USA. Her academic interests include material feminist theory and research, children's literature, and post structural feminisms theory. Mindy's articles have appeared in journals such as *The International Journal of Learning* and *Gender & Education.*

Celia Lury is Professor of Sociology and Director of the Centre for Interdisciplinary Methodologies at the University of Warwick, UK. Her research explores feminist and cultural theory, interdisciplinary methodologies, sociology of culture, and branding and consumer culture. Celia is co-author of the book, *Inventive Methods*: *The Happening of the Social (Culture, Economy, and the Social)* (Routledge, 2013).

Lisa A. Mazzei is Associate Professor of Education Studies at the University of Oregon, Eugene, USA. Her areas of teaching and research include qualitative research methodology and curriculum theory. Lisa is author *of Inhabited Silence in Qualitative Research*: *Putting Poststructural Theory to Work* (Peter Lang, 2007), co-author of *Thinking with Theory in Qualitative Research*: *Viewing Data Across Multiple Perspectives* (Routledge, 2012), and *Voice in Qualitative Inquiry*: *Challenging Conventional, Interpretive, and Critical Conceptions in Qualitative Research* (Routledge, 2009).

Anna Palmer is Assistant Professor in the Department of Child and Youth Studies at Stockholm University, Sweden. Anna specializes in feminist material theory and methodology in relation to early-childhood education.

Donna Kalmbach Phillips received her PhD from Oregon State University, Corvallis, USA, and teaches in literacy at Pacific University, Forest Grove, USA. Her current research focuses on literacy and teacher identity acquisition. Prior to her studies in this field, Donna taught literacy in middle schools.

Jocey Quinn is Professor of Education at Plymouth University, UK. Her research interests include education and culture, feminist ideas, and lifelong learning outside formal education. Her latest book, *Education and Culture*, was published by Routledge in 2015.

Emma Renold is Professor in Childhood Studies at the School of Social Sciences, Cardiff University, Wales. Her current research focuses on young sexualities, equalities, and wellbeing. Emma has published extensively in her field. Her works include *Girls, Boys and Junior Sexualities* (Routledge 2005) and *Children, Sexuality and the Sexualisation of Culture* (Palgrave 2015).

Hillevi Lenz Taguchi is Professor of Education and Child and Youth Studies in the Department of Child and Youth Studies at Stockholm University, Sweden. Her research focuses on feminist theories and continental philosophy in relation to higher education, teacher education and early childhood practices. Hillevi has contributed numerous works to her field, including her book, *Going Beyond the Theory/Practice Divide in Early Childhood Education: Introducing an intra-active pedagogy* (Routledge, 2010).

Carol A. Taylor is a Reader in the Sheffield Institute of Education at Sheffield Hallam University, UK. Her research focuses on space, gender and bodies, mundane materialities, student engagement, and ethics. She has recently co-edited two journal special issues: one on New Material Feminisms for *Gender and Education* (with Gabrielle Ivinson) and one on student engagement and ethics for the *Journal of Applied Research in Higher Education* (with Carol Robinson). Her work has been published in *Cultural Studies* ⇔ *Critical Methodologies*, *Studies in Higher Education,* and *Gender and Education.*

INTRODUCTION

Material feminisms: new directions for education

The radical shifts occurring across the social sciences make this an exciting time for educational research. New material feminisms, post-humanism, actor network theory, complexity theory, science and technology studies, material culture studies and Deleuzian philosophy name just some of the main strands that call us to reappraise what counts as knowledge and to re-examine the purpose of education. Together these strands shift the focus away from individualised acts of cognition and encourage us to view education in terms of change, flows, mobilities, multiplicities, assemblages, materialities and processes.

New material feminisms offer ways of looking at how students and teachers are constituted by focusing on the materialities of bodies, things and spaces within education. They make available new analytical tools to help re-think the co-constitutive entanglements of and between knowledge domains, practices, subjects, objects and things of all kinds. Central to the strands mentioned above is the critical endeavour of inter- or post-disciplinarity. Thinking 'with' resources made available by a number of theoretical fields can widen the scope for interrogating educational practices and problems, encourage new accounts of theory-practice relations and provide a basis for some new feminist insights. As a counter-movement to the increasingly neo-positivist outcomes-based, ever-intensifying (it seems) neo-liberal political and economic climate of education, such a post-disciplinary approach can, perhaps, offer some potentially ethical and political, as well as intellectual, resources. Alongside this, we are seeing the emergence of 'post-qualitative research' (Lather and St Pierre 2013) in terms of new methodological orientations that some refer to as 'New Empiricism'. This special issue on material feminisms can be read in relation to these broader theoretical and methodological currents.

In this special issue, authors draw on Karen Barad's (2007) work in particular as well as Alaimo and Hekman (2008), Bennett (2010), Coole and Frost (2010) and others, as springboards for thinking about educational practices in new ways. All the authors share an orientation towards new feminist materialisms as a means to 'establish a radical break with both universalism and dualism as they theorise the co-constitutiveness of cultural discourse and materiality' (Lenz Taguchi 2013, 707). Barad's (2007, 3) insight that 'matter and meaning are not separate entities' is crucial and addresses a question often posed about 'new' material feminisms, namely what is new about 'new' materialism?

But first, claims about newness have to be put in context. While 'new' material feminisms offer innovative ways of conceptualising and analysing issues about gender inequality, discrimination and violence (symbolic and not) in education, we recognise that these concerns have always been central to feminism. The perception of 'newness' is, as Jones and Kawehau Hoskins (2013) remind us, conditioned by culture, history and place. For example, in traditional Maori thought the human-natural world is an entangled continuity: objects are respected and alive, and object-human energy exchanges are experienced and enjoyed as a material manifestation of conjoined becomings. We need to remember that the subject/object split inflicted by the legacy of Descartes is a western ontological problem exported via colonialism.

So what is new? In new material feminism matter and discourse are co-constitutive and neither is foundational. This position differs from Marxist-inflected materialism which reads consciousness and ideology as a reflection of prior economic organisation and posits the centrality of the human as the organising force in capitalist consumption and use of natural and material resources. In 'new' materialism, matter is not inert, neither does it form an empty stage for, or background space to, human activity. Instead, matter is conceptualised as agentic and all sorts of bodies, not just human bodies, are recognised as having agency. Attributing some form of agency to matter is what differentiates 'new' material feminisms from what Lenz Taguchi (2013, 711) calls 'renewed' materialist accounts. While both share the premise that materiality matters profoundly in the constitution of subjectivity, 'renewed' materialism continues to install the human subject as the intermediary between matter and meaning and thus reworks a 'negative and dialectical ontology'. In contrast, 'new' material feminisms displace the human as the principal ground for knowledge and, instead, embrace all manner of bodies, objects and things within a confederacy of meaning-making. By accepting a flattened, non-hierarchical, human–non-human form of knowledge production, 'new' materialism takes matter seriously and accepts that matter is alive. In Barad's (2007) and Bennett's (2010) work, human and non-human bodies are considered as intra-actively entangled. That is, they come into being as agentic phenomena only and always through dynamic, co-constitutive emergence. This is a radical ontological move that decentres the human and emphases the co-constitutive power of matter. It urges us to take a much greater responsibility for our capabilities as humans and especially when 'disposing' of those bodies and things that we all too conveniently designate as our 'others'. More than that, it requires us to recognise the power of things (Bennett 2010) and to lose some of our hubris as humans in order to see, understand and take into account the forces, capacities and energies possessed by matter, including non-humans, other-than-humans and more-than-humans (Braidotti 2013), Such an ontology has particular epistemological implications.

Barad, Braidotti, Haraway and other material feminists make it clear that we cannot separate the materiality of the world from our knowledge of it (Coole and Frost 2010). By properly recognising that we have no bird's-eye position from which to look back or down at our world, we have to take seriously our own messy, implicated, connected, embodied involvement in knowledge production – what Barad (2007) calls our 'onto-epistemology'. In recognising and affirming that it is our being in the world that allows us to have knowledge, new material feminisms foreground ethics as an engaged practice and displace objectivity as a central value in social and natural scientific studies. Such moves reinforce earlier feminist theories (Butler 1990; Grosz 1994), and speak back to the second corporeal turn in social theory (e.g. Bourdieu and Wacquant 1992; Foucault 1979; Merleau-Ponty 1962, 1968; Shilling 2008) and within education (Evans, Rich, and Davies 2009; James 2000; Prout 2000; Walkerdine 2009).

The re-turn to a focus on matter as vibrant (Bennett's 2010) marks an epistemological and ontological sea change that challenges deeply entrenched scientific categories such as student, teacher, classroom, school, government, text, table, desk, PC, ipad, mobile phone as separable phenomena. Material feminism provokes us to think of meanings as emergent within dynamic entanglements of all manner of elements. This leads to questions concerning how categories, persons, and things come to matter differently (Fenwick, Edwards, and Sawchuk 2011). Barad's (2007) ethico-onto-epistemology is both provocative and generative for education because it forces us to pay attention to which kinds of matter, human and non-human, matters.

The articles in this special issues show how, by placing a focus on materiality and how matter affects and is affected by other living phenomena, we may gain significant purchase in the feminist quest to understand how academic institutions reproduce, sustain and shift gender inequalities. By questioning how boundaries between categories, people or things get made, we are forced to grapple with our own position, voice and intentions and, more than this, to accept uncertainty. The contingency of knowledge is, of course, not a new epistemological problem, yet it is placed centre stage by new material feminisms.

We hope the articles included here will help foreground how matter comes to matter within educational practices. The articles aim to show how class, gender, race and power operate in material assemblages in often submerged or hitherto 'unseen' ways. Some articles begin to explore possibilities for new forms of feminist praxis. Many of the articles show how new materialist accounts of educational instances can produce lively new forms of feminist knowledge. They highlight how feminist scholars, researchers and teachers are not only ethically implicated in the world but become ethically responsible, via the material-discursive 'cuts' they make and the interventions they enact. These cuts produce the world we inhabit. The emphasis in new material feminism on 'becoming-in-relation' to/with matter and meaning has the potential to re-cast and reinvigorate an ethics of care by installing an ecological perspective – rooted in a respect for the vitality of all matter – at its heart. As Barad (2007, 392–393) says:

> We (but not only 'we humans') are always already responsible to the others with whom or which we are entangled, not through conscious intent but thorough the various ontological entanglements that materiality entails.

This post-human ethic of 'worlding' is not a matter of choice, will or intent but a matter of our 'incarnate relation' that precedes consciousness and individualism, borne of our being in and of the world. Material feminisms, then, make us realise not just how necessary it is to revise what we understand as causality, motivation, agency and subjectivity, all of which are central terms in educational theory and pedagogy, but also to devise new, practical and ethical acts of engagement which motivate and enact change in the material continuum that constitutes educational practice. The following articles show that these tasks are profoundly challenging and that we are only at the early stages of recognising the potential of these theories for feminist praxis. Even so, new material feminisms encourage us to look (again) at the micro-political level, at what is happening in a specific material context. By recognising the micro intensities of *here and now*, 'new' material feminisms invite us to reaffirm that the personal is as political as it ever was.

While second wave feminism worked well in western societies to challenge patriarchal structures in modernity, it does not work well in sub Saharan Africa or modern Palestine nor, indeed, does it work for the current generation of young women in western societies. By focusing on what becomes perceptible, detectable, recognisable, salient or significant as matter, new material feminists effectively widen the purview of scale; they refuse to delineate the boundaries around the contexts in which humans and other entities dynamically exist. So while the student enters the classroom as a classed, gendered and ethnic being, she or he also enters as a being who breathes in air, air that circulates through the air conditioning system, that whistles in through a cracked window pane, that carries the smell of freshly cut grass, that was part of the storm that broke the tree in the playground last week, etc. All teachers know that the bodies that enter the classroom after a wet and windy break time need to be managed in a different way to those that arrive straight from the history lesson. They know that bodies with asthma have to be given special provision to use inhalers. And they know that children who arrive with no overcoat and leaky shoes attend to the maths equation in different ways to those who are well heeled. The forces and powers at work in classrooms operate through the bodies and things of the classroom, its space and its many materialities. The classroom as material assemblage, bodies as matter to be managed, and the materialities which impact on knowing, affect how learning takes place. New material feminisms put these everyday things on the radar and values them within 'educational theory'. Material feminisms legitimate these matters as part the social and scientific construction of 'the student' in processes of learning and living. Recognising that matter is part of meaning can only expand and enrich our understanding of gender and education.

The articles at the beginning of the issue provide close empirical foci on practices, doings and actions while the papers towards the end become increasingly theoretically engaged. Hillevi Lenz Taguchi and Anna Palmer focus on the way educational practices promote and discipline girls' ill- and well-being. They work with diffraction as 'an experimental achievement of the "power to wonder" [which produces] an event of knowing things differently'. The next four papers illustrate how space, place and objects intra-act co-constitutively with bodies to afford different kinds of agency. Carol Taylor illustrates how mundane objects including clothes contribute to a male teacher's authority in his classroom. She invites us to pay greater attention to the power of things as part of the process through which authority is instantiated materially in pedagogic intra-actions. Gabrielle Ivinson and Emma Renold draw attention to place, including the history of a place, to rethink relationships between teen girls' bodies and agency. They suggest how the history of a post-industrial place influenced girls' body-movement repertoires. Jocey Quinn tackles the social marginalisation of young people. She describes their engagement in nature through a post-humanist lens while cautioning that a focus on materiality must not eclipse the enduring power of social inequalities. Malou Juelskjaer works with spacetimemattering diffractively to trouble post-structuralist ideas about subjectivity and question the notion of 'new' beginnings in a Danish school.

Lisa Mazzei discusses the methodological implications of diffraction, a concept for 'reading insights through one another', which Barad (2007, 25) developed from Haraway (1997). This provokes her to ponder critically her own 'seduction by theory' and, subsequently, her embodiment as researcher becoming-with the data. She encourages us to think of data's intra-active materiality and how it may re-work us as researchers. Mindy Legard–Larsson and Donna Kalmbach-Phillips highlight the intra-active responsibilities which emerge through diffraction and discuss how to promote social justice in classrooms. Alecia Jackson urges us to propagate 'free acts'. She posits freedom as a matter of acting and doing rather than being. Through a reading of Grosz and Bergson, she envisages the possibilities for transformation and change that materialise when 'subjectivity and freedom are enacted through the materiality that the living and the nonliving share'. Christina Hughes and Celia Lury elaborate an ecological perspective which re-turns us to epistemological feminist questions about how we envisage situatedness and difference in a more-than-human world.

We thank the authors included in this special issue for their lively engagement with some of the empirical, theoretical and methodological possibilities raised by 'new' material feminisms. We would like to extend our thanks to the reviewers who worked with us on this special issue. We are grateful not just for the detailed and developmental advice but also for the speed with which reviews were turned around. A special thank you goes to Helen Rowlands who ensured we kept to our tight timescale through impeccable organisation and always tactful reminders. Thanks, too, to Liz Eades for seeing the issue through the production process so swiftly and painlessly for us.

References

Alaimo, S., and S. Hekman, eds. 2008. *Material Feminisms*. Bloomington: Indiana University Press.

Barad, K. 2007. *Meeting the Universe Halfway: Quantum Physics and the Entanglement of Matter and Meaning*. London: Duke University Press.

Bennett, J. 2010. *Vibrant Matter: A Political Ecology of Things*. London: Duke University Press.

Bourdieu, P., and L. J. D. Wacquant. 1992. *An Invitation to Reflexive Sociology*. Cambridge: Polity Press.

Braidotti, R. 2013. *The Posthuman*. Cambridge: Polity.

Butler, J. 1990. *Gender Trouble: Feminism and the Subversion of Identity*. New York: Routledge.

Coole, D., and S. Frost. 2010. *New Materialisms: Ontology, Agency, Politics*. Durham, NC: Duke University Press.

Evans, J., E. Rich, and B. Davies. 2009. "The Body Made Flesh: Embodied Learning and the Corporeal Device." *British Journal of Sociology of Education* 30 (4): 389–391.

Fenwick, T., R. Edwards, and P. Sawchuk. 2011. *Emerging Approaches to Educational Research: Tracing the Socio-Material*. London: Routledge.

Foucault, F. 1979. *Discipline and Punish: The Birth of the Prison*. London: Peregrine Books.

Grosz, E. 1994. *Volatile Bodies: Toward a Corporeal Feminism*. Bloomington: Indiana University Press.

Haraway, D. 1997. *Modest_Witness@Second_Millennium. FemaleMan© _ Meets OncoMouse: Feminism and Technoscience*. New York: Routledge.

James, A. 2000. "Embodied Being(s): Understanding the Self and Body in Childhood." In *The Body, Childhood and Society*, edited by A. Prout, 1–18. Basingstoke: Palgrave MacMillan.

Jones, A., and T. Kawehau Hoskins. 2013. "Object Lessons: Vital Materiality and Indigenous-Settler Engagement." Keynote Presentation, Summer Institute in Qualitative Research, Manchester Metropolitan University, 22–26 July.

Lather, P., and E. St Pierre. 2013. "Post-Qualitative Research." *International Journal of Qualitative Studies in Education* 26 (6): 629–633.

Lenz Taguchi, H. 2013. "Images of Thinking in Feminist Materialisms: Ontological Divergences and the Production of Researcher Subjectivities." International *Journal of Qualitative Studies in Education* 26 (6): 706–716.

Merleau-Ponty, M. 1962. *The Primacy of Perception*. London: Routledge and Kegan Paul.

Merleau-Ponty, M. 1968. *The Visible and the Invisible*. Evanston, IL: Northwestern University Press.

Prout, A. 2000. *The Body, Childhood and Society*. Basingstoke: Palgrave MacMillan.
Shilling, C. 2008. *Changing Bodies*. London: Sage.
Walkerdine, V. 2009. "Biopedagogies and Beyond." In *Biopolitics and the 'Obesity Epidemic'*, edited by J. Wright and V. Harwood, 199–207. London: Routledge.

Carol A. Taylor

Gabrielle Ivinson

A more 'livable' school? A diffractive analysis of the performative enactments of girls' ill-/well-being with(in) school environments

Hillevi Lenz Taguchi and Anna Palmer

Department of Child and Youth Studies, Stockholm University, Stockholm, Sweden

School girls in Sweden are reported to develop psychological (ill)health in relation to their school behaviour and over-achievements. The methods offered as prevention and treatments are aimed at the individual girl's self-management of stress, health and psychological state, putting the responsibility on the girls themselves. This feminist agential realist study aims to explore how the material-discursive school environment, that is, the entanglement of architecture, materialities, bodies, discourses and discursive practices – including the discourses on girls' health in research and media texts – are collectively responsible for, co-constitutive of and enacting female students' ill- and well-being. Doing a diffractive analysis, we register how we as researchers are involved and co-productive of this complex apparatus of knowing of school-related ill-/well-being. A diffractive analysis aims to not only analyse how this apparatus is made and what it produces, but also how it can be productive of new possible realities that might produce more livable school environments.

Introduction

It has been argued that any production of knowledge is actually a production of reality with very specific material consequences for the agents involved in that particular reality (Barad 2007; Hekman 2010; Law 2004; Mol 2002). When, for example, the 'boys' problem', that is, boys finding it unmanly and feminising to study, is blamed on over-achieving girls and the female teachers who privilege girls' learning styles in research (Nyström 2012), this will inevitably produce one of multiple realities that will have material consequences for the agents involved (Hekman 2010). In the context of the extensive scientific reporting in media on young Swedish school girls' increasing psychological (ill)health, and of the increasing amount of preventive pro-grammes and self-treatments being implemented in schools around Sweden to enhance the individual girl's self-management of stress and psychological problems, it is only fair to ask how such knowledge production becomes part of a larger and extended apparatus (Barad 2007) of producing school girls' (multiple) realities and their enactments of ill- or well-being in those realities. The question is, in what ways do reported scientific findings (based on various psychological, psychoanalytical and neuro-cognitive theories) become co-constitutive agents in the production of the phenomenon of school girls' ill- or well-being together with other performative agents? Such agents are here understood to be entanglements of discourses, places, materialities and embodied practices in or connected to the school environment. All of these involve socio-historical aspects of gender, ethnicity, class, age, etc. in various situated ways. Although this study focusses primarily on the materiality of language (MacLure 2013) as the strongest agent in these intra-active entanglements, our analysis also shows how various other material agents, such as the school building and architecture, which we usually take to be the fixed material backdrop of human agency, are themselves strong co-constitutive agents of school-related ill- or well-being.

From an agential realist (Barad 1999, 2007) stance, the aim of this paper is thus to explore how the material-discursive school environment, with all its various agents and the plurality and diverging character of practices (Stengers 2007), can be understood to be collectively responsible for, co-constitutive of and collaboratively enacting the phenomenon of Swedish female students' ill-/well-being. These enactments are understood to emerge as effects of an open-ended *material-discursive apparatus of knowing* (Barad 2007, 149–150), in which we as researchers constitute significant performative agents as well. This means that we are not looking for answers located 'inside' of the pre-existing subject, as the psychological and neuro-cognitive epistemologies suggest. Instead we analyse events of encounters of multiple material-discursive agents and situated practices, and what emerges as *differences* in these events: that is, how matter *matters* in an ongoing process of material-discursive mattering (Barad 2007, 145–147). In terms of methodology, this can be understood to put to work what Barad (2007, 73–94) and Haraway (1997, 268–274) have called a *diffractive analysis*. For our analysis, we will make very specific agential and provisional cuts in the multiple realities produced by the apparatus that we understand to be productive of girls' school-related ill-/well-being. These cuts and how they are diffractively produced in the research process will constitute our analysis in the core section of the paper called *Enacting a diffractive analysis*.

What a diffractive analysis might entail will be unfolded shortly. We wish, however, to point to the diffractive analysis as, what Stengers (2007) has called, an experimental achievement of 'the power to wonder' that can be celebrated as an event of knowing things differently (5). The 'power of wonder', says Stengers, is about constructing relevant problems that provide relevant other ways of knowing as well as new imaginings that can escape the knowledge economy that buys right into the state machine of managing public order (Stengers 2007, 6). In this case, such knowing might be able to interfere with the seemingly unanimous discourses and practices that put the cause and responsibility of ill-/well-being on the girls themselves. Hence, this is a methodology that experiments with controversy and the fact that 'it could be otherwise', as Mol suggests (2009).

Agential realism and how phenomena are produced by an apparatus of knowing

How will we, as two collaborating researchers, be able to identify 'which specific material practices matter, and *how* they matter' (Barad 2007, 168, italics added)? To do this we first need to know more about the wider, multiple and open-ended *apparatus of knowing* that we take to be productive of the phenomenon. It is in the *events of encounter* with the different agents of this apparatus – including the affective responses and memories of our own – that we can make intelligible how this phenomenon will come to matter as an effect of the material-discursive intra-activities taking place in this apparatus. Before showing how this specific apparatus is assembled and how it is possible to produce knowing together with and as constituted by this apparatus, we will discuss a couple of key concepts in Barad's agential realism: phenomenon and apparatus.

Constructionism and realism can be said to be brought together in agential realism as a relational ontology (Barad 2007, 332–336). This means that instead of thinking about a world of physical stable objects out there and language and concepts to represent the meaning of these bodies, it is *phenomena,* as an ongoing process of mutual intelligible-making of matter and meaning, that are constitutive of reality (139, 333). The phenomenon of, in this case, girls' school-related ill- or well-being, is thus to be understood as material-discursive intra-active enactments. In this study we show how the materiality of, for example, a panicking girl-body is attached with a specific meaning of ill-being in a specific situated event of intra-activities in a wider apparatus of girls' school-related ill-/well-being. Thus, the primary ontological unit (e.g. the body of the girl) is no longer an object with inherent boundaries and fixed properties, as in classical physics and philosophy. Rather, the ontological unit is understood as a *phenomenon*; defined as 'the ontological inseparability/entanglement of intra-action "agencies"' (Barad 2007, 139). In the example of the panicking girl-body, this can be understood as an event of an entanglement of multiple performative agencies: the agencies of discourses of schooling and ill- or well-being as well as the agency of the physical school building and practices of schooling. These are collectively intra-acting in situated events where the phenomenon of school-related ill-being is produced and subsequently reported on in media. Hence, phenomena are enacted (or produced) in specific agential intra-actions, where 'the boundaries and properties of the components of phenomena become determinate' as the particular concept that we attach to that phenomena becomes meaningful in the very same event (Barad 2007, 139). This is why Barad (2007, 334–335) suggests for us to talk of concepts not as linguistic entities but as 'specific material arrangements' and of 'discursive practices' that should not be confused with discursive speech acts, where discourse is merely a synonym for language. Hereby, writes Barad, *material-discursive intra-activity* will replace the dominant notion of language as representations of a reality separated from meaning-making Barad (2007, 141). Thus, in a Baradian agential realist account, matter and meaning are always already co-constituted:

> Neither discursive practice nor material phenomena are ontologically or epistemologically prior. Neither can be explained in terms of the other. Neither is reducible to the other. Neither has privileged status in determining the other. Neither is articulated or articulable in the absence of the other; matter and meaning are mutually articulated. (2007, 152)

If matter and meaning are seen as co-constitutive of each other, then so is being/becoming (ontology) and knowing (epistemology). This is how Barad's agential realism can be understood in terms of an onto-epistem-ology (2007, 185).

'What is an apparatus?' Barad asks herself this question in the opening phrase of a central section of her book by putting it side by side with other more familiar concepts (2007, 141). If it is not a Kantian grid of intelligibility, or an Aristotelian schemata, and not the same as Althusserian apparatuses, or Foucault's discursive practices or *dispositive*, then, what is it? Barad's theory on apparatuses of knowing relies on Niels Bohr's thinking from quantum physics. Apparatuses, writes Barad, are specific material-discursive practices that become productive of phenomena by ways of specific boundary-making cuts (2007, 333–224). '[A]pparatuses are macroscopic material arrangements through which particular concepts are given definition, to the exclusion of others, and through which particular phenomena with particular determinate physical properties are produced' (Barad 2007, 142). As researchers, we make a cut in a world made up of phenomena that are *not manifest in themselves* but that become temporarily manifest through this practice of the scientific knowledge production (Barad 2007, 335–336). And this is what makes is possible to write scientific texts with provisional descriptions of the phenomenon.

A crucial part of understanding the apparatus as a material-discursive practice is that we as researchers (irrespective of research disciplines) inevitably become an entangled part of these apparatuses, as we set them up and become productive of the boundary-making agential cuts that will then be written up as scientific knowledge. Thus, we can no longer be seen simply as the agency of observation, observing an object at distance, distinctly (as well as ontologically) separated from us. The subject–object distinction is invalidated in Bohr's and Barad's thinking. The production of knowing is constituted by the process by which this larger material arrangement (*of which we are an entangled part*) produces differences and enacts specific cuts that are boundary-making and meaning-making; that is, that 'determinate the boundaries and properties of objects and meanings of embodied concepts within a phenomenon' (Barad 2007, 143, 143–147, 332–336). This will have consequences for how we understand ourselves as researchers, as we will expand on below and as previous material feminist studies have already shown (Lenz Taguchi 2012, 2013; Palmer 2011; Banerjee and Blaise 2013; MacLure 2013; Mazzei 2013).

Setting up the apparatus of knowing for a diffractive analysis

It was with an increased wish for a critical and innovative discussion about young school girls' (ill)health in Sweden today that we set up this apparatus of knowing. During the last years, there has been an intensified media discussion with reference to various research studies in medicine, psychology and neuro-cognition that unanimously situate the cause of ill-being within the girls themselves or their families. For example, a newspaper interview, drawing on psychological studies, reports that young female students' stress problems and ill-health refer almost exclusively to high-achieving girls with a 'good-girl' syndrome (Alfvén, Caverius, Karling, and Olsson 2010). Reports in media on young girls developing fibromyalgia are exclusively connected to girls with high-achieving performance anxiety (Ant Jacobsson 2012). Recently, the governmentally appointed commission on gender equality in schooling concluded that girls' reports of health problems have to be taken seriously (SOU 2010, 99).[1] The preventive programmes and treatments aimed at girls with stress problems are, without exceptions, self-treatments, putting the responsibility of change and well-being on the girls themselves (Eldh and Ingvar 2012; Wilson and Murrel 2011).

When we as researching agents enter into and simultaneously become productive of this apparatus of knowing, we are engaged with all of our own previous and ongoing experiences of these kinds of realities of young girls' illness in and outside school that are described in media and various research reports. We both know young girls who have suffered/suffer from some of these problems, and both of us are high-achieving academics who navigate with various exercise- and self-treatment programmes to prevent the damaging effects of work-related stress. As Barad (2007, 168) writes, we are, as researching agents, not 'fully formed, pre-existing subjects, but as subjects intra-actively co-constituted through the material-discursive practice that /.../ [we] engage in'. This means that the way this apparatus is set up depends not only on the kinds of data we encounter, 'find' and 'collect', but also on the differences that get made in our embodied engagements with these data in the apparatus of knowing. This means that it matters that we are white, middle-class, heterosexual women in the production of knowing, but this does also matter for how we will be transformed in new events of encounter in the researching process (Lenz Taguchi 2012, 2013).

Apart from reading and engaging with various kinds of research reports and following the media discussion, we chose to meet and engage with the stories produced by two young school girls, Alice (grade 7) and Emma (grade 10).[2] We first met with Alice and Emma at a coffee shop where the girls usually hang out to make them feel comfortable. The first meeting was all about information and getting informed consent from the girls.[3] During the upcoming two meetings, the girls told us memory stories and showed us photos that they had taken with their smart phones. To get away from discursive descriptions of physical and psychological symptoms or diagnosis, and to, instead, get to the material-discursive situatedness of the phenomenon, we asked about specific spaces, places, things and practices or activities that mattered to experiences of ill- or well-being. 'Something must always take place somewhere', as Mol (2009) says in relation to the situatedness of material-discursive phenomena. For example, where in, or outside, the school buildings and while doing what would they feel well, ill, comfortable or anxious? Could they describe smells, sounds or other details in these places or practices that affected the way they felt? The girls had no problems talking about these events and then writing on them at home, adding more details and sent them to us by e-mail the same or the next day. We also asked them to take photographs of these or other places or situations where they experienced ill- or well-being. The girls told us that the photos helped them write on the stories and that they felt differently about these events after having written about them and discussed them with us.

In the events of engagement with the data produced by the two girls and the various research reports, articles and media clips, memories and critical incidents of our own would emerge. The two of us would sit together in one of our studies, surrounded by all the data: the articles and books, written stories, photographs and images, or different web-sites on the internet on the screen in front of us. We read data out loud to each other or put the photographs into different software to highlight or downplay parts of them. We thus enacted agentic cuts in the construction of various encounters with data, while talking and telling each other stories or experiences, as a way to collaboratively produce knowing in this rhizomatic zigzagging flow. This process felt as if we passed ourselves over to a flow of entangled social, material and discursive forces in the apparatus of knowing, where one text would link, connect or collide with another, and produce something new or different. This might be a memory or experience evoked in one of us, or associating to another field of research, such as architecture or art, or connecting different data to each other in previously unexpected ways. It was these events of engagement with data in the apparatus of knowing that made us physically experience the workings of a diffractive analysis. We felt like surfers taking advantage of 'the diffraction patterns created by the rocks or pieces of land that stick out near the shore/.../literally riding the diffractive patterns, wave after wave in different directions', as Barad writes (2007, 80). In this way, the analysis constituted events where minds and bodies, thinking and feeling cannot be understood as separated but entangled in a 'spacetimemattering' practice (Barad 2007, 179).

The doing of diffractive analysis

When we claim to do what Barad (2007, 73–94) and Haraway (1997, 268–274) have called a diffractive analysis, what does this mean? Diffraction, as a concept from physics, can be illustrated by the rolling, pushing and transformation of waves in, for example, the sea, as in Barad's quote above. However, in physics it can be any kind of wave, sound waves or light waves. A diffractive analysis can be understood as a wave-like motion that takes into account that thinking, seeing and knowing are never done in isolation but are always affected by different forces coming together, or, to use Barad's words; '… knowing is a matter of part of the world making itself intelligible to another part of the world' (Barad 2007, 185).

For Haraway and Barad, diffractive analysis basically constitutes an alternative methodology to critical reflection (Lenz Taguchi 2012). While reflection basically mirrors reality as a more or less fixed phenomenon seen from a distance, diffraction is about engaging in the world and its differential becomings (Barad 2007, 87–91). A diffractive way of doing analysis, then, is not about a researcher interpreting what the data means, where the analysis is supposed to be 'out there' to be studied, reflected upon and deriving meaning/knowing from (Barad 2007, 29, 81). Rather, a diffractive analysis can be understood as an enactment of flows of differences, where *differences get made* in the process of reading data into each other, and identifying what diffractive patterns emerge in these readings.

A diffractive style of reading allows for the researchers to identify the intra-activities that emerge in between the researchers and the data. These shifts do not happen completely at random; new directions are marked out in the very intersection between the data, theory, methodology and the researcher. In these diffractive crossroads, the original 'wave' partly remains within the new wave after its transformation into a new one, and so on, wave after wave (Barad 2007, 71–83). The new disturbs, intervenes and calls for attention and in this event something new can be created with the data and new data might be produced. In this Baradian (2007) way of thinking, intention, as we know it, cannot be ascribed to a single human subject as a pre-existing determinate mental state. Rather, writes Barad, intention is something distributed that emerges from a complex network of human and nonhuman agents, including historically specific sets of material conditions, thus exceeding the notion of being assigned to an individual who produces intention that pre-exists an activity (2007, 23).

However, in this process, we also found that our own gender-, class- and ethnic performativity was an important factor in the production of the diffractive analysis: how we inter-related to each other's (gendered, classed, ethnic, aged) experiences, connections and memories, and how we negotiated and came to decide on how to perform the specific agential cuts we made. Thus, the diffractive analysis unfolded below consists of cuts produced in a predominantly ethnic, white, middle-class reality of girls and women that have all the opportunities of a western democracy in a progressive nation-state of Northern Europe, and it is exactly this socio-material historical situatedness that became productive of this specific school-related ill- or well-being produced in these cuts. Last but not least, it was in the writing of the analysis/paper and in the hands-on production of the power point to be presented that the diffractive analysis, more than any place else, took place. This is where new additional cuts were made and where different data were literally written into each other.

Enacting a diffractive analysis

The photograph and the story below, as part of this larger apparatus of knowing, both call our attention to research on the liberal school reforms of the 1990s, implementing 'free choice of schools' (Bunar 2010). Thus, in rush hour you will find thousands of children and youth, and especially girls, of different ethnicity, class, skin colour or religion, travelling, sometime for an hour, to an inner-city school 'of their own choice'. They hope to get a better education in predominantly ethnic Swedish, middle-class (white) high schools, in order to enter a good university programme (Bunar 2010). The girl in the story, just as we ourselves as female academics and researchers, together with many women since the late nineteenth century, seems to have understood that education is the only way to compete with men in the labour market.

> The subway starts and stops; station after station. I feel the anxiety growing in my chest; my heart beating harder and quicker and my breathing as if on top on my lungs. I feel sick: maybe I must get off at the next stop to throw up? I can't make it. I will get off at the next stop! The air smells grossly of sweat. I cannot breathe too deeply. Cannot get any disgusting bacteria into my body. Only two more stations to go. But I have to get out. Cannot miss maths today – must pass maths to get into the university. The sound of the breaks as the train prepares to stop cuts through my head. I hate this train! Why do I throw up almost every day before school? (Alice's story)

The blurry image of people in a hurry or blocking the way on the subway platform in the photograph intra-acts, as narrated in the story, with the molecules of sweat and smell from other bodies, and the penetrating sound waves generated from the breaks of the train as it arrives at a station (Figure 1). All of these different material agents are entangled with discourses on school achievement, mathematics and anxiety about the future. They become, in the story, productive of bodily contractions of the stomach, a speeding heart rate and breathing pushed to the top of the lungs.

'Human concepts [such as mathematics] are clearly embodied' writes Barad (2007, 154). They should not be understood as abstract and immaterial, or 'ideational' according to Barad based on Bohr, but rather as 'actual physical arrangements' that intra-act with other matter (Barad 2007, 147). In this specific apparatus of knowing, concepts such as mathematics become productive of *difference* that will come to *matter* in the experiences of the girl in the story, as bodily sickness and increased anxiety. And as part of this specific apparatus of school-related ill- or well-being, concepts and practices of mathematics, or even simply the experience of using public transport during rush hours to get to work every day, will come to matter in our own bodies as researching subjects, as intrusive feelings of sickness in the event of engagement with this data. Things, places, emotions and bodily reactions described in the story intervene, connect and take action in our own bodies, evoking memories of a mathematical practice neither of us could ever properly master. We become *with* this data in an event of engagement and become, in a sense, different from what we just were.

This story intra-acts in painful ways to another story about Paulina, reported in a major daily newspaper. The headline reads: 'Paulina had cold-sweats every time she came even close to the school building.' The article continues:

> When Paulina [after a three month break] tried to go to school she had attacks again. Her legs trembled so badly she had to sit down on the sidewalk. [Three years later] – I still have difficulties going into school environments and often have light forms of panic attacks in the classrooms of my community college, but it works. (Lerner and Lofors 2010).

Figure 1.   The central station in rush hour. Photo by Alice 10th grade.

How can the school environment become such a powerful performative agent in enacting Paulina's failed sense of well-being that she does not even need to be inside of it to feel bad? In an agential realist sense, the school environment is making itself intelligible to Paulina in ways that do not enact her well-being, but rather quite the opposite.

Paulina's story can be read into research on children who refuse going to school. What can this research teach us about the school environment? And what differences are made in relation to girls' illness and well-being when reading into the stories above? In a report on a programme for girls with extensive truancy (up to two years of school absence), the researcher concludes that all of these girls (ten girls in a school of over 600) desire an education and basically want to go to school; they just have not found the right way to do it (Bodén 2010). While mainstream research on truancy shows that truancy is either caused by individual psychological problems, sometimes expressed in 'school-fobia' (Kearney and Bensaheb 2006), or family problems (National School Agency 2010; Reid 1999; 2006), Bodén (in press) suggests that truancy can instead be understood as material-discursive intra-actions of many different performative agents such as the formal structures of schools, architecture, the computer technology to register absence and presence, as well as human agents. In Bodén's (2010) report she shows how the postmodern transparent glass constructions of a school, even at the level of the individual classrooms, intra-act with a particular girl to cause frequent anxiety attacks. This girl feels as if she is always watched and can never escape the eyes of the other children or teachers. While the teachers and some other children would report on the beauty of this architecture and appreciating the light, most children asked would complain about the feeling of not being able to find spaces of integrity within the school building (Bodén 2010).

The piece of data below activates a diffractive movement that evokes a theorising of how schools have been architecturally constructed in a way to enable adults' surveillance and children's self-regulation (Foucault 1991). In the history of architecture, there is a strong connection between schools, army stations, prisons, hospitals and mental institutions (Foucault 1991). Many schools take pride in their large hallways sometimes called their 'hall of light' or 'the open market place' for communication and interaction. This theorising of self-regulation practices and feelings of severe stress in situations of open threat connects diffractively to Emma's story and the photograph she took presented in Figure 2.

Don't look up, don't look up! It takes about 30 seconds to walk through that light-hall in school. It is a risky 30 seconds! Without having to look, I know there are plenty of older students up there, mostly guys, who lean over the rails of the balconies. If you for only half of a second look up there is a risk that you will get a gob of spittle right in your face. Or a rubber in your eye, or a comment about your behind. The walk through the

Figure 2.   The light hall. Photo by Emma 7th grade.

light-hall is dangerous but has to be done several times a day. There is no other way to get to the classrooms on the other side. (Emma's story)

In the event of reading these data into each other, the materiality of the architecture in the photograph and the anticipated embodied materialities and emotional responses in the story become multiple performative agents that enact ill-being together with discursive practices of gender, sexuality and age in this situated space of the school. When we as researchers engage with these data and acknowledge all of these entangled performative agents, 'we do not stand outside of the world, we are instead part of the world in its ongoing intra-activity' (Barad 2007, 146). We read into this story research and reports on bullying in hallways. Bullying is frequent among students, but adults assaulting students is also more frequent in the hallways than in classrooms (Human Rights Watch 2001, 2010).

However, other photographs and stories of the participating girls in our study intervene and force us to read into the above horrifying data another image of the hallway. The hallway provides, for some girls, one of the very few spaces in school of personal integrity: the personal locker. Emma and Alice tell us that the locker is the only space in school you can call your own. At best the locker works as a secret hide-away for your stuff and yourself, but it can also become a central part of your enactment as school girl, and pose high demands on your ability to decorate your locker in the right way (Figure 3). Alice (grade 10) writes:

> The locker. It was probably the most important thing when I chose upper secondary school. I wanted a locker – just as in High school musical or Glee. Just the thought of having a locker of my own, with a code – was irresistible. There were several other schools that were closer to my home. Other programs that seemed interesting and fun. But there you had to carry your things around in your bag all day long. It felt unthinkable. No, I would rather travel a bit longer and have a locker of my own. A place of my own. Just as in Glee. (Alice's story)

Alice and Emma talk about how many Swedish teenagers live in close relationships with TV shows (such as *Glee, Gossip girl* or *High school musical*) that seem to intensify and have transformative effects on concrete school situations in their everyday life. The school environment in *Glee* can, as one of the girls says, constitute a different image of what going to high school might be, which feeds into and transforms the everyday experience of going to high school in Sweden. As 'modest witnesses' (Haraway 1997) of this scenery that our participant girls narrate to us, we can – as researchers – perfectly imagine similar material-discursive imaginaries in our own lives, which make our days in the academy transform into something else. Like when intra-acting with the memories from scenes from the unisex bathrooms in *Ally McBeal* while preparing for a lecture, or images from *L.A. Lawyers*, when trying to convince the head of department of why your particular research contributes highly to the programme you are about to construct. These mediated images from television intra-act in our everyday lives. They are entangled with our bodies, clothes, gestures, emotions and talk, and can thus have transformative effects in the production of our realities, for better and for worse: as normalising, self-managing discursive practices, or as occasional escapes, but sometimes as offering possible inventive leakages and enhancement of transformative and productive change.

The above analysis shows that school environments constitute spaces that produce stress of different kinds, and both ill- and well-being as a result. In our readings about

Figure 3.   The personal locker. Photo by Alice 10th grade.

school- and work-related stress, we understand how stress can be both positive and negative, and that stress can work on your body and mind in ambivalent and sometimes paradoxical ways: there is a very thin line between 'good' and 'bad' stress and they sometimes overlap (Hasson 2008). There has been a lot of attention on girls' school-related stress problems during the last five years in Sweden. Girls claim to feel worried and anxious in school due to stress, but they also brag about and use this stress to enact who they want to, and/or feel forced to, become as school girls: 'I was in the natural science program in high school and the girls there were obsessed with studying. It was natural to be stressed in order to get high grades and good test-scores. It was almost a sport.' (Lerner and Lofors 2010). We read this quote diffractively into the realities of (female) academics. We often express an agitated and almost aggressive stress, claiming to work 60–80 hour weeks seven days a week. This seems to be the way to enact a successful or even just good enough scholar in the reality of the academy today. Based on her research, the psychologist Malin Bergström states in an interview that 'the connection is clear between demands of individual school performances [self-imposed or imposed by parents] and psychological illness' (Mlik 2010). The girls she treats are generally 'overambitious' and 'need to lower the demands on themselves to a more reasonable level to achieve a balanced life' (Mlik 2010). This is also in line with the experiences of the welfare officers Susanne Håkanson and Åsa Gotte, who are working in two of the largest schools in the inner city area of Stockholm (Mlik 2010). They state that girls are over-represented in relation to stress-related problems and often ask for help after already having developed eating disorders, anxiety, pain problems or depression. They think that these girls need to get out of 'the achievement tunnel' and formulate to themselves other values with life than education. They should not be so fixated with becoming a lawyer, doctor or any other high-achievement vocation (Mlik 2010). These statements can be read into a newspaper article, where the psychotherapist, Irena Markower, claims that it is sad that high-achieving girls

> do not plan their studying in a smart way /.../ To get the highest grade and be perfect these girls think that they cannot make priorities. They read everything from the first page and every detail is as important as the other. (Carling 2011)

When we read the adults' gender-biased notions on over-ambitious girls diffractively into one of the researcher's own memory plugged in below, it is possible to evoke another possible enactment of girls' well-being in school. This enactment is based instead on emancipatory feminist goals within, and with an awareness of, the patriarchal brute reality that young girls/women are still living in. The other reality expressed in the memory below is a reality of a competent and equally smart high-achieving school girl, but who – importantly – does not perceive herself as a victim of her high achievements, as in the statements by the adult doctors, psychologists and counselors above. High achievement is here, as it is in the work environment of the academy, enacted as something good, useful and respectful, (albeit its adherence to masculine norms), rather than something to be looked down upon as a risk behaviour for girls' psychological ill-health. Therefore, let us read diffractively into the data above of the memory of a girl who puts to use her imaginary faculties to enact possible future realities as a strategy, both for learning and of becoming in various ways:

> The way to motivate myself to study was to imagine that every fact and turn of the words in the book was needed for something someday in my life: something that I could often visualize as a possible future scenario where I needed to know this particular thing/fact that made learning more fun. Going to the test not knowing everything was simply to fail, the way I saw it. You never knew what this particular teacher would ask or try to trick you around: you had to outsmart her/him: this was an equally important goal. When a teacher one day told me to study 'smart' instead – like the guys – and just learn the basics and overalls, this was like a disrespectful spit in my face: how could this be 'smarter' than knowing everything? Just think about all those things I had imagined I could do knowing this or that: becoming a biologist or famous diplomat, or whatever! I could never again trust or respect this teacher. (Researcher's story)

In the reading of these data, it is possible to unfold a different reality of ambition and high achievement that merge with this girl's well-being. This is a reality where a young girl tries out different possibilities of becoming an adult and a professional in different fields, in relation to the stuff she needs to learn in school. This is an active engagement of transformation and *becoming-different-in-herself*, using your imaginative powers to do so. Such a practice makes new realities emerge, although so far in her imagination only. Such a practice of imagining can, as in the example from our participating girl referring to the media discourses of *Glee* and *High School Musical*, enhance the girl's possibilities to do well both in school and later in life as well. Relating to Barad (2007), the 'I' isn't separated from the word but *of* the world of material things, places, dreams and imaginaries.

The 20-year-old girl, Malin, used to be an over-achieving girl 'who asked for help too late' (Mlik 2010). Similar to around one percent of Swedish school children, she let many years of stress and pains have her brain put the switch to the level of constant and chronic pain. She was diagnosed with fibromyalgia at the age of 18 (Ant Jacobsson 2012).[4] This chronic pain syndrome is usually associated with middle-aged women degradingly called 'ace-and-burn-hags' among doctors. You cannot observe or diagnose a physical cause 'in the body', rather, the pain is said to be 'all in your head' (Wilson and Murrel 2011). Malin describes how she cannot even cook herself a meal because of the pain she feels in her hands while handling pots and pans. The doctors tell her: 'Since we can't help you – it's your problem … ' (Ant Jacobsson 2012). She has to, as the doctors keep saying, 'take command over her own pain' (Eldh and Ingvar 2012). Girls and women with fibromyalgia 'need to make their own effort and to learn how to use the powers of their own brain', writes the neurologist Martin Ingvar in his new book with the witty title: *Brain-control your pain* (Eldh and Ingvar 2012). Evidently, the good-girl syndrome needs to be cured with girls getting to be even better at enacting an even more self- and brained-controlled subjectivity. If you cannot do it, you can only blame yourself.

Barad (2007) writes on responsibility the following way: 'is not a commitment that a subject chooses but rather an incarnate relation that precedes the intentionality of consciousness' (392). In relation to the story of Malin, this means that Malin's pain, her diagnose and her daily routines cannot be a matter of an individual choice for her to navigate completely on her own. Rather, the phenomenon of schoolgirls' ill-/well-being is constituted by a larger apparatus of multiple discursive practices. This way of theorising makes it possible to understand Malin's condition as a complex process of multiple intra-acting agents that are collectively productive of and responsible for her ill-being (compare Mol 2002).

We read the story of Malin into reports from the Swedish state-health institute describing the treatment programmes offered to Swedish schools and health centres. All these programmes are focused on 'self-help', and most commonly based on *Cognitive Behavioural Therapy*, *Dialectical Behavioural Therapy* or *Acceptance and Commitment Therapy* (ACT). The latter treatment is recommended by basically all Swedish University hospitals and clinics. The ACT treatment understands language and thinking both as the source of illness but also, by ways of formulating new 'higher values', the way to health (Wilson and Murrel 2011). Basically, you need to get away from thinking too much, since thinking is saturated with valuing: and acceptance is about refraining from valuing. The call to girls and women with low self-esteem, or in chronic pain, is to 'defuse yourself from thinking and language' and 'establish a transcendent sense of self' (Hayes and Shenk 2004). Hence, it is *not* about trying to think differently to *become* different in yourself; but rather to *detach* yourself from your thinking, *accept* the hardships of life and connect to a transcendental self *beyond* your body (Hayes and Shenk 2004). But do we really want to tell our youth that their thinking about the future, whether in success, mediocrity or drop-out failure, is not real and cannot become possible future realities?

Concluding discussion

Girls' well-being in schools is a multiple phenomenon (Mol 2002). As researching 'modest witnesses' (Haraway 1997) we are part of an apparatus of knowing that consists of multiple performative agents; photographs, images, research, media-texts, our own memories, etc. We have only been able to make a few provisional cuts in this complex and dense multiplicity of ongoing intra-activities that are part of a larger apparatus, producing the phenomenon of school girls' ill- and well-being. Because we do the choosing of those cuts, as Barad (2007, 178) points out, we are responsible for the boundary-making that takes place. These cuts depend on what is 'given' in that instance, in terms of who and what we think we are as white, middle-class, female academics and mothers of daughters, but also on our imaginary faculties. It is upon this ontologically co-constitutive and ethical relationship that the diffractive patterns depend, as they emerge in our writing of this paper. Therefore, how have we come to know the phenomenon of girls' ill- and well-being throughout this process? And have we, in this experimental achievement, been able to construct a problem relevant enough to produce other ways of knowing and even some new imaginings, as Stengers (2007) suggests? That is, knowledge and imaginings that can help us interfere with and escape from the notions of a regulating knowledge economy that puts the blame and responsibility on the girls themselves (Eldh and Ingvar 2012; Hasson 2008). And finally, how might our analysis suggest that 'it could be otherwise' (Mol 2009)?

In this diffractive analysis, we have seen how ill- and well-being emerge as enactments of (material-discursive) intra-activities between entangled material environments and discursive notions in different and situated ways. One material-discursive practice of doing schoolwork and studying might evoke ill-being in one situated context, but it might also evoke a sense of well-being, control and even a sense of emancipation for the same girl in another situation. Some girls are on the threshold of what produces ill- or well-being: a threshold that is never clear or definite but situated and shifting. Such are the diffractive patterns that emerge in this analysis: indeterminate from a wider perspective, but determinate in the situated local cuts we make. This is what Barad (2007, 175) describes as 'the resolution of the ontological indeterminacy' – a provisional agential reparability *within* the phenomenon where the local and situated cut is made: The cut that makes it possible for us to at all write about the phenomenon despite its indeterminacy. This also means that '[d]ifferent agential cuts produce different phenomena' (Barad 2007). In terms of ethics, we will have to take the local situatedness into account every time we evaluate what material consequences the knowing we produce of a specific phenomenon will have for the agents involved. Thus, we need to be careful before we draw conclusions about individual school girls' apparent over-achieving behaviour and what they might be productive of.

However, the overall diffractive pattern that emerges from this collective analysis shows that the phenomenon of school-related ill-/well-being can never be an individual affair; it is rather a collective and distributed phenomenon that engages multiple performative agents that are collectively responsible for counteracting practices as well as prevention. Opposed to what the dominant notions and practices suggest, we should as human agents *not* try to free or defuse ourselves from thinking. On the contrary, we need to think more, but think *differently* and together with other material-discursive agents in the school environment. Children, youth and adults need to collaboratively engage in practices of intra-active engagements of imagination, where multiple images and discourses about the school environment, ill- and well-being, are allowed to be expressed, enunciated and actualised. Such enunciations might enhance well-being and make the school environment become a more livable place.

Acknowledgements

We would like to sincerely thank Alice and Emma who agreed to participate in this pilot study.

Notes

1. National School Agency (2009) concludes that almost 50% of the girls and 20% of the boys claim to feel stressed frequently in school. Figures show that 24% of the girls and 10% of the boys aged 16–24 claim to feel moderate or strong stress. Forty-six per cent of the girls and 25% of the boys feel anxiety and/or panic attacks regularly. Fifty-eight per cent of the girls and 42% of the boys have problems with feeling tired and 27% of the girls and 19% of the boys have sleeping problems. See also Bragée (2009).
2. Emma and Alice are not the girls' real names.
3. Since Emma and Alice are under 18 we first contacted their parents and informed them about the study and asked for their permission to contact the girls. We made clear that the participation was voluntary, we described how the data would be used (as data in a research article), and that they would have access to our writing throughout the process. We also said that they could read the article before it was published and that the article would be written in English. However, the talk was carried out in Swedish and the data that were produced were translated to English by us. After giving this information we asked if they would consider participating in the study.
4. Fifteen per cent of school children in Stockholm state that they often suffer from bodily pain in the stomach, head, back and shoulders, and 4% or 5% have severe pains almost every day. One per cent of the school children develop chronic pain syndromes like fibromyalgia and irritable colon syndrome. This makes them physically and psychologically impaired to study and work, sometimes for life: chronic pain syndromes that cost the Swedish society ten million Swedish crowns per year (Mlik 2010).

References

Alfvén, G., U. Caverius, M. Karling, and G. L. Olsson. 2010. "Barn med smärta osynlig grupp" [Children with pain is an invisible group]. *Svenska Dagbladet, Brännpunkt*, October 4.

Ant Jacobsson, P. 2012. "Smärtlindring utan piller. Att ta kommandot över det som gör ont." [Pain Release without Pills. To Take Control Over Your Pain.] *Dagens Nyheter*, March 11.

Banerjee, B., and M. Blaise. 2013. "There's Something in the Air: Becoming-with Research Practices." *Cultural Studies = Critical Methodologies*, online publishing May 19. doi:10.1177/1532708613487867

Barad, K. 1999. "Agential Realism: Feminist Intervenstions in Understanding Scientific Practices." In *The Science Studies Reader*, edited by M. Biagioli, 1–12. New York and London: Routledge.

Barad, K. 2007. *Meeting the Universe Halfway. Quantum Physics and the Entanglement of Matter and Meaning*. Durham: Duke University Press.

Bodén, L. 2010. "Rapport ELLEN." [Report on the Ellen Project on Longtime Truant Girls] Botkyrka kommun [Botkyrka Municipality in Stockholm, Sweden].

Bodén, L. In press. "Seeing Red? The Agency of Computer Software in the Production and Management of Students' School Absence." Submitted to *International Journal of Qualitative Studies in Education*.

Bragée, W.-B. 2009. "Kroppens mening. Studier i psykosomatiska lösningar." [The meaning of the body. Studies in psychosomatic solutions.]. Dissertation, Stockholm University.

Bunar, N. 2010. "Choosing for Quality or Inequality: Current Perspectives on the Implementation of School Choice Policy in Sweden." *Journal of Education Policy* 25 (1): 1–18.

Carling, M. 2011. "Prestationer kan vara ett sätt att dämpa ångest." [High Achievement Can be a Strategy of Anxiety Reduction] *Svenska Dagbladet*, September 13.

Eldh, G., and I. Ingvar. 2012. *Hjärnkoll på värk och smärta* [Controle Your Pain and Distress]. Stockholm: Natur & Kultur förlag.

Foucault, M. 1991. *Discipline and Punish: The Birth of the Prison.* Harmondsworth: Pinguin.

Haraway, D. 1997. *Modest_Witness@second_Millenium. Female-Man©_meets_Onco Mouse™. Feminism and Technoscience.* New York: Routlegde.

Hasson, D. 2008. *Stressa rätt!* [Stress in the right way]. Stockholm: VIVA.

Hayes, S. C., and C. Shenk. 2004. "Operationalizing Mindfulness without Unnecessary Attachments." *Clinical Psychology: Science and Practice* 11 (3): 249–254.

Hekman, S. 2010. *The Material of Knowledge. Feminist Disclosures.* Indiana: Indiana University Press.

Human Rights Watch. 2001. "Submission from Human Rights Watch to the Committee on the Rights of the Child for its Day of General Discussion September 28, Violence Against Children in Schools." http://www.crin.org/docs/resources/treaties/crc.28/HRW.pdf

Human Rights Watch. 2010. "Violence and Discrimination against Lesbian, Gay, Bisexual." http://www.hrw.org/news/2010/10/01/us-hatred-hallways

Kearney, C. A., and A. Bensaheb. 2006. "School Absenteeism and School Refusal Behavior: A Review and Suggestions for School-Based Health Professionals." *Journal of School Health* 76 (1): 3–7.

Law, J. 2004. *After Method: Mess in Social Science Research.* London: Routledge.

Lenz Taguchi, H. 2012. "A Diffractive and Deleuzian Approach to Analyzing Interview-data." *Journal of Feminist Theory* 13 (3): 265–281.

Lenz Taguchi, H. 2013. "Images of Thinking in Feminist Materialisms: Ontological Divergencies and the Production of Researcher Subjectivities." *International Journal of Qualitative Studies in Education* 26 (6): 706–716.

Lerner, T., and E. Lofors. 2010. "Paulina blev kallsvetting varje gång hon kom i närheten av skolan" [Paulina had Coldsweats of Anxiety Every Time She Came Near Her School] *Dagens Nyheter*, March 11.

MacLure, M. 2013. "Researching without Representation? Language and Materiality in Post-qualitative Methodology." *International Journal of Qualitative Studies in Education* 26 (6): 658–667.

Mazzei, L. 2013. "A Voice without Organs: Interviewing in Posthumanist Research." *International Journal of Qualitative Studies in Education* 26 (6): 732–740.

Mlik, N. 2010. "Det finns ett samband mellan höga prestationskrav och psykisk ohälsa hos unga" [There is a Connection Between High Achievement Demands and Young People's Psychological Illhealth] *Dagens Nyheter*, October 25.

Mol, A. 2002. *The Body Multiple. Ontology in Medical Practice.* Durham: Duke University Press.

Mol, A. 2009. "What Methods Do." Lecture by Annemarie Mol. *Alexander von Humboldt Lecture Series, 2008–2009 on "Reflexive Methodology: On Doing Qualitative, Post-Positivist Research".* February 5, University of Amsterdam, The Neatherlands.

National School Agency. 2009. "Attityder till skolan. Elevernas och lärarnas attityder till skolan." [Attitudes towards school. Pupils and teachers attitudes towards school.] Report 344.

National School Agency. 2010. "Skolfrånvaro och vägen tillbaka. Långvarig ogiltig frånvaro i grundskolan" [Truancy and the Way Back. Long-Time, Invalid Truancy in Compulsory School]. Report 341, Fritzes, Stockholm.

Nyström, A. 2012. "Att synas och lära utan att synas lära: En studie om underprestation och pri-vilegierade unga mäns identitetsförhandlingar i gymnasieskolan." [To be seen and to Learn, without being seen to Learn. A Study of Under-Achievement and Identity-Negotiation among Privileged Young Men in Upper-Secondary School]. Dissertation, Uppsala University.

Palmer, A. 2011. "'How Many Sums can I Do'? Performative Strategies and Diffractive Thinking as Methodological Tools for Rethinking Mathematical Subjectivity." *Reconceptualizing Educational Research Methodology* 1 (1): 3–18.

Reid, K. 1999. *Tackling Truancy in Schools.* London: Routledge Falmer.

Reid, K. 2006. "An Evaluation of the Views of Secondary Staff towards School Attendance Issues." *Oxford Review of Education* 32 (3): 303–324.

SOU. 2010. "Flickor, pojkar, individer - om betydelsen av jämställdhet för kunskap och utveck-ling i skolan." [Girls, boys, individuals – about the importance of equality for learning and development in school.]. Fritzes, Stockholm.

Stengers, I. 2007. "Diderot's egg. Divorcing Materialism from Eliminativism." A Revised Version of a Paper Presented to the *Radical Philosophy Conference, Materials and Materialism*, London, May 12.

Wilson, K. G., and A. R. Murrel. 2011. "Values work in Acceptence and Commitment Therapy: Setting a Course for Behavioural Treatment." In *Mindfulness and Acceptance: Expanding the Cognitive-Behavioral Tradition*, edited by S. C. Hayes, V. M. Follette, and M. M. Linehan, 120–151. New York: Guilford Press.

Objects, bodies and space: gender and embodied practices of mattering in the classroom

Carol A. Taylor

Sheffield Institute of Education, Sheffield Hallam University, Sheffield, UK

This article focuses on objects, bodies and space to explore how the mundane materialities of classrooms do crucial but often unnoticed performative work in enacting gendered power. Drawing on ethnographic data from a UK sixth form college study, the article analyses a series of 'material moments' to elaborate a material feminist analysis of embodied practices of mattering. I argue that 'practices, doings and actions' (Barad, K. 2007. *Meeting the Universe Halfway: Quantum Physics and the Entanglement of Matter and Meaning*. London: Duke University Press), while often hidden or taken for granted, are a constitutive material force in producing what and who matters within classrooms. By highlighting objects, bodies and space as entangled material agencies, the article raises new questions about gendered pedagogic practices. It proposes the necessity to rethink classroom space as an emergent intersection of multiple, mobile materialities, and argues that doing so is a crucial task for a material feminist praxis.

1. Introduction

This article focuses on objects, bodies and space as vital materialities which possess active, dynamic agency. Through an analysis of the complex choreographies within which object and bodily materialisations are enacted, power relations are mobilised and educational space is continually re-constructed, the article sheds light on how material cultures of everyday classroom life are both active and constitutive in processes that recreate gender inequalities. Drawing on an ethnographic case study of a UK A Level Sociology classroom, the article elaborates a material feminist analysis which empirically takes forward Barad's (2007, 170) argument that 'bodies do not simply take their place in the world ... rather "environments" and "bodies" are intra-actively constituted'. In doing so, it shows that space is not simply a physical container; objects and things are not inert, fixed or passive matter awaiting 'use' by human intervention; nor is the body a mere corporeal vehicle to be moved by the mind. The article draws new attention to how objects, bodies and spaces do crucial but often unnoticed performative work as vital materialities within the classroom. To explore how objects and bodies work to produce the classroom as a gendered space of differential matterings, I focus on a number of 'material moments' – including the manner in which a chair is occupied, the irregular use of a pen and the wearing of a particular t-shirt – to illuminate how that which is resolutely mundane within everyday pedagogic practice nevertheless possesses a surprising material force. My central argument is that bringing to the fore how material things act on and with us reveals educational practices to be a constellation of human–nonhuman agencies, forces and events.

The arguments I put forward are informed by post-human material feminist theorisations of matter (Barad 2007), understandings of objects from material culture (Bissell 2009; Miller 2010) and analyses of space which originate in human geography (Hubbard, Kitchin, and Valentine 2004; Massey 2005). Drawing together these interdisciplinary threads provides an analytical purchase on the detailed specificity and density of the material moments and enables us to grasp the force of the material in its speed and evanescence. This close empirical focus on embodied practices of mattering discloses how 'bodies are understood and lived spatially as much as are topographical sites in the landscape' (Shields 1997, 186) and I put Barad's (2007) concepts of 'intra-action', 'cut', 'phenomena' and 'apparatus' to work in developing a material feminist analysis of the body in the 'fullness of its materiality'. The article thus contributes a distinctive feminist intervention in the emerging field of 'Barad studies'. Furthermore, in its deployment of a 'diffractive' approach the article works as a methodologically strategic act of experimentation which unsettles some of the usual conventions of article writing, and I do this to demonstrate how a post-human research practice brings to the surface our ethical entanglement as researchers in enacting practices of knowledge production.

The article begins with a discussion of the main theoretical confluences which inform the ensuing empirical analysis. After an account of the data, and a discussion of the importance of utilising a diffractive methodology within material feminist analyses, the article turns to a detailed empirical exploration of a number of material moments to show how objects–bodies–spaces 'work' within the spatial assemblage of the classroom. A performative account of instantiating a diffractive methodology as an act of experimentation, and the differences this makes to the production of knowledge, is woven through the empirical analysis. The article concludes by highlighting the importance of things and bodies as vital players through which gender gets done, power is worked and inequalities re-embedded within the space of the classroom.

2. Theoretical contexts: space, objects, bodies and materiality

This section provides an account of the theories which inform the subsequent empirical analysis. Both here and later, my aim is to bring material culture studies (Miller 2010) and material feminism (Barad 2007; Bennett 2010; Coole and Frost 2010) into relation with spatial understandings (Massey 2005) to indicate, theoretically and empirically, what educational analyses have to gain from viewing classrooms as an entangled 'mosaic' of 'vital matter' (Bennett 2010, 22). This interdisciplinary theoretical enterprise is, I suggest, generative for understanding the agentic force of material objects, analysing the minutiae of bodily practices, and highlighting what can be gained from this novel way of apprehending objects–bodies–space as intra-actively entailed material agencies within the assemblage of the classroom.

Borrowing from human geography, I have found Massey's (2005, 9) notion of space as a 'practiced place' which is always open, contemporaneously plural, emergent and 'under construction' useful. Her theorisation of space as 'the sphere of relations, negotiations, practices of engagement, power in all its forms' (Massey 2005, 99) helps raise some new questions about the micro-practices of matter, bodies and space and reveal what an intensely political, contested and unequal space the gendered classroom can be. The recent 'spatial turn' has brought renewed attention to educational space, as demonstrated by recent edited collections by Boys (2010) and Brooks, Fuller, and Waters (2012) and studies by Allen (2012), Hirst and Cooper (2008), Jones (2013b) and Mahony, Hextall, and Richardson (2011). It is perhaps worth remembering that a rich seam of analyses which touches on space already exists, albeit emanating from other research traditions, including classroom ethnographies (for example, Delamont and Galton 1986), and studies from within critical pedagogy of schools, politics and place (Di Leo and Jacobs 2004). Foucault's (1979, 1984) discursive genealogies also offer radical re-evaluations of modern institutional space and have informed studies on educational architecture (Burke and Grosvenor 2008), teachers' discursive practices within classroom and staffroom space (McGregor 2001), as well as feminist studies of space (Dunne 2007; Quinn 2003; Tamboukou 1999). However, the 'spatial turn' has usefully refocused attention on micro-level spatial practices, and brought theories of space into productive relation with studies of pedagogy and materialities (Fenwick and Landri 2012; Ivinson 2012; Mulcahy 2012; Palmer 2011; Zembylas 2007). Studies such as these lend support to my argument for understanding space as a material 'multiplicity' (Massey 2005, 9).

Analyses which focus on the contemporaneous plurality of spatial practices resonate with recent shifts towards recognising the force of 'thing-power' (Bennett 2010). Giving due regard to the material force of objects, and seeing objects not as commodities and artefacts but as things with their own sense of agency is, I suggest, a valuable move towards a post-human understanding that 'objects make us, as part of the very same process by which we make them' (Miller 2010, 60). While it is not my intention to argue that the agency of objects is 'like' human agency in degree or kind, thing-power discloses agency as 'congregational' or 'confederate' (Bennett 2010, 20) rather than a matter of individual human will, and this opens up new ways of seeing and thinking about how classroom space is made, transformed and continually re-made through the concerted co-constitutive acts of objects–bodies–spaces. Likewise, I argue that the body is a vital material agency in the classroom. Taking forward Shields's (1997, 186) view that 'bodies are understood and lived spatially as much as are topographical sites in the landscape', I develop a material feminist account which includes in its frame Foucault's (1979, 1984, 1988) considerations of bodily discipline and Butler's (1990, 1993) notions of gender performativity, as reformulated by Barad (2007) to include a post-human recognition that all bodies, things and matter – not just human bodies – are active material-discursive agents. Embodied practices, doings and actions are central to the account I develop because, as Stengers (2007) reminds us, practices are always collective.

As indicated earlier, the article also works as an act of methodological experimentation to indicate the potential of material feminism to unsettle conventional ways of thinking about and reporting research. In its use of a diffractive methodology to show that knowledge is an emergent and embodied 'practice of knowing in being' (Jackson and Mazzei 2012, 116), the article brings to the fore our ontological, epistemological and ethical responsibilities as producers of knowledge, which is what I turn to now.

3. Diffracting the methodology: reflecting on data

To highlight what new openings material feminism offers as a way of producing knowledge, I begin by presenting a familiar account of my data as a qualitative research case study. I follow this by highlighting some of the key differences that doing a material feminist diffractive analysis might make.

There are currently more than 150,000 students studying at sixth form colleges (Igoe and Kewin 2013). As post-compulsory educational institutions, sixth forms are often but not always places of greater relative freedom than schools but, like many other classrooms, they are redolent with material-discursive practices of gendered power. The empirical data I draw on were part of a wider ethnographic case study of the strategies sixth form students deploy in forming their identities in relation to A Level curriculum subjects, knowledge hierarchies, pedagogic practices and spatial for-mations, both inside and outside their college location. The data were collected during 2005–2006 in two sixth form colleges in South-East England. Both colleges had a pre-dominantly white student and teacher population and, in both colleges, young women outnumbered male students by 2:1 in the seven curriculum subjects sampled. In its entirety, the data set includes classroom observations, interviews with students, tea-chers and Principal Examiners, my research diary and field notes. The data extracts included here originate in six two-hour observations in an A Level Sociology class at Seaside College, and a teacher interview, chosen because of the acute concerns they raise about the 'micro-physics' of gendered power in classroom space. The account just given lays out clearly the scope of the study, its sample, and the rationale for choice of data extracts to be used in the ensuing meaning-making procedures. So, what new ways of looking at research practice does a diffractive approach make possible?

Research protocols often remain caught within assumptions of a transparent relay between data and meaning in which data is envisaged as inert, passive 'stuff' we (humans) go out and 'collect', return with and then pore over to analyse, code and the-matise. In treating data as 'evidence' in this way, data is rendered, contained, con-trolled, indeed it is condemned to the death-like status of object (Koro-Ljungberg and MacLure 2013). In contrast, a vital materialism prompts us to think of data as lively matter – as a material actant – and research practices as 'encounters between ontologically diverse actants, some human, some not, though all thoroughly material' (Bennett 2010, xiii–xiv). I bring out the import of these material entwinings in my reflections on observation notes in the following section. A second novel implication of the use of a diffractive methodology turns on the difference it makes to acknowledge our capacity to be affected by data. Such concerns are usually excised from written research accounts but many of us as researchers feel haunted by 'our' data long after collecting 'it', and I take up this idea later to show how and why these affective engage-ments matter. And thinking data's liveliness leads to a third point, the often insistent invitation data makes to us to follow it on nomadic theoretical journeyings, on to-and-fro zig-zags and 'backwards' readings as we work 'on' it to make sense of it. Fol-lowing the data-theory in this way interferes radically both with the presumed linearity of 'rational' sense-making procedures, and even the iterative accounts of post-structur-alism which still usually 'end' in forms of transparent representability. Instead, a dif-fractive methodology helps highlight 'knowledge-ing' as a messy multiplicity, a point I pick up again later. Fourth, and added to this, a diffractive methodology is most persistent in calling us to account in new ways for the choices we make by includ-ing *these* data and *these* incidents and not others. I follow this line of thinking through in relation to Barad's (2007) concept of the 'agential cut', an analytic practice which both separates out 'something' – an object, practice, person – for analysis from the ongoing flow of spacetimemattering, but which, at the same time as separating and excluding, entangles us ontologically with/in and as the phenomena produced by the cut we make. I show the ethical import of cuts which hold us to account in my later analysis of Malky, 'Sheila', and 'Brains', cuts which make it apparent that in an entangled materialist ontology 'knowing does not come from standing at a distance and representing but rather from a direct material engagement with the world' (Barad 2007, 49).

A diffractive methodology, then, encourages new ways of thinking about and relating to data and meaning-making. It offers a critical practice of interference which pays attention to what we don't normally see, to what is excluded; as such, it urges 'a commitment to understanding which differences matter, how they matter, and for whom' (Barad 2007, 90). In addition, it offers to be a creative methodology which opens ways of undoing traditional, humanist epistemic codes so we may do, present and write research differently. In the next section, I put a diffractive methodology to work, and thread the somewhat abstract methodological points made just now into the ensuing empirical analysis where I focus on those 'small but consequential differences' (Barad 2007, 29) from which knowledge about objects, bodies and spaces is produced in the gendered practices of everyday classrooms.

4. His magisterial chair

That teachers control the 'action zone' at the front of the (their) classroom is a commonplace, of a piece with Bourdieu, Passeron, and Saint Martin's (1965, 10) observation, made some time ago, that 'space is a source of pedagogical distance'. However, their subsequent comment – that pedagogic authority is conferred by the 'magisterial chair which consecrates him' – has largely gone unnoticed, although Jones's (2013b) article is a notable exception. Asking the question 'what does a chair do?' prompts a reconceptualisation of things, bodies and pedagogic space as an assemblage of intra-active, ongoing and productive happenings entailing multiple agencies.

> Malky had his desk and chair at the front and his resources laid out around him on adjoining tables and didn't move out of his zone. Straight in front of his desk, the students' desks were in a complete square and it was not possible to get inside it, so physical movement towards and proximity to students was out of the question. (Observation No. 1 Notes)

> He had his 'instruments' laid out like a pilot's flight deck around him. He glided in his chair between his things, pushing himself off with his heels from a still point with speed and grace, like a practiced dancer. His body language is totally relaxed and expansive. (Observation No. 2 Notes)

> I'm getting more of a feel for Malky and how he conducts his lessons … He is leaning back in his chair and controlling the space at a distance. He decides who should talk and when they should talk. He's like a radiating star … everything comes from him and goes back to him. When the students discuss things in pairs this is set off by Malky and he controls how long they talk to each other. Other than that the whole focus of the class is on Malky. (Observation No. 3 Notes)

I said in the previous section that data was 'lively matter' and that agential cuts work both to separate and entangle. In integrating these observation notes at this point I enact an agential cut which focuses attention on the chair-body assemblage. This cut counts as a meaning-making practice in precisely these ways: it separates the chair-body assemblage from the ongoing 'context'; it foregrounds the material agency of my observation notes in producing this particular textual incarnation; and it entangles me, and you as reader, materially, cognitively and sensorially with the data and, through the data, with the participants and the classroom they emerged from. Thus, the data have done and continue to do their agentic work *with* me on this page: they assist me to make the cut. Why is this significant? In both separating out (chair-body) and suturing together (me, objects, participants, you), the cut's significance is that it constitutes ontologically entangled phenomena, it installs a relational materiality at the heart of this account and, Barad would argue, at the heart of all worldly events. I pick up some implications of this further on. Now, I return to the data to trace what emerges from making the cut regarding Malky's chair-body assemblage.

Malky's chair was no mere piece of furniture. As an object with thing-power, it took its place as a material-discursive agency within a classroom space saturated with gendered meanings. It was a seat positioned for a material performative of gendered bodily power, as well as a physical location from which the teacher could direct his gaze at his students and ensure all were looking at him at all times. As the data extract indicates, the mobility of Malky's chair-body assemblage worked to materialise what Mulvey (1975) calls the male gaze, a visual technology of power which gave Malky visual freedom to roam over the static bodies of the students fixed as they were behind immobile desks in unmoving chairs. In Malky's classroom, the small-scale panoptics enacted through the arrangement of tables and chairs served as a material reminder of Foucault's (1979, 25) point that 'it is always the body that is at issue – the body and its forces, their utility and their docility, their distribution and their submission'.

The materiality of the chair – an elegant, black and chrome, decidedly 'office' chair, on casters and with a tilting facility, the only one of its kind in classrooms throughout the college, all the others being fixed and upright, moulded red or orange plastic – conditioned the possibilities of mobility and stasis. Unless exiting the chair for the occasional virtuoso performance like the ones I discuss below, Malky remained seated in his chair throughout the class. The chair and his body formed a human–nonhuman assemblage which freed him up to glide, slide, spin, twirl, tilt, lean, roll and spring. The vitalism of the chair-body assemblage created momentary eruptions in the lessons (my observation notes record) which disrupted traditional notions of how teachers sit, stand and physically behave as, for example, when chair-and-Malky whizzed to the computer to display a powerpoint in which 'Max [Weber] goes walkabout', or when Malky leaned back in the chair to the tipping point in an embodied display of adult hegemonic masculine nonchalance (young men and boys, unlike girls, routinely tip backwards in chairs to embody resistance and/or aggression in pedagogic authority contexts). The variability, flexibility and mobility instantaneously enacted by the teacher's chair-body assemblage contrasted markedly with the obdurate materialities of the students' chairs and desks, the walls with their posters of the 'founding fathers' of Sociology, windows and a classroom door which Malky closed with a flourish at the start of each lesson. These harder, more solid materialities and their immobile moorings (Urry 2003) enacted physical barriers which constrained who was free to move (the teacher) and, crucially, who couldn't (the students). Ivinson (2012, 490) notes that such regulative disciplining of educational bodies into stasis has its roots in a monastic legacy which sought to separate the contemplative and the intellectual life from 'the dirt and labour of mundane life', a point I return to below.

It was not simply that Malky occupied the 'chair', his manner of occupation was important. Notes from the second observation record that:

The power clearly resides with him. He is totally relaxed and expansive in his body language, leaning back in his chair and controlling the space at a distance.

I wrote that 'he never leaned forward' and there are repeated comments on his 'even, quiet and controlled' tone of voice. I record that he often 'adopted the open bodily stance of a genial, chat show host', and that this relaxed, embodied stance remained in vibrant tension with the eruptive dynamism of chair-body movement and the occasional, exuberant out-of-chair performance (see below). Ironic humour was central to Malky's embodied and vocal practices. He interlaced extended stories, jokes and anecdotes with information about key sociological figures, their research and the pre-eminence of Sociology as a mode of knowledge production. My fieldwork diary records that, from his chair, he choreographed his lessons as a 'stand-up comedy routine', that his lessons were a 'wise-cracking performance' and that his 'repartee' was delivered in a 'sardonic tone reminiscent of Jack Dee'. I aimed to capture the 'logic of sense' of one lesson as follows:

> Malky covered topics as various as a J. K. Galbraith, a Lyndon Johnson 'piss story', a man who hallucinated on the 'jazz woodbines', moonies, smoking, pub quizzes, student dreams, chair design, renaissance female artists, the ugliness of Southampton, the church's abolition of limbo, postmodern relativism, contemporary musicals, ice cream and sex, and 15% mortgage rates under the Tories. All of this with a deadpan delivery in an atmosphere in which you could hear a pin drop as he was talking, followed by out-bursts of extended laughter from students at each punch line. (Research Diary)

Then, as researcher, I was 'taken up' by all of this and I relished the potentially rich, if difficult, data this would give me. *Now* (revisiting the data via a diffractive method-ology) I see not only how Malky's embodied practices work by his agential cuts in the spacetimematter of the classroom which enact a spatially authoritative, urbanely flexible and powerfully dominant masculine performative, but also, what my data does as an 'ontologically diverse actant' to use Bennett's phrase cited earlier: it hails me, it hauls me in and perplexes me with its material embrace.

Barad (2007, 159) argues that 'bodies in the making are never separate from their apparatuses of bodily production' and, as I have noted above, chair, objects and bodies are entangled intra-active forces in the spatial assemblage of the classroom. The concept of intra-activity is particularly useful in making sense of Malky's embodied doings because it encourages us to contend directly with material practices which bring into being subjects and objects. As Barad (2007) notes, agencies do not precede their interaction but emerge through an intra-active process. Thus, Malky's individualistic and idiosyncratic flair, the material force of the chair-body assemblage and the spatiali-sation of his capacity to entertain and hold students' attention emerge as intra-active con-stituting forces in the ongoing flow of spacetimemattering. These intra-active materialisations enact tropes of masculine confidence, power and authority vis-à-vis stu-dents, they produce boundaries between his chair-body physical ease and their immobile attention, his voice and their silence, his wit and their receptivity to his humour, his knowledge and their lack. This is why Malky's (and by extension all teachers') intra-active cuts count: they enact 'differentness' (Barad 2007, 137), maintain hierarchies and instantiate gendered power. Of course, boundary-making practices are endemic in teaching contexts. However, seeing Malky's embodied practices as intra-active cuts which enact micro-level gendered differentiations encourage us to rethink teacher–student–space–object relations as an intra-active co-constitutive accomplishment which show materially that some bodies (and some chairs!) matter more than others. Focusing on Malky's chair brings to the surface the usually unnoticed dynamic force of things and their capacity for confederate intra-action with human agencies. It encourages us to notice how much the thing-power of the chair contributes to Malky's gendered practices and how the chair-body assemblage together choreographs a material practice of mattering in this classroom space. Having asked 'what does a chair do?' in the classroom in the following section I ask 'what do things do?'

5. 'Come here Sheila'

My observation notes above remark on how Malky's panoply of materialities – objects, coursework, resources, desk furniture, along with chair and desk arrangements – separated him spatially from the students. More than that, what was interesting was how Malky pressed various material 'instruments' into action in an embodied orchestration of gendered pedagogic action. Three instances of mattering within the human–nonhuman assemblage of the classroom are worthy of note.

'Sheila' occupied a position on the right hand side of Malky's desk, spending most of the time unnoticed and unobserved until summoned into action by Malky with the commanding phrase 'come here Sheila'. In this, 'Sheila' was just like the many other things which inhabit our spaces but which we often don't 'see' because the 'work' they do accords with our sense of what is natural, commonplace and culturally familiar. Their very invisibility determines expectations and produces the required effects of normality. My observation notes record two 'come here Sheila' moments when 'Sheila', the flipchart stand with paper displaying a pre-drawn sociological model or theory, was hauled or dragged over by Malky to front centre stage. Malky performed his man-handling of 'Sheila' with physically expansive aplomb in an exhibitive spatial display which each time generated laughter from the students. Re-positioned, revealed and brought to sight, 'Sheila' exhibited all the virtues of a compliant Stepford wife and dutiful hand-maiden to the man, shocked into silence by her unexpected and unwanted visibility.

Mundane as this example is, it is no little matter that the flipchart was given the name 'Sheila' because, while the anthropomorphisation of matter has a long and complex cultural history, in this instance, it tells us a lot about the gendered dynamics of this classroom in which control of space is key, and the appropriation, use and movement of things is so very clearly and visibly (albeit humorously) put into the service of a masculine performative of ownership. And more than that, we can see that it installs the notion of binarised space within the classroom, in which the sexual specificity of gendered identities are predicated on an essentialist normative male/female binary, which ontologically articulates male to action, thought and Logos and female to stasis, matter and mute passivity (Grosz 1994). Likewise, it is a matter of note that the flipchart was given the name 'Sheila' which is derogatory slang for woman in Australia. Seen diffractively through the lens of post-human materialist feminism, Malky's repeated embodied practice of possessing, containing and mobilising 'Sheila' is perhaps an indication of hegemonic masculine anxiety in the face of thing-power, or perhaps a gendered need to establish and display authority in the potentially unruly space of the classroom (even if it did carry shades of a knowingly exaggerated post-modern performance of authority). Nevertheless it shows how things make people and how people make things (Miller 2010) as well as how things work within a spatial assemblage of lively material events.

A second material moment concerns past students' coursework which sat in three large piles on the left hand side of the desk and from which Malky regularly extracted work graded A (the highest grade) to read out or refer to. While human endeavour was no doubt required to activate the coursework, we could also say that the coursework 'issued a call' (the phrase is Bennett's 2010, 4) which summoned human agency into response. Many teachers use past students' coursework as exemplars to motivate and challenge current students, and such uses are undoubtedly effective pedagogic practice (Gibbs, 2010, notes that high expectations work well in engaging students). But perhaps we also need to keep in mind coursework as matter which inhabits class-rooms, desks, drawers, cabinets and cupboards, which regulations demand we keep, which we posit future pedagogic use for and thus don't/can't throw away. Seen in this way, coursework as matter acts in confederation with space, objects and bodies as an apparatus, that is as a 'practice of mattering through which intelligibility and materiality are constituted' (Barad 2007, 170). In the instance under discussion, course-work serves to materialise and insistently memorialise the credentialism, high grades culture and intensification of national A Level meritocratic educational regimes here and now in the proximate space of the classroom. And there is, too, a very particular gendered inflection to the summons issued by coursework, one which plays into young women's anxieties to produce themselves as 'good girls' and 'good students' by materialising themselves as coherent subjects within dominant neoliberal discourses of 'successful girl' (Ringrose 2007; Taylor 2011).

Pens mattered in Malky's classroom. My observation notes contain a surprising number of references to students' pens which leads me to suggest that it is worth taking notice of pens as material agencies within 'object assemblages which make things happen' (Bissell 2009, 112). The following exchange with a male student occurred during the first observation:

Malky: If you don't stop whistling down that pen top I'll have to punch you.
Student: Sorry.

And this one in the second observation, said to female student holding a pen with a fluffy top to it:

Malky: Spongy, is that a sociologist's pen?
Student: No (laughter).

Pens as singular items of matter may be considered inconsequential, peripheral to pro-cesses of cognition and intellection, a mere adjunct to and device for recording the dis-cussions arising in collaborative pair or group learning contexts, or nowadays as increasingly redundant in the face of iPads, tablets and other mobile learning devices. This, though, would be to mistake the identity investments students make in and publicly attach to such mundane material articles as pens, pencil cases and bags, albeit that these patterns of consumption, display and use are highly gendered. Both examples I discuss highlight what can be at stake in having and holding a pen. The second example designates a fluffy-top pen as obviously inappropriate to the matter of being a serious, cerebral (and, by implication, male) sociologist, and uses a comedic put-down to make a powerful point about the gendered hierarchies of aca-demic knowledge, a point I return to later.

However, the whistling noise made in an un-thought way by pen-mouth-hand assemblage in the first example was clearly sufficient to provoke Malky into offering an extreme and violent retribution as payback for the momentary auditory annoyance it caused (I hadn't even registered it as a noise). In this example, both cuts – that made by the pen/noise and that made by Malky's comment – produce rapid, successive interventions which constitute the dynamic of mattering very differently for the individuals involved. The student, on the one hand, felt compelled to provide an immediate apology; publicly positioned as 'wrong' and verbally chastened/threatened he enacts an embodied, instantaneous and felt recognition that his momentary capture of auditory space is something not to be tolerated: this is, after all, Malky's classroom. On the other hand, threatening as this comment is especially in written form above, *in situ* Malky's tone and verbal delivery, given from a relaxed reclining sideways position in his chair, was mild, courteous and calm, and elicited class laughter. His cut was not embodied materially or spatially as a particularly threatening cut, nevertheless it intra-actively instantiated a threat. In drawing attention to the materiality of this instance of incipient gendered violence called into action by a pen, a material feminist account helps complicate some of the universalistic theorisations of gendered violence which would position Malky's response as hegemonic masculinity, the student's apology as dominated, and the class response as complicit (Connell 1995). No doubt that is also the case but I want to emphasise how this mundane example of the pen's materialisation in a human–nonhuman apparatus of mattering brings to the fore the conduct of human relations between people in a classroom, in all their visceral, emotional and ethical import.

The agential cuts I enact in this section have produced empirical instances which illuminate what things do, how things work within gendered relations of power, and how things materialise actions and relations in human–nonhuman apparatuses which complicate notions of human agency and human relationality. I have suggested that mundane things choreograph an 'invisible pedagogy' (Bernstein 2004) of relations which matter; and I have shown how things as mobile elements enfold matter and meaning at a micro-level in a complex spatial web within classrooms. Furthermore, in 'diffracting the methodology' above, I noted the invitations data offers for theoretical journeyings and that these nomadic zig-zags disclose knowledge-ing as a messy multiplicity. As illustration of this, the three instances discussed in this section emerged and concretised through 'backwards', 'circular' and 'forward' readings in which I sited the lively data (for example, 'Sheila') alongside Butler alongside Foucault alongside Deleuze and Guattari alongside Barad, reading each theoretical account diffractively through the others. This is not a particularly idiosyncratic or unusual approach to meaning-making (is it?). However, with its lines of flight, heterogeneous bricolage and fortuitous findings, it follows a logic of sense and intuition rather than a logic of rationality and deduction. I use this to illustrate that, in its undoing of linearity, and in highlighting 'knowledge-ing' as a messy multiplicity, always mediated through the material body of the researcher, a diffractive methodology is valuable in enabling us to notice, pinpoint and perhaps value more openly than we usually might, how that which is utterly provisional (knowledge) is smoothed, soothed and straight-jacketed into a 'finished' academic article which, whether in its solid paper materiality or virtual online im/materiality, offers (as I do above with 'Sheila' and the pen-mouth-hand assemblage) a 'final' account.

Returning from this diffractive interference, and having raised some important concerns about objects in this section, the discussion next turns to clothes.

6. 'If these were brains, I'd be a genius'

The data in this section have been the most troubling/troublesome. MacLure (2013) talks about the wonder of data, of data which 'glow', and it is certainly the case that the data I dice with here feel like shining points or 'hotspots'. I referred earlier ('diffracting the methodology') to data's affective power, its capacity to haunt us through ongoing entanglements. The agential cuts I have made which have produced these data and these phenomena testify to the power of Malky's glamour (in the archaic sense of casting a spell), which caught me out (as novice researcher) and caught up the students (another funny day in class) in its allure.

Clothes as markers of class, status and identity, and the communicative function of clothes, have been discussed within Cultural Studies, Material Culture studies and Anthropology for some time, and there is a growing body of feminist scholarship on how clothes produce gendered and aged subjectivities (Jones 2013a; Pilcher 2013; Renold 2005). In studies of education, however, clothes have mostly received attention in relation to how pupils express individuality, conformity and resistance to the homogenisation effected by school uniforms (Park 2013). In Sixth Form College settings clothing is crucial, as sixth forms are usually much less regulated spaces than schools for the expression of young people's individuality, sexuality and peer group or sub-cultural affiliations. Many of the participants in my study said they partly chose Sixth Form College over school sixth form because it enabled them to leave school uniform behind. In this section, I pursue a material feminist analysis of clothes. By focusing on clothes as 'vital players' (Bennett 2010, 4) in classroom space, I bring new attention to the powerful but usually unremarked material-discursive work they do in installing gendered practices through their entanglement with bodies and space.

Butler (1997, 5) has spoken of the 'inaugurative' power of naming both as a means for a person to be recognised as a viable subject in discourse and as a process which produces a 'fundamental dependency on the address of the Other'. 'Brains' functioned as one such name. 'Brains' was the nickname Malky used to a young woman who had once worn a t-shirt with the logo 'if these were brains I'd be a genius'. Other students also had nicknames and, while students did not use these names, neither did they contest their usage in class (although in interviews two students expressed their disapproval of the naming of other students). Malky used the names in class in a humorous, bantering tone accompanied by praise and positive feedback. While recognising the social and performative power of names, the name 'Brains' is of particular interest when considering clothes from a material feminist angle. That such naming is a form of gendered 'power over' (Kreisberg 1992) is obvious but how does this 'power over' do its work materially? Much like Sera and her suit (Jackson and Mazzei 2012), the t-shirt and the student interact in a mutual production of agency, the t-shirt has thing-power, it has a life of its own and we can see how the t-shirt–body–classroom apparatus works in an intra-active dynamism. We can, however, take things further.

I suggest that the repeated naming of 'Brains' functions as a micro-practice of the power of the male gaze. 'Brains' calls attention to one part of this particular student's body (her breasts), while at the same time the name – *'Brains'* – materially *dis*-embodies the body. The power of this name designates the body as partial, reduced to placid, receptive matter and, as in pornography, insistently summoned up in fragmented form, in a spatial field of dispersed panoptics, which regulates this individual student body and, undoubtedly, serves the larger purpose of regulating all student bodies in that proximate space. But the material feminist reading I have just offered is, when thinking diffractively, complicated by other material feminist possibilities. The student chose to wear this t-shirt with its material alliance of breast-brains-genius, and this prompts me to suggest that what this t-shirt seeks to do is entangle feminist with post-feminist discourses in a materiality which knowingly sexualises the feminist body as a paradoxical means to demonstrate sexual and intellectual autonomy under/from the male gaze. In that case, like Aschenbrand (cited in Genz 2006, 345) who says 'I am on a mission to change things – one pair of tits at a time', this particular t-shirt–body–name–space assemblage becomes an unruly, energetic and threatening irruption in the classroom space, and one which materialises broader concerns about sexualisation and 'pornification' of young people's cultures (Renold and Ringrose 2011; Ringrose and Renold 2012). In drawing attention to how clothes matter material feminism, like feminism more generally, is a valuable resource which opens an emergent field of analytical possibilities, some of which may be in tension. A material feminist reading of the 'if these were brains' t-shirt example undoubtedly undoes the dualistic presumption of the Enlightenment ego that clothing is exterior to us, mere cover, or surface, there to hide or represent the 'real me' within. It shows how clothes as materialities become with us as we become with them in an open, contingent unfolding of mattering.

I include now, as my data compel me to, a discussion of Malky's clothing. Malky, on every occasion I observed his lessons, was smartly dressed in a dark grey or navy tailored suit, with white shirt, tie and leather shoes. His suited neatness and close-cropped hair expressed 'classic' understated masculine elegance, and these material elements worked in confederation to ensure his body remained at all times the 'clean body' of the 'privileged subject' (Ahmed 2000, 93). That Malky's suit worked in a choreography of materialities in much the same way as his desk – as border and boundary to separate him from the students – became apparent with his comment in interview: 'if I see one more belly top I'll puke' (short, tight t-shirts, which made girls' midriffs visible, were in fashion at that time), a comment which, as glowing data hotspot, invites me to conjecture that his physical loathing of young women's display of flesh is tied to the materialisation of their abjection (as in the name 'Brains') and to the spatial arrangements of his room. Pursuing this line leads me to propose Malky's clothes as a material 'intensification of [his] being' (Simmel, cited in Carter 2012, 352).

So much for t-shirts and suits. What about jumpers? On more than one occasion Malky criticised, and encouraged students to laugh at, the male Physics teacher's jumpers (Observations 2 and 3), commenting 'oh you are a bitch you' in response to one male student's laughter (which provoked yet more class hilarity). And in one lesson I observed, Malky had the students crying with laughter as he gave a virtuoso embodied performance of 'Physics student', in which he slouched around caveman-style at the front of the class, dribbling, with his knuckles touching the floor, speaking incomprehensible words. This performance was followed by a verbal diatribe about Physics students which exhibited perfect comic timing:

> Geeks, with spots, who wear clothes bought by their Mum, they don't see daylight, they only talk to other geeks on the web, they wear trainers with no logos on them, also bought by their Mum. (Observation 3)

In this momentary transformation of classroom space into an arena of entertainment, however uncomfortable I felt, how could I remain 'outside' the laughter? As novice researcher, what would you have done? The materially embodied spatialisation of

Malky's production and reproduction of 'Physics' as an undesirable, even despicable, 'other' to Sociology had, by this point in the educational lifecycle of this teacher and his students, becomes routinised, acceptable and fun. 'Sociology', sociological knowledge, Sociology students and teachers were, incontrovertibly, superior physically, socially and intellectually, to everything and everyone pertaining to 'Physics'. The very materiality of Malky's stylishly suited body in this Bakhtinian, carnivalesque performative was sufficiently incongruous to make the point. Malky's material enactment of comedic routines pathologised 'Physics' through powerful categories of normalisation and exclusion. In this way he spatially reconstructed *his* classroom as serious, theoretical and analytical, and materially installed himself in that space as 'authentic knower and keeper of knowledge' which, as Francis (2008, 113) notes, is a 'profoundly masculine' enactment. Based on the data discussed here I propose that one good answer to the question 'what do clothes do?' is that clothing produces 'pleasure, exuberance and vertigo' (Caillois 2003, 49). In this instance, clothing's 'vertigo' works materially as a regulative ontological and epistemological disciplining which, as I noted early, separates the cleanness of an authentic intellectual life from the grubby social ineptitude of its despised 'others'. The practices enacted by Malky's clothed body show that 'nothing is more material, physical, corporal than the exercise of power' (Foucault 1980, 57).

And so, another cut has been made; and this cut puts the data which has troubled me so long on the page from where it continues to glower at me, even scold me. I noted earlier the profound responsibility that comes with making cuts in a material feminist diffractive approach. This is because 'the primary ontological unit is not independent objects with inherent boundaries and properties but rather phenomena', whereby 'phenomena are the ontological inseparability/entanglement of intra-acting agencies' (Barad 2007, 139). These intra-active entanglements make ethical relationality a touchstone, a key to the process of 'worlding' which involves us all, humans and non-human agencies together. The 'Physics' instance indicates the material force of classroom space to homogenise consent, provoke collective endeavour and marginalise dissent. In bringing to the fore that our ethical responsibilities arise from our entangled ontologies a diffractive methodology can prompt new ethical attention to our 'direct material engagement with the world' (Barad 2007, 49). This, undoubtedly, has profound implications for how we conduct research *in situ*.

7. Materialising a diffractive analysis

My aim has been to write this article as an accessible and practical illustration of what it means to undertake and write about how a diffractive methodology, inside a feminist materialist approach to how gender matters, can work, and what it can do. Choosing to weave diffractive interferences into the empirical account the article no doubt offers an irruptive reading experience, as does the direct address to 'you' the reader, in your entangled materiality, as I invite a comment, reflection or even judgement.

This act of experimentation in writing diffractively has been my attempt to instantiate both the critical and the creative potential of this approach. Thinking about data as matter returns me to Koro-Ljungberg's (2012) question '*what do data want?*' Perhaps, I suggest, what data want is a risky encounter. Recognising data's troublesome agency, its affective scope to unsettle our grooved, established research practices, may help us 'think with the uncertainties of knowing' (Lather 2007, 156) and open research to new ways of seeing and more plural, innovative practices.

8. Towards a conclusion

This article has contributed to moving forward educational analyses of objects, bodies and space through its use of a material feminist analysis of embodied practices of mattering in the classroom. In disclosing empirically the material multiplicity of classroom space, the article has indicated how space works as, at one and the same moment, entertainment space, performative space, epistemological space, ontological space and pedagogic space. Through a focus on objects and matter within the classroom, new attention has been drawn to space as a distributed confederacy of agentic materialities, within which differential gendered subjectivities are produced and enacted co-constitutively in vital human–nonhuman assemblages. By asking the questions 'what does a chair do?', 'what does a body do?', 'what do things do?' and 'what do clothes do?' I have illustrated matter's thing-power and the importance of attending to that which is so often unnoticed, unremarked, or passed over as mundane in the materiality of the classroom.

My argument has been that the confederacy of materialities means we can no longer think of agency as an individual, willed and bounded human property; agency is, instead, distributed, confederate, brought into being though the co-constitutive enactments of human–nonhuman apparatuses. This has profound ontological and ethical implications for classroom practices. In relation to gender, I have shown how the spatial multiplicity of the classroom in question was 'cut' by powerful gendered performatives of masculinity and how, in the space of entertainment, it was the player who occupied 'the chair' who was able to have the most fun.

The article has also made an original methodological contribution by instantiating one way of doing a diffractive analysis. This has enabled me to illustrate how a diffractive methodology enables a livelier, emergent and more open interaction between data and researcher and thus how it may suggest 'critical practice[s] for making a difference in the world' (Barad 2007, 90). In foregrounding Malky's glamour and my cuts I noted my material entanglement as researcher with data which was and still is troubling. This led me to propose the advantages to be gained in deploying a material feminist approach both as an ethical research practice and as a final nail in the coffin of objectivist, rationalist Enlightenment presumptions. In putting to work various concepts as tools for thinking from Barad – intra-action, entanglement, phenomena, apparatus, cut – I argued the necessity of plunging into particularity, of getting down and dirty in the empirical details. In this way, we can create a space for material feminism to work its way into our lives and embodied educational practice as we seek not just to fight the familiar but to change it through our feminist praxis.

References

Ahmed, S. 2000. *Strange Encounters: Embodied Others in Post-coloniality*. London: Routledge.

Allen, L. 2012. "Behind the Bike Sheds: Sexual Geographies of Schooling." *British Journal of Sociology of Education* 34 (1): 56–75.

Barad, K. 2007. *Meeting the Universe Halfway: Quantum Physics and the Entanglement of Matter and Meaning*. London: Duke University Press.

Bennett, J. 2010. *Vibrant Matter: A Political Ecology of Things*. London: Duke University Press.

Bernstein, B. 2004. *Pedagogy, Symbolic Control and Identity: Theory, Research, Critique*. Revised ed. Oxford: Rowman.

Bissell, D. 2009. "Inconsequential Materialities: The Movements of Lost Effects." *Space and Culture* 12 (1): 95–115.

Bourdieu, P., J. C. Passeron, and M. de Saint Martin. 1965. *Academic Discourse*. Oxford: Polity Press.

Boys, J. 2010. *Towards Creative Learning Spaces: Re-thinking the Architecture of Post-compulsory Education*. London: Routledge.

Brooks, R., A. Fuller, and J. Waters, eds. 2012. *Changing Spaces of Education: New Perspectives on the Nature of Learning*. London: Routledge.

Burke, C., and I. Grosvenor. 2008. *School: Iconic Architecture*. London: Reaktion.

Butler, J. 1990. *Gender Trouble: Feminism and the Subversion of Identity*. New York: Routledge.

Butler, J. 1993. *Bodies that Matter: On the Discursive Limits of 'Sex'*. New York: Routledge.

Butler, J. 1997. *Excitable Speech: A Politics of the Performative*. New York: Routledge.

Caillois, R. 2003. *The Edge of Surrealism, A Roger Caillois Reader*. Durham, NC: Duke University Press.

Carter, M. 2012. "Stuff and Nonsense: The Limits of the Linguistic Model of Clothing." *Fashion Theory* 16 (3): 343–354.

Connell, R. 1995. *Masculinities*. California: University of California Press.

Coole, D., and S. Frost. 2010. *New Materialisms: Ontology, Agency, Politics*. Durham, NC: Duke University Press.

Delamont, S., and M. Galton. 1986. *Inside the Secondary Classroom*. London: Routledge and Kegan Paul.

Di Leo, J., and W. Jacobs. 2004. *If Classrooms Matter: Progressive Visions of Educational Environments*. New York: Routledge.

Dunne, M. 2007. "Gender, Sexuality and Schooling: Everyday Life in Junior Secondary Schools in Botswana and Ghana." *International Journal of Educational Development* 27 (5): 499–511.

Fenwick, T., and P. Landri. 2012. "Introduction: Materialities, Textures and Pedagogies: Socio-Material Assemblages in Education." *Pedagogy, Culture & Society* 20 (1): 1–7.

Foucault, F. 1979. *Discipline and Punish: The Birth of the Prison*. London: Peregrine Books.

Foucault, M. 1980. *Power/Knowledge: Selected Interviews and Other Writings 1972–1977*. New York: Harvester Wheatsheaf.

Foucault, M. 1984. "Space, Knowledge, and Power." In *The Foucault Reader*, edited by P. Rabinow, 239–256. London: Penguin.

Foucault, M. 1988. *The History of Sexuality*. Vol. 3. *The Care of the Self*. Harmondworth: Viking.

Francis, B. 2008. "Teaching Manfully? Exploring Gendered Subjectivities and Power via Analysis of Men Teachers' Gender Performance." *Gender and Education* 20 (2): 109–122.

Genz, S. 2006. "Third Way/ve: The Politics of Postfeminism." *Feminist Theory* 7 (3): 333–353.

Gibbs, G. 2010. *Dimensions of Quality*. York: Higher Education Academy.

Grosz, E. 1994. *Volatile Bodies: Toward a Corporeal Feminism*. Bloomington, IN: Indiana University Press.

Hirst, E., and M. Cooper. 2008. "Keeping Them in Line: Choreographing Classroom Spaces." *Teachers and Teaching: Theory and Practice* 14 (5–6): 431–445.

Hubbard, P., R. Kitchin, and G. Valentine. 2004. *Key Thinkers on Space and Place*. London: Sage.

Igoe, D., and J. Kewin. 2013. Creating a Level Playing Field in Sixth Form Education, White Paper, Sixth Form Colleges Association.

Ivinson, G. 2012. "The Body and Pedagogy: Beyond Absent, Moving Bodies in Pedagogic Practice." *British Journal of Sociology of Education* 33 (4): 489–506.

Jackson, A. J., and A. Mazzei. 2012. *Thinking with Theory in Qualitative Research*. Oxon: Routledge.

Jones, L. 2013a. "Becoming Child: Becoming Dress." *Global Studies of Childhood* 3 (3): 289–296.

Jones, L. 2013b. "Children's Encounters with Things: Schooling the Body." *Qualitative Inquiry*. doi:10.1177/1077800413494348

Koro-Ljungberg, M. 2012. "What do data want?" Conference presentation, American Educational Research Association Annual Meeting, Vancouver, Canada.

Koro-Ljungberg, M., and M. MacLure. 2013. "Provocations, Re-Un-Visions, Death, and Other Possibilities of 'Data'." *Cultural Studies=Critical Methodologies.* doi:10.1177/1532708613487861

Kreisberg, S. 1992. *Transforming Power: Domination, Empowerment and Education.* Albany, NY: SUNY Press.

Lather, P. 2007. *Getting Lost: Feminist Efforts Toward a Double(d) Science.* Albany, NY: SUNY Press.

MacLure, M. 2013. "Classification or Wonder? Coding as an Analytic Practice in Qualitative Research." In *Deleuze and Research Methodologies,* edited by B. Coleman and J. Ringrose, 164–183. Edinburgh: Edinburgh University Press.

Mahony, P., I. Hextall, and M. Richardson. 2011. "'Building Schools for the Future': Reflections on a New Social Architecture." *Journal of Education Policy* 26 (3): 341–360.

Massey, D. 2005. *For Space.* London: Sage.

McGregor, J. 2001. "Making Spaces: Teacher Workplace Topologies." Paper presented at the British Educational Research Association Annual Conference, Leeds University, September 13–15.

Miller, D. 2010. *Stuff.* Cambridge: Polity Press.

Mulcahy. D. 2012. "Affective Assemblages: Body Matters in the Pedagogic Practices of Contemporary School Classrooms." *Pedagogy, Culture & Society* 20 (1): 9–27.

Mulvey, L. 1975. "Visual Pleasure and Narrative Cinema." In *Feminist Film Theory: A Reader,* edited by S. Thornham, 58–69. Edinburgh: Edinburgh University Press.

Palmer, A. 2011. "Performative Strategies and Diffractive Thinking as Methodological Tools for Rethinking Mathematical Subjectivity." *Reconceptualizing Educational Research Methodology* 1 (1): 3–18.

Park, J. 2013. "Do School Uniforms Lead to Uniform Minds? School Uniforms and Appearance Restrictions in Korean Middle Schools and High Schools." *Fashion Theory* 17 (2): 159–178.

Pilcher, J. 2013. "'Small But Very Determined' A Novel Theorisation of Children's Consumption of Clothing." *Cultural Sociology* 7 (1): 86–100.

Quinn, J. 2003. "The Dynamics of Protected Space: Spatial Concepts and Women Students." *British Journal of Sociology of Education* 24 (4): 449–461.

Renold, E. 2005. *Girls, Boys and Junior Sexualities: Exploring Children's Gender and Sexual Relations in the Primary School.* London: RoutledgeFalmer.

Renold, E., and Ringrose, J. 2011. "Schizoid Subjectivities: Re-Theorising Teen-Girls' Sexual Cultures in an Era of Sexualisation." *Journal of Sociology* 47 (4): 389–409.

Ringrose, J. 2007. "Successful Girls? Complicating Post-Feminist, Neoliberal Discourses of Educational Achievement and Gender Equality." *Gender and Education* 19 (4): 471–489.

Ringrose, J., and E. Renold. 2012. "Slut Shaming, Girl Power and 'Sexualisation': Thinking Through the Politics of the International Slutwalks with Teen Girls." *Gender and Education* 24 (3): 333–343.

Shields, R. 1997. "Spatial Stress and Resistance: Social Meanings of Spatialization." In *Space and Social Theory: Interpreting Modernity and Postmodernity,* edited by G. Benko and U. Strohmayer, 186–202. Oxford: Blackwell.

Stengers, I. 2007. "Diderot's Egg: Divorcing Materialism from Eliminativism." *Radical Philosophy* 144 (July/August): 7–15.

Tamboukou, M. 1999. "Spacing Herself: Women in Education." *Gender and Education* 11 (2): 125–139.

Taylor, C. 2011. "'Hope in Failure': A Level Students, Discursive Agency, Post-Feminism and Feminism." *Gender and Education* 23 (7): 825–841.

Urry, J. 2003. *Global Complexity.* Cambridge: Polity.

Zembylas, M. 2007. "Risks and Pleasures: A Deleuzo–Guattarian Pedagogy of Desire in Education." *British Educational Research Journal* 33 (3): 331–349.

Valleys' girls: re-theorising bodies and agency in a semi-rural post-industrial locale

Gabrielle Ivinson[a] and Emma Renold[b]

[a]School of Education, University of Aberdeen, Aberdeen, UK; [b]School of Social Sciences, Cardiff University, Cardiff, UK

This paper draws on materialist feminist theories to rethink relationships between girls' bodies and agency. New feminist onto-epistemologies redefine agency as 'becomings' that dynamically emerge through assemblages comprising moving bodies, material, mechanical, organic, virtual, affective and less-than-conscious elements. Vignettes from a multi-modal, ethnographic study conducted over three years are used to demonstrate how place influenced young teen girls' body-movement repertoires. The place was a former coal-mining locale with a proud tradition of masculine, working-class labour. The vignettes focus on corporeality and demonstrate wide variations and fluctuations in girls' experiences of agency, which we theorise through the Deleuzeo-Guatarrian concept of 'becoming'. We discuss how material feminism(s) helps us to understand girls' becomings as emergent within assemblages that carry legacies of the past. Some girls experienced becomings that could not easily be spoken about yet which allowed them to imagine expansive futures while others felt unable to move on in life.

Introduction

Historical legacies of gender and patriarchy continue to influence the lives of young people, yet the places where they grow up can vary the intensity of these effects (McDowell and Massey 1984; Taylor 2012). This paper draws upon ethnographic research which explores young people and place and how such gender legacies continue to play out and affect young teenage girls in a South Wales Valleys' community.[1] General findings from the broader study revealed strong differences in the patterns of corporeal movement between young teen boys and girls inside and outside school (Ivinson 2012, 2013; Renold and Ivinson 2012a, 2012b). An anecdote from our fieldnotes illustrates these differences:

> At break-times girls tended to inhabit the school yards surrounding a Victorian building. Whenever we walked through the yard, we passed girls sitting: they sat in groups on stone steps; in corners propped against brick walls and when it rained, they sat directly on the wooden floor of the main hall. Girls sometimes said they feared the gossip flowing between groups while boys told us their greatest fear at break times was that someone would hit them or trip them up. When we walked across the yard used by the boys that flanked a 1960s flat roofed building we had to walk around groups of boys standing together, swerve to dodge boys running or duck to miss a flying football.

These contrasting images from school break times depict comparatively docile, female and active, male bodies. The general patterns of movement between the girls and boys we interviewed in the first phase of the study broadly reflected these gendered patterns of movement. We were struck by the differences in the ways boys and girls *talked* about movement; boys spoke at length and with animation about physical activities in interviews which were often long and entertaining, while the interviews with girls were less elaborated and far less animated. However, we learned a great deal more about the girls' physical activities in later stages of the research project especially during walking tours and film-making activities, that is, when we used methods other than seated interviews conducted in school time. In the later phases of the research, girls revealed that at times they enjoyed running fast, speeding down mountains on bikes, rolling down muddy banks, creating new street-dance moves, splashing into swimming pools or flipping into backward somersaults. These accounts were often animated, hinting that at such times they felt truly alive. In order to understand why boys and girls spoke so differently about physical activities in the first phase of the research project, we were drawn to consider the specific history of the place and the gendered legacies that might have been influencing what can legitimately be talked about in relation to corporeal physicality.

We came to recognise that the specificities of the history of the place may be important to our analysis. In South Wales, many valleys' communities have experienced the trauma of the end of industrial productivity, mass unemployment, poverty, social marginalisation and lower levels of educational achievement than in other parts of the UK. Despite these radical changes, gendered legacies inherited from the industrial past such as strongly demarcated and reciprocal gender roles and associations between corporeal strength, movement and masculinity remain active (cf. Mannay 2013; Marshall 2008; Walkerdine and Jimenez 2011). The questions we wish to tackle are how does gender exert its influence on what girls (and boys) do, what they aspire to become and how they imagine their futures? In this paper, we explore these questions by focusing on feelings of agency relating to corporeality that seem to be experienced by girls, yet which girls talked about less easily than the boys in our study. Eventually, we would like to be able to explore how experiences of agency relating to corporeality can be harnessed for educational purposes and used to bridge between activities that motivate girls outside school and pedagogic practices in school. However, this paper focuses primarily on exploring girls' agency, theorised as 'becomings' by focusing on their movements outside school.

We have three main tasks in the paper. First, we turn to new material feminist philosophers to theorise agency beyond notions of will and intentionality associated with minds and rationality. We pay attention to the gendered history of the locale and how this was experienced as conscious and unconscious affects that continue to mediate girls' movements and activities. We try to understand how gender is transmitted intergenerationally in everyday practices, influenced by the gendered history of place and here we turn to psychosocial work on 'affective practices' (Walkerdine 2010). In order to illustrate how agency was experienced through movement and how these movements were sometimes inflected with gender values, we present some of our empirical data as vignettes. The vignettes illustrate how four 13–15-year-old girls experienced agency through movements that were part of their everyday practices. By drawing from a range of data sources we demonstrate the wide variation in girls' experiences of agency which we theorise below as 'becomings' (Braidotti 2002/2005; Deleuze and Guattari 1987; Probyn 1996). In the discussion, we suggest how material feminism(s) can help us to understand how girls living in places of high unemployment with a strong industrial past experienced becomings that enabled some to imagine expansive futures, while others struggled to do so.

Material feminism(s): agency 'in-between'

As readers of this journal will be all too familiar with, contemporary debates around gender and educational achievement often make a virtue of girls' compliant, containing and still bodies (e.g. Gordon, Holland, and Lahelma 2000a). When we think about schools as places that discipline bodies (e.g. Foucault [1978]1990), corporeal passivity is often promoted as a feature of ideal educational subjectivity (Walkerdine 1990). However, girls' corporeal stillness is also often interpreted as lacking agency and 'boring' in comparison to boys' 'exciting' movement (cf. Ivinson and Murphy 2007; Murphy and Gipps 1996). Boys' non-compliance is frequently associated with agency and bad behaviour where excessive movement is tolerated as a legitimate expression of masculinity captured by phrases such as 'boys will be boys' (Francis 2000).

There is an enduring tension between active bodies and constructions of femininity that has long been the focus of theoretical and empirical, feminist work. Young (2005) distinguishes between the ways boys and girls move their bodies by drawing attention to the historical legacies of Western culture that demand girls be compliant, sedate and passive. She suggests that boys throw themselves into movement, while girls stand on the edge in hesitation. For example, within classrooms girls have been observed to move less, speak less and break the rules lesser than boys in general (see Gordon, Holland, and Lahelma 2000b; Renold 2006). Formal sports education research shows how many girls have a fraught relationship with the active, athletic body (Azzarito 2010) reflected in the ways girls participate in organised leisure activities (Evans 2006; Smyth, Mooney, and Casey 2011). Many girls in our study told us how they gradually gave up their sporting activities and outdoor hobbies specifically around the ages of 11–13 years as they transitioned from primary (elementary) to secondary (high) school and from girlhood to adolescence. Within the hidden geographies of the 'fourth environment' (Matthews and Limb 1999), that is, where young people spend time *not* in classrooms, playgrounds or homes, research suggests that girls tend not to take up space in public domains and instead negotiate in and around boys' leisure zones (Matthews and Tucker 2001). Even in studies of rural locations, that evoke the romanticised idyll of wild spaces, the subject is yet again imagined to be male: rural girls are imagined to be tomboys (Jones 2010) and girls 'hanging out' on the street to escape domesticity or boredom are frequently constructed as 'out of place' (Skelton 2000).

Because femininity has so often been the object of male science, feminist philosophers such as Simone de Beauvoir, Elizabeth Grosz, Gayle Rubin and Monique Wittig have worked to distance it from associations with nature, matter and corporeality in order to make the point that women and girls are as much mind/agency as body/matter and produce knowledge as well as offspring. To overcome associations of femininity with passive/matter and masculinity with agency/will (or spirit), some have argued that feminists had moved too far in the opposite direction (Alaimo and Hekman 2008, 4) and left what some refer to as the fleshy or alive body of blood and bones (e.g. Birke 1999) out of the picture, thus maintaining enduring binaries such as mind or matter, subject or object and signifier or signified. Even Judith

Bulter's notion of performativity, like other Foucauldian inspired concepts, has a tendency to collapse agency back into either side of these binaries (see Barad 2007, 150–153; Van der Tuim 2011). Along with others (e.g. Alaimo and Hekman 2008; Barad 2007; Braidotti 2002/2005, 2006; Deleuze and Guattari 1983, 1987; Haraway 1991) we are searching for ways out of this impasse. One route is to follow Barad's onto-epistemology which posits agency as an emergent force *between* elements such as nature and culture, matter and representation (meaning) and signifier and signified (Barad 1996, 188). Working from her position as a physicist, Barad rejects the notion that knowledge resides in the mind of the scientist as he [*sic*] stands above the apparatus. Instead she opens up a way to understand agency as emergent between elements of assemblages, where assemblages form as part of dynamic movement and include material elements such as the apparatus involved in scientific experiments. In a similar vein, Deleuze and Guattari (1983, 1987) contend that assemblages can be made up of all manner of matter: corporeal, technological, mechanical, virtual, discursive and imaginary. And it is within assemblages that agency or 'becomings' emerge. We can use these conceptual moves to understand the way girls alluded to the aliveness of their bodies as a form of becoming, experienced through bodily practices (and not only through their minds) as they became entangled in movements with bikes, skateboards and other objects in various terrains and landscapes beyond the school walls.

The importance of place in the inter-generational transmission of gender

Entanglements of intra-acting phenomena (Barad 2007) are always located in time, history and place. So, when we consider the practices that young people undertake in locales, we have to see these as practices that have histories that carry traces of the past, and in this locale it was an industrial past. Communities and families developed routines and practices to survive harsh conditions in relatively remote places. While men worked below ground in dangerous jobs that required muscular strength, women organised life within the community above ground and forged bonds of sociality through which they organised the daily routines of cooking, caring and cleaning (Bruley 2007; Marshall 2008; Penlington 2010). For example, wives battled against dirt, as thick coal dust from mine entrances, chimneys, streets and returning husbands curled around doors to settle in sitting rooms, kitchens and on clothes (Penlington 2010). One historically rooted pattern of practice was the need for dichotomous and reciprocal roles relating to activities above and below ground essential for community survival (Walkerdine and Jimenez 2011).

We worked with young people in the locale at a time when all the mines had finally closed down following brave attempts on behalf of miners and unions to keep them open during the 1980s. Anxieties surrounding enforced conditions of worklessness infuse traditional gender roles with a new set of contradictory and complex values and associations. Long-term unemployed men are forced to live out their days in domestic sites such as kitchens, gardens and in local streets. There are few public spaces for young people to meet except the school and the only youth club in the town closed during the course of our study. The town and its surrounding valleys stretch out into a vast expanse of wilderness. Many of the young people in the study said they felt unsafe yet to varying degrees. In these newly gendered contradictory places, girls were growing up with the endured difficulties associated with poverty such as sexual violence, predatory men, illness, accidents and loss. The specific legacies of industrialisation together with the geography of the place facilitate communal and individual movement practices.

To capture all these dimension of community life we can draw on the concept of a relational matrix (Latour 2005; Arendt 1958 cited in Walkerdine 2010) in which buildings, streets and the everyday movements, rhythms and rituals that take place in them have affective dimensions (Henriques 2010) which Walkerdine defines as 'affective practices' (2010, 100). Indeed, many everyday practices have historical legacies that reach back to the industrial era when people had to manage economic uncertainty and to ensure the community's survival in tough times. Subjectivities emerge within these everyday, repeated, affective practices as dynamic assemblages. Corporeality is central to such acting assemblages because affects pass through bodies and not only through minds. In this paper, we draw attention to the importance of place (cf. Walkerdine 2013) and the entanglement of girls' becomings as emplaced. Furthermore, we explore how the habitual practices associated with the history of places (cf. Wulf 2013) carry affects that are often experienced unconsciously through bodily rhythms.

Researching bodies-in-place

A longitudinal, ethnographic study employed multiple methods to capture young people's body-movement practices. The vignettes presented below came from research carried out as part of a large-scale research programme that aimed to use a wide range of quantitative and qualitative measures to map locales in Wales (*WISERD*). The Young People and Place project was conducted in a location chosen by the wider research programme and its central aim was to explore place on numerous levels (e.g. as physical environment, as a source of symbolic resources, as social and material constructions and in terms of affects). Our methods used photographs, films, walking tours, seated and mobile interviews and fieldnotes to generate a range of multimedia data that have informed us about the way young people created, appropriated and negotiated local spaces.

Each vignette is informed by semi-structured narrative interviews conducted in the first phase of the project and which used specially created photographs of places in and around the town (photographs of buildings such as the supermarket, skate park, railway station and library; of various streets in the satellite housing estates; places in the school, such as the yard, art room, science laboratory and dining room and places in the home such as kitchen, bedroom, garden and bathroom) as a sorting task. Participants sorted photographs of places into groups and explained why the groupings were chosen. In the first phase, 64 boys and girls aged 13/14 including Kayleigh, Arwydd, Rowan and Sharman were interviewed on school premises and a smaller group, including Rowan participated in visual and audio-recorded walking tours during which they took us to some of their significant places and spoke about them (see Ross et al. 2009). Two years further into the study we returned to the same cohort and invited young people including Arwydd to participate in an experimental film-making project working with an independent film maker over a period of one week to make short films about activities that they valued (see Renold and Ivinson 2013).

Data analysis was informed by concepts of assemblage and becoming (Braidotti 2002/2005; Deleuze and Guattari 1987) and we paid attention to elements such as landscapes, public and private spaces, body movements, tools and artefacts, virtual media as well as persons such as friends and extended family members. In interview accounts we specifically focused on vivid stories that revealed feelings, desire and intense connections (cf. Walkerdine, Olsvold, and Rudberg 2013; Probyn 1996; Young 2005). We present vignettes to illustrate the different ways that girls seemed to experience 'becomings' emergent within assemblages that involved their moving bodies. The vignettes captured moments in the everyday lives of the four participants. We have deliberately presented interpretations within the vignettes as tentative suggestions. Kayleigh had suffered from a childhood illness and was being stigmatised as sexually available because her BEBO account had been hacked into by local peer networks. Some of her accounts epitomise being 'stuck' and unable to move forward physically or psychically. We caught Arwydd in transition from a state of grieving for her mother who died when she was 10 years old, to glimpsing a new becoming as her body recalled an earlier joy associated with dancing. We meet Rowan, a high-achieving student with her sights set on university, who repeatedly climbed local mountains to offset a profound fear of being trapped. In the final vignette, we see how Sharman who had experienced multiple setbacks in her life, managed to reclaim a sense of liberation through enjoying mud fights with boys and dressing-up parties with girls, benefiting from activities in both wild and domestic places in the locale.

Arrested movement: Kayleigh's fantasy others

Kayleigh lives in the town centre with her mum, her mum's boyfriend and an older teenage sister in a small-terraced house next to the police station. When we met Kayleigh with her friends, she was keen to be interviewed and from the very outset had a lot to say about growing up in the locale. The narrative weaves many trails that dip in and out of a range of time–space realities and multiple traumatic events, including: survival of a serious infection as a young child; parental separation; the death of her infant nephew in her arms at age 8 and a number of sexual assaults and physically violent peer-group conflicts at home, in virtual space and in various public places around the town. Not surprisingly, safety and danger were identified as key categories in the photo sort and the picture of the bedroom was immediately honed in on to represent a 'safe space'. From here, the narrative moved swiftly between expressions of feeling safe and unsafe:

> Kayleigh: It's, I like going shopping, coz, I dunno, I feel, if I'm with the girls and everything, I feel safe, and that . . . but when I'm on my own I don't, I don't really go (out?) and that really.
> (. . .)
> ER: So what do you think will happen if you're on your own then?
> Kayleigh: I don't know, I just feel like I'd get taken or something, coz if I went [Emma: Hmm] shopping to Cardiff and it's so crowded in the shops and that, I just feel like, all closed up by everyone and that.
> ER: OK.
> Kayleigh: So, that's why I have to go with other people.
> ER: Yeah, yeah, and is that just Cardiff, or is that like, in town as well?
> Kayleigh: Everywhere.
> . . .
> ER: Have you always felt like that about being on your own?
> Kayleigh: Yeah, I hate it.
> . . .
> Kayleigh: (. . .) like when I'd go shopping and If I'm on my own and that, like, you know like when you go shopping with your friends and say 'oh I'll go down here, you stay up

here', I don't, and if they do go, I'll hide away and I'll just look around and I'll go white and everything/

Kayleigh's talk about needing and creating togetherness to be 'safe' ('I have to go with someone') was more strongly expressed than in other girls' narratives and extended to 'hating being on your own'. She offered many examples of where 'being with' seemed vital to her well-being. She described following her mum to the shops or to a neighbour's house rather than being alone in the house; sharing a room with her sister rather than sleeping in her own bedroom and having her girl-friends sleep next to her, rather than in the bunk below. Indeed, Kayleigh's fear of 'not being' emerges in many of her narratives, even when she spoke of communal spaces where the fear of being left made her skin 'go white'. She used tomb/death metaphors for both her psychological sense and her embodied practices of 'hiding away' as if her life force was draining away making her unable to take part in every-day routines. She described not going out for an entire summer as she negotiated complex social–virtual relations resulting from her BEBO profile being hijacked and messages purporting her sexual availability being sent to boys and girls without her consent or knowledge.

Her need to feel safe was experienced both in terms of the local (e.g. town centre) and 'everywhere' (e.g. friends, family and wider community). The others she needed to 'be with' were sometimes named and sometimes became 'somebody', 'anybody' revealing the extent of her anxiety. Indeed, throughout the interview Kayleigh seemed to dis-inhabit her body in a number of ways and discussed at length how she had created a compensatory inner fantasy world where she could talk to herself so as to 'feel like somebody's next to me all the time'. Indeed, she talked openly about a range of imagined others that included close and extended family members, her deceased nephew, TV characters and even the moon and the stars.

Kayleigh created a rich inner world of imagined and lost others; a psychic space to cope with the traumatic events that life had thrown her way. Although providing an effective strategy for survival, Kayleigh's story was also very much one of stuckness rather than of becoming. She became all interiority, all mind, while dislocating her per-ception from her moving body. Creating a fantasy of others was perhaps Kayleigh's way of 'being held, contained, alive' and keeping feelings of 'being uncontained and unsafe' at bay (see Walkerdine 2010, 95). Despite her passion for education, evidenced by remarks such as 'I really like school ... I love learning', Kayleigh did not appear to invest in further education, but remained stuck in her relatively still and unmoving body.

Kayleigh was more stuck than the other girls. This may have been due to her early illness or because a hyper-surveillance furnished by her stolen BEBO account had stigmatised her body as a sexual object. She seemed to have lost control of her body image to others, as if it had floated off on the airwaves of a virtual yet public media (see Ringrose et al. 2013). She used images of her body in hiding, entombed and dead. Kayleigh expended effort and energy on repeating the practices that pre-vented her being alone as if she feared she would disintegrate without the presence of others. Walkerdine (2010) reminds us that to move on and create sustainable becomings, people first have to feel safe and Kayleigh did not feel safe at all. The possibility of forming positive images of the future appeared blocked by her inability to inhabit her body.

In transition: Arwydd moves again

Arwydd lives with her father and one of her three older brothers. Three years ago before we met her, her mother with whom she had a very close relationship inexplicably became ill and died a few days before Christmas. We identified three startling features of her interview: her obsession with birthdates and ages when introducing new characters, especially babies and children; a need to talk about food and thirdly, that she sorted the photographs into two distinct groups, children's and adults' activities. It was about half way through the interview before Arwydd described her mother's death by saying:

> The thing that happened with my grandfather was, he was poorly and then he died and then the week after I, we had his funeral and the day after his funeral my mother died and then two days later it was Christmas, so it all happened in one month, four weeks time so . . . It was quite sad at the time but like it's been three years, all the girls have helped me through it and.

The timing of these events is striking. Her mother had died 'the day after' her grandfather's funeral and two days before Christmas. She had no explanation for her mother's death. We came to recognise that it was as if time had stopped when her mother died and paying close attention to birthdates and ages was a way of explicitly marking the passage of time; a way to keep time going on:

> And then we're going to go to Cardiff again and take my cousin Jason to see the museum, he just turned eight in April and then we're going to be taking my baby cousin which turned three in May, down to Pen-y-parc.

Having lost her mother when she was 10 it is not surprising that many of her comments focused on food and it seemed important that her dad and her nan cooked for her. Many of her comments relating to children also mentioned food. We were able to trace connections between food, caring, children, mothering and time. She described babysitting:

> My cousin hasn't long learnt to go in the toilet either because I, like her mother, I was like her mother for a couple of weeks because I use to babysit her because her mother was in work all the time but her mother has changed her shifts now because the baby is in school, so she's there all the time for the baby now, so but I still see her and babysit on the weekends sometimes.

Arwydd's ambition was to become a midwife or a crèche teacher and becoming an adult seemed to mark an important transition into a new being, beyond the pain of loss:

> Well I can't wait to get out because then I will be an adult and I get to work and know what it's like to be older then.

One story, however, stood out as different. We see this story of swimming outside in the rain as an entry point into a different modality of being, which foregrounds corporeality:

> Well it was nice and fine and we went and got changed into our bathers in the toilets and we came out and it was hammering down but we thought oh well we're still have a good time, so we went into the pool and it was a bit chilly, then because I said girls just stick

your head under and you get warmer then so that's what they all done, they listened and then we got really warm and then we went out of the pool and went into the park and we went on the slides, because it was slippery I went nearly flying, then we went onto the other side of the park where all the wood was and . . . . . . We went into the wood chippings after we went into the sand and we went on the slide and it was faster than the sand one, so the sand one is for quite young children and I went flying across the park because it was really fast but Kayleigh and Meghan wouldn't push themselves . . . and went down and I went down swimming.

The passage conveys joyous sensations and is full of fine-grained details about her body such as her descriptions of speed, slipping and 'nearly going flying'. Arwydd had spoken with animation and intensity. This was an unusually vivid description of her moving body, which later we came to recognise as mimetically referencing (Wulf 2013) her earlier life. While making a film about friendship with us two years later, Arwydd revealed that her mother had taken her to dance classes since the age of 3 and that she had only stopped dancing when her mother died when she was 10 years old. There had been no mention of dancing in the initial interview. In a poignant episode in the film-making activity she brought in three of her ballet costumes made by her mum for special performances when she was aged 3, 5 and 7 and laid them out on the school gym floor so we could film them. Afterwards, Arwydd took her friends to a stack of crash mats at the back of the gym and performed somersaults. She told us that she was trying to get back to dancing with help of her friends and hoped for 'a fresh start' during the summer. Arwydd's description of swimming provides a tiny glimpse into the joyous affects that she experienced through bodily movement and seemed to mimetically reference an earlier being before the trauma of death cut her off from dancing.

Carol Anshaw (cited in Probyn 1996, 41) captures this kind of transcendent being when she described the corporeality of swimming. 'Swimming works only when the swimmer and the water become other than their separate functions. The body translates matter into energy that becomes velocity . . . legs pumping, arms pulling, back straining, muscles melding' (Probyn 1996, 41). The body becomes a fully functioning part of the machinery of movement and through physical activity the swimmer 'leaves herself behind'. In this moment of transcendence or 'singularity' (Deleuze and Guattari 1987) the swimmer or dancer becomes 'what she can do'. It seemed that for Arwydd, the affects associated with dance were stored through years of repeated practice in her muscles and movement repertoires. While swimming and somersaulting, her vital, moving body seemed to make connections across a gulf before and after death; across her past as a child to becoming an adult and from a time when she was fed by her mother to her present feeling of safety and being nurtured by friends and relatives.

Arwydd did not mention dancing at all in the first interview. Dancing seemed to have been associated with her mum to the extent that when she lost her mum, she stopped dancing. It may be that giving up dancing allowed Arwydd not to feel some of the most acute pain of loss. When Arwydd gave details of her body flying and slipping we catch a glimpse of the joy associated with the movements of her body. It was as if the movements revitalised a kind of corporeal memory (Mortimer-Sandilands 2008) of her dancing as a child. When we met her for the second time her knowing-dancing body was reawakening and beginning to move beyond the immobilising pain of grief towards a transformative becoming.

Nature–culture entangled: Rowan aims high

Since the age of 2, Rowan has lived in Cwm Valley, an ex-mining village where her grandfather and great grandfather used to work, in a small-terraced house with her mother, father and 10-year-old brother. She was part of a close-knit extended family; her gran and grandad lived a couple of doors away and her auntie over the road. Of significance to Rowan's 'growing up girl' (Walkerdine, Lucy, and Melody 2001) is the interconnectedness of her plans to go to university and travel, and her local outdoors. The ubiquitous fear of being colonised came across strongly in Rowan's interview.

> Rowan: I'm aiming high so I think I will get there if I like, aim for it
> ER: Yeah?
> Rowan: Sort of thing, so yeah, I want to get out of here, I don't like it . . . it's always the same, like, you see people going to work, coming back, cooking dinner and stuff
> ER: Mmm
> Rowan: I don't wanna be just stuck here with like, loads of kids and stuff, I wanna like, go around sort, the world sort of thing.

Rowan feared being trapped in 'this place' where 'useless' men tie girls into relationships that would inevitably lead to kids and cooking. These domestic rhythms seemed to carry negative affects experienced as being trapped.

Mountains, streams, forests, trails and lakes provide her immediate backyard. Walk to the end of her street and you enter the wild. Indeed, the life-affirming energies of the local landscape permeate Rowan's narrative:

> Rowan: Yeah I started, I came up just in the pathway first, then I went further into like the zone that hasn't got a path and that's probably the most part I enjoy because. . .
> ER: Being off the track?
> Rowan: . . . yes, you're like you don't know where you're going . . . so it's like something new or something.
> . . .
> Rowan: This is one of my favourite parts of the walk . . . sometimes I go on a long one so I go up the mountain twice . . . I try to go different places sometimes, not just always up here but this is like my favourite of all the mountains.

Rowan loved being outside, building dens, speeding on her bike, walking untrodden paths and creating special enclosed places where she felt happy. Rowan's love of movement might have been a counter action to this fear.

She liked to write about and photograph the 'smallest things' in nature which was part of the way she cared for the environment. She spoke about being a young explorer, going on adventures, enjoying being off track and discovering 'something new'. These stories revealed her desire to escape the valleys and see the world, as a scientist or an engineer. She was located at the very edges of the village – a village at the very edges of the valley – where the wild merged into the built environment. Garden terraces melded imperceptible into the landscape. The wild offered rich resource for Rowan who imagined futures where she could explore in a world that was more expansive than the immediate one where women were bound by cooking and kids. In this assemblage comprising nature and culture, women such as her grandmother create, build and are ultimately responsible for their dwelling (Young 2005):

> I don't depend on people that much . . . I like to do things in my own . . . I get it from my grandmother . . . we are all like that, the woman at least . . . the men are wimps . . . my

grandmother built the house and the men sat there and did nothing . . . and used to make me angry and stuff.

Rowan talked animatedly about forging her own path since the age of 9 at first with her grandmother and then on her own. She described adventures and a compulsion to find her 'own way', away from 'the crowd', forging 'a self made path . . . where nobody goes' such as a den in the 'DIY (do-it-yourself) tree' which is 'high up' and 'enclosed'.

In contrast to the wild she described the town as a place of 'drinking, sex and drugs'. Rowan felt the rush and pull of these and alluded to her desire for 'boys, boys, boys . . . drinking and clubbing'. Yet she resisted this saying she 'must wait . . . I've got different things to worry about now . . . like my future . . . I got time to drink and stuff when I'm older'. Straight after this she showed us a photograph of her favourite tree:

> Rowan: There's the tree, I think it's the one, its all twisty and stuff [. . .] it's just like . . . you know when trees usually go up and stuff, I dunno it's just like it's unique I guess, and that's why I like it . . . I always take pictures of little things like this . . . my friends don't get it . . . really I like stuff like this.

It seemed important that she described the tree as 'twisty' as if it reflected the complexity of her own becomings. She described the first time she ventured out into the wild, aged 9 and got stuck in the grassy mounds:

> Once I come up here on my bike for the first time and I went in there and I got stuck and it took me an hour to pull my bike up . . . it was horrible . . . I turned and thought it was a short cut and went down there and I was stuck in there for like about an hour . . . I went all the way down on my bike and then it was like, you know like when you have lots of grass mounds, and I couldn't push it up and I was getting all scared and panicky, I'm just like that, I panic about everything.

This vivid description alludes to the visceral 'panic' of being trapped. This fear was strongly articulated when she described riding fast on her bike. She talked of 'being watched, being looked at'. When this sense of surveillance became too intense, she retreated into nature by diving into bushes, hiding behind trees and sometimes waiting there for up to an hour at a time. She talked of avoiding the 'short cuts' for fear of 'getting stuck' and furthermore of avoiding contact with boys, 'in case I fancy them' and physical closeness with girls ('not into hugs . . . not sickly like that'). Avoiding physical contact seemed to work as a defence against being contaminated by a peer culture where contact also alludes to sexual contact and the threat of pregnancy and kids. Unlike Kayleigh, who defends against a feeling of possible disintegration by invoking an imaginative world of others, Rowan avoids others and defends herself by retreating into the wild spaces of nature where she feels autonomous.

While climbing she seemed to relive her anxiety and every time she came down safely her movements incorporated a feeling of future liberation. Her bodily practices mimetically referenced her nan's building project in line with historical legacies of capable women who build communities in harsh conditions. This desire was revitalised and kept psychically alive by climbing mountains or speeding on her bike. Rowan's becomings seemed to capture a yearning to be other (Deleuze and Guattari 1987, 2983; Probyn 1996) and to escape the traditional gender roles of the community: the luminous figure of the 'valleys' girl/wife' trapped by boys, kids and cooking.

Crossing boundaries: Sharman's abundant becomings

We meet Sharman a few months after she had moved from an area that she described as violent and alienating to a village near the town centre and a new school. She constantly referred to her new place as a gentler environment where she found friendly adults, loyal friends and good teachers. Even so, at the beginning of the interview she described her life as weird, explaining that 'many things have happened to me':

> Well I don't know, because my life has been really weird and not normal, it's just not safe for me.

She told stories of mishaps such as when she hurt her knee cheer-leading, when she fell out of a tree onto a needle, when her brother was bullied and when her mother's friend got killed by a train. When she talked about her mother suffering from a brain tumour and being taken into hospital for six weeks, she communicated a sense of being left. At the beginning of the interview she talked explicitly of places where she still did not feel safe, such as on the internet and in other people's homes:

> I don't like the feeling of them so I don't go into a stranger's house' [….] I just don't feel like I am welcome, I am not very safe, there is just something about it.

She avoided social networking sites because she was afraid that her father would track her down. When she had a BEBO account she says that strange men kept sending her unwanted messages. Yet, her ability to defend herself is captured by a forceful act of self-preservation when she 'smash[es]' her phone to cut off the disturbing connection with unknown others.

Towards the end of the interview she told of the time when she was beaten up by a group of older kids leaving her with scars on her shoulder and on her elbow. She says that these scars still hurt but that at least they are not on her face. Her ability to reflect on and talk about the bad things that have happened to her was remarkable because of the way she also described good things. Even as she described her mother's illness she talked of the friends who looked after her and the huge party her mum had thrown for her after they moved.

Indeed, her interview was animated with vivid descriptions of events, places and playing. She explained her ability to tune into boys' play:

> Um, well when I moved over here, I was like 7, so I went to primary school in Cwm Parc and I just bonded well with the boys cos I got brothers and I know what they are like and on their birthdays I know what to get them, and like all my friends that are girls know mostly boys, so I am friends with them as well, so … I just get along with them.

Affects related to being with boys and moving the way they do were expressed in her pleasure while playing in mud:

> Yeah. Get my hoodie on, get my tracksuit, old trainers, not my new ones and go out in the mud. Don't bother about my hair and makeup … we go up the country park, or anywhere where it its muddy […] We make mud slides and slide down them, get mud all down our backs and […] Yeah, we sort of throw mud at each other, its fun.

She hinted at her ability to 'become boy' (*Yeah, I know a boy more than I know a girl*) and her smooth negotiation of masculine and feminine territories is captured by her descriptions of clothes and dressing up:

51

Me and the girls talk in the toilets sometimes put mascara on, sort of talk.
Um me and boys on clothes, like I said, we dressed Andrew up in my glittery dress, he tried on some eyeliner as well, I mean he got to try something.

Sharman demonstrated an ability to switch back and forth playfully between groups of friends helping them also to disregard the normalised boundaries between gendered worlds. She moved between fear and security, cleanliness (order) and mud (abundance) and male and female territories. There were still some people and places that she excluded as no-go areas, such as strangers' homes, social networking sites and her father. Yet, she was able to gather friends and relatives around her through her ability to enter reciprocally into their worlds. Even although her body has been scarred and hurt such as the knee that did not work properly, she did not allow these impediments to prevent her from moving physically, affectively and in tune with others. These attunements meant that she became at times a 'boy' and at times a 'girl'. She found ways to be held by others and by the landscape, through activities of skateboarding, BMXing and drumming. Her talk of activities and bodily movements seemed to invoke affects that she felt intensely sometimes as pain and sometimes as joy. Her ability to de-integrate and then re-integrate through constant movement seemed to assure that while stuck in some places, she was predominantly moving forward away from adversity.

Sharman's interview exemplified many positive feelings as she embraced the new: a new home, a new school and a new town and distanced herself from a past that involved violence, bullying and harassment. These new ways suggest possible future becomings that break free from past rhythms of life: becomings (Deleuze and Guattari 1983, 1987) that may or may not come to fruition for Sharman. Her interview was full of vivid descriptions such as the joy of throwing mud. Sharman could 'throw like a boy' and her movements mimetically referenced the imaginary world of boys' fun, liberty and abundance that is not easily socially available to girls (Renold 2008; Young 2005). Even so, she retained fears that her father might find her or that older men would appropriate her.

Discussion: bodily knowing, affect and gendered becomings

The vignettes present a variety of feelings and many of the girls' descriptions reveal how their moving bodies were entangled with places, objects and others in dynamic assemblages.

Young (2005) maintains that bodies inhabit space influenced by deep historical legacies such as patriarchy. She argues that in everyday life, girls are constantly reminded of the dangers of movement. Indeed, negative feelings of being under surveillance, fears of predatory men or that you 'will be taken' weave in and out of these accounts and were enduring themes in the data sets of the larger study (Renold and Ivinson 2012a). We also detected considerable self-consciousness in girls' accounts of movement. However, while each girl feared invasion, or sometime felt oppressed, they also seemed to have experienced positive feelings and moments of liberation albeit in very different ways. For example, Rowan's account of riding her bike fast seemed to involve a joyous transcendence and at the same time an awareness of a ubiquitous (masculine) gaze positioning her as one who was transgressing the historical norms of feminine (im)mobility. While Sharman explicitly stated in her interview, 'I don't care what they think of me', Rowan remained compromised, evidenced by her comment, 'I know I should have relationships but'. This hesitancy was typical of girls' descriptions of bodily movements, in contrast to boys' descriptions that demonstrated their ability to plunge into actions (cf. Ivinson 2013).

Each vignette gives a sense of how becomings involved fluctuating affects experienced as gradations on a spectrum of agency from empowering to disempowering. There were occasions when each girl felt stuck and unable to move forward. We have tried also to show that the patterning of these momentary fluctuations varied across the four participants so that we can say that some girls seemed to experience many expansive becomings while others were comparatively more stuck and less able to imagine themselves forward.

We have tried to demonstrate a wide range of expansive and blocked becomings (Delueze and Guattari 1983, 1987) through the vignettes and how expectations from others in their immediate lives allowed girls to resist or mimetically recreate gender practices. We have sought to understand why some girls managed to find ways to imagine themselves forward while other girls, with similar life stories and social contexts experienced so much 'stuckness' that their ability to imagine themselves forward was negligible. In striving to understand how this happens we detected an agency that is more to do with affect than cognition: one that is experienced yet cannot easily be spoken about. In making visible how girls' bodies are entangled with bikes, water, mud and other elements in moving assemblages, we have tried to demonstrate how becomings emerge *in-between*. At times, girls' movements capture a positive sense of being transported beyond themselves that at times hinted at a yearning to be other (Probyn 1996). Along with material feminists, we hope to shift the emphasis away from women's bodies as only objects for the gaze of others and to stress that within assemblages, bodies were integral elements in girls' becomings.

Conclusion

This paper has connected Deleuzeo-Guattarian's concept of becoming with new materialist feminist onto-epistemologies which in many ways challenge the very foundations of how subjectivity and agency have come to be theorised and researched within the social sciences.[2] Positive experiences are often felt rather than understood as cognitive or rational, because affect goes through bodies and not only through minds. Thus we can expand traditional understandings of agency beyond will, spirit or mind and recognise agency as emergent within moving assemblages in which bodies and other elements are intra-actively entangled (Barad 2007).

We have tried to show how agency emerges in the intra-action of bodies, places and all forms of matter including landscapes, water, bikes and others. Specifically we have tried to show how body-movement assemblages afforded girls different kinds of agency. At the heart of these philosophical moves lies a reconceptualisation of agency from linear to complex. Thus, cause and in this case, human motivation or agency can no longer be said to reside on one side of a binary, motivated by will, spirit or 'masculinity'. Instead, causality is said to emerge *between* elements in dynamic intra-acting relations (Barad 2007, 244–246). This shift has radical implications because it overthrows Cartesian images of the universe as dead matter that only moves according to the application of mechanical forces applied from outside and reinstates matter as alive (e.g. Bennett 2010). Barad defines matter 'like meaning' as 'always already (having) an ongoing historicity' (2003, 821, cited in Van der Tuim 2011, 32). Significantly then, matter is afforded a temporal dimension and a trajectory of its own. Matter is said to have dynamic movement and a life of its own with traces of its past (cf. Bennett 2010; Birke 1999; Fox 2012). Thus, all matter including corporeal matter has the potential to have effects along with other elements. If we transpose this complex causality onto humans, agency emerges within intra-acting entanglements of elements (all having their own properties) as assemblages. Furthermore, agency is about 'possibility' (Barad 2007, 218) or what Deleuze and Guattari theorise as 'becoming' which can wax and wane depending on the artefacts, instruments and contexts that make up assemblages as they incessantly form and reform as part of the dynamic movement of life. Accordingly, human agency when conceptualised as becoming can be understood as 'volitional choices as complex, contradictory and multi-faceted' (Braidotti 2002/2005, 61). In turn this approach suggests that subjectivity is complex, dynamic and plural and cannot be separated from places, history and corporeality.

All the young women (and young men) we worked with had aspirations and dreams. They also had multiple experiences of difficulties that related to living in a post-industrial place marked by poverty. Even so, through movement, some girls found ways to imagine futures and some of the most playful movements were also the most liberating. While our vignettes show how traumatic memories can restrict movement, they also illustrate how corporeal memories were re-invoked and reworked through movement that, for example, allowed Arwydd to overcome difficulties. Understanding becomings as emergent between elements of assemblages that include moving bodies can provide some powerful insights into resources and barriers that girls encounter in their everyday lives and in fulfilling their aspirations. Aspiration broadly defined involves having a sense of hope and hope constitutes having a sense of moving forward. Post-Oedipal understandings of desires (Deleuze and Guattari 1983) recognise desire as self-expansion (Grosz 1994) embracing plenitude and abundance and not only feelings of lack and melancholy (Alaimo and Hekman 2008). If girls do not move they also do not explore, take risks, experiment and therefore miss out on ways of being and becoming that may open up new imaginative worlds including worlds in which they build houses, work abroad and, dare we say it, desire.

Notes

1. This publication is based on research supported by the Wales Institute of Social and Economic Research, Data and Methods (WISERD) funded by the UK Economic and Social Research Council (Grant number: RES-576-25-0021) and the Higher Education Funding Council for Wales.
2. For how we might research and conceptualise future theorisations of girls (and boys) gendered becomings, see also Coleman (2009), Coleman and Ringrose (2013), Gonick and Gannon (2013), Renold and Ringrose (2008, 2011) and Ivinson and Renold (2013).

References

Alaimo, S., and S. Hekman, eds. 2008. *Material Feminisms*. Bloomington: Indiana University Press.
Azzarito, L. 2010. "Future Girls, Transcendent Femininities and New Pedagogies: Toward Girls' Hybrid Bodies?" *Sport, Education and Society* 15 (3): 261–275.
Barad, K. 1996. "Meeting the Universe Halfway: Realism and Social Constructivism without Contradiction." In *Feminism, Science and the Philosophy of Science*, edited by N.H. Nelson and J. Nelson, 161–194. Dortrecht: Kluwer Academic Publishers.

Barad, K. 2007. *Meeting the Universe Halfway: Quantum Physics and the Entanglement of Matter and Meaning*. Durham: Duke University Press.

Bennett, J. 2010. *Vibrant Matter: A Political Ecology of Things*. Durham and London: Duke University Press.

Birke, L. 1999. "Bodies and Biology." In *Feminist Theory and the Body: Reader*, edited by Janet Price and Margrit Shildrick, 42–49. New York: Routledge.

Braidotti, R. 2002/2005. *Metamorphoses: Towards a Material Theory of Becoming*. Cambridge: Polity Press.

Braidotti, R. 2006. *Transpositions: On Nomadic Ethics*. Cambridge: Polity Press.

Bruley, S. 2007. "The Politics of Food: Gender, Family, Community and Collective Feeding in South Wales in the General Strike and Miners' Lockout of 1926." *Twentieth Century British History* 18 (1): 54–77.

Coleman, B. 2009. *The Becoming of Bodies: Girls, Images, Experience*. Manchester: Manchester University Press.

Coleman, R., and J Ringrose. 2013. *Deleuze and Research Methodologies*. Edinburgh: Edinburgh University Press.

Deleuze, G., and F. Guattari. 1983. *Anti-Oedipus: Capitalism and Schizophrenia*. Translated by R. Hurley, M. Seem, and H. R. Lane. Minneapolis: University of Minnesota Press.

Deleuze, G., and F. Guattari. 1987. *A Thousand Plateaus: Capitalism and Schizophrenia*. Minneapolis: University of Minnesota Press.

Evans, B. 2006. "'I'd Feel Ashamed': Girls' Bodies and Sports Participation." *Gender, Place and Culture* 13 (5): 547–561.

Foucault, M. [1978]1990. *The History of Sexuality. Volume I: An Introduction*. Translated by R. Hurley. New York: Vintage Books.

Fox, N. 2012. *The Body*. Cambridge: Polity Press.

Francis, B. 2000. *Boys, Girls and Achievement: Addressing the Classroom Issues*. London: Routledge Falmer.

Gonick, M., and S. Gannon. 2013. "Collective Biography: An Introduction." *Girlhood Studies* 6 (1): 7–12.

Gordon, T., J. Holland, and E. Lahelma. 2000a. *Making Spaces: Citizenship and Difference in Schools*. Basingstoke: Palgrave Macmillan.

Gordon, T., J. Holland, and E. Lahelma. 2000b. "Moving Bodies/Still Bodies: Embodiment and Agency in Schools." In *Organizing Bodies: Policy, Institutions and Work*, edited by L. McKie and N. Watson, 81–101. Basingstoke: Palgrave MacMillan.

Grosz, E. 1994. *Volatile Bodies: Towards a Corporeal Feminism*. Bloomington: Indiana University Press.

Haraway, D. 1991. *Simians, Cyborgs and Women: The Reinvention of Nature*. London: Free Association Press.

Henriques, J. 2010. "The Vibrations of Affect and Their Propagation on a Night Out on Kindston's Dancehall Scene." *Body & Society* 16 (1): 57–89.

Ivinson, G. 2012. "The Body and Pedagogy: Beyond Absent, Moving Bodies in Pedagogic Practice." *British Journal of Sociology of Education* 33 (4): 489–506.

Ivinson, G. 2013. "Skills in Motion: Boys' Motor Biking Activities as Transitions into Working Class Masculinity." *Sport, Education and Society*, 1–16. http://www.tandfonline.com/doi/abs/10.1080/13573322.2012.692669#.UiXsX83UqjQ

Ivinson, G., and P. Murphy. 2007. *Rethinking Single-Sex Teaching: Gender, School Subjects and Learning*. Berkshire: Open University Press McGraw Hill.

Ivinson, G., and E. Renold. 2013. "Transversal Subjectivity: Thinking with Deleuze and Guattari's BwO to Theorise a Young Girl's Becoming in a Post Industrial Locale." *Subjectivity* 6 (4): 1–22.

Jones, O. 2010. "Tomboy Tales: The Rural, Nature and the Gender of Childhood." *Gender, Place and Culture* 6 (2): 117–136.

Latour, B. 2005. *Reassembling the Social*. Oxford: Oxford University Press.

Mannay, D. 2013. "'Keeping Close and Spoiling': Exploring Discourses of Social Reproduction and the Impossibility of Negotiating Change and Maintaining Continuity in Urban South Wales." *Gender and Education* 25 (1): 91–107.

Marshall, J. 2008. "Experience of Learning: A Generational Study." Doctoral thesis, Cardiff University.

Matthews, H., and M. Limb. 1999. "Defning an Agenda for the Geography of Children." *Progress in Human Geography* 23 (1): 61–90.

Matthews, H., and F. Tucker. 2001. "They Don't Like Girls Hanging Around There: Conflicts Over Recreational Space in Rural Northamptonshire." *Area* 33 (2): 161–168.

McDowell, L., and D. Massey. 1984. "A Woman's Place?" In *Geography Matters! A Reader*, edited by D. Massey and J. Allen, 124–147. Cambridge: Cambridge University Press in Association with the Open University.

Mortimer-Sandilands, C. 2008. "Landscape, Memory and Forgetting: Thinking Through (My Mother's) Body and Place." In *Material Feminisms*, edited by S. Alaimo and S. Hekman, 265–291. Bloomington: Indiana University Press.

Murphy, D., and C. Gipps. 1996. *Equity in the Classroom: Towards Effective Pedagogy for Girls and Boys*. London: Falmer Press.

Penlington, N. 2010. "Masculinity and Domesticity in 1930s South Wales: Did Unemployment Change the Domestic Division of Labour?" *Twentieth Century British History* 21 (3): 281–299.

Probyn, E. 1996. *Outside Belongings*. London: Routledge.

Renold, E. 2006. "Chapter 12: Gendered Classroom Experiences." In *The Handbook of Gender and Education*, edited by C. Skelton, B. Francis, and L. Smulyan, 439–453. London: SAGE.

Renold, E. 2008. "Queering Masculinity: Re-theorising Contemporary Tomboyism in the Schizoid Space of Innocent/Heterosexualized Young Femininities." *Girlhood Studies* 1 (2): 129–151.

Renold, E., and G. Ivinson. 2012a. "Girls, Sexuality and Sexual Objectification." Paper presented at 'Sexual Exploitation, Sexual Objectification and Sexual Abuse: Engaging with Research: Policy and Practice', Cardiff University/Barnardos, April 30.

Renold, E., and G. Ivinson. 2012b. "Young People and Sexual Assemblages: Changing Theories, Changing Subjectivities in Changing Times." Invited Panel: 'Studying Gender and Sexuality Psychosocially: Dialogue Across Perspectives', Open University, May 15.

Renold, E., and G. Ivinson. 2013. "Girls, Camera, (intra)Action: Applying a Diffractive Analysis to Teen Girls' Engagement with Visual Participatory Methodologies in Ethnographic Research on Gender, Identity and Place." Paper presented at America Education Research Association, San Francisco, April 27–May 1.

Renold, E., and J. Ringrose. 2008. "Regulation and Rupture: Mapping Tween and Teenage Girls' Resistance to the Heterosexual Matrix." *Feminist Theory* 9 (3): 335–360.

Renold, E., and J. Ringrose. 2011. "Schizoid Subjectivities: Re-theorising Teen-Girls' Sexual Cultures in an Era of Sexualisation." *Journal of Sociology, Special Issue on 'Youth identities, Cultures and Transitions'* 47 (4): 389–409.

Ringrose, J., L. Harvey, R. Gill, and S. Livingstone. 2013. "Teen Girls, Sexual Double Standards and 'Sexting': Gendered Value in Digital Image Exchange." *Feminist Theory* 14 (3).

Ross, N. J., E. Renold, S. Holland, and N. Hillman. 2009. "Moving Stories: Using Mobile Methods to Explore the Everyday Lives of Young People in Public Care." *Qualitative Research* 9 (5): 605–623.

Skelton, T. 2000. "Nothing to Do, Nowhere to Go? Teenage Girls and 'Public' Space in the Rhondda Valleys, South Wales." In *Children's Geographies: Playing, Living, Learning*, edited by S. Holloway and G. Valentine, 80–99. London: Routledge.

Smyth, J., A. Mooney, and M. Casey. 2011. "Where has Class Gone? The Pervasiveness of Class in Girls' Physical Activity in a Rural Town." *Sport, Education and Society* 1–18. doi:10.1080/13573322.2011.619525.

Taylor, Y. 2012. *Fitting into Place? Classed and Gendered Geographies and Temporalities*. Surrey: Ashgate.

Van der Tuim, I. 2011. "'A Different Starting Point, a Different Metaphysics.' Reading Bergson and Barad Diffractively." *Hypatia* 26 (1): 22–33.

Walkerdine, V. 1990. *Schoolgirl Fictions*. London: Verso.

Walkerdine, V. 2010. "Communal Beingness and Affect: An Exploration of Trauma in an Ex Industrial Community." *Body & Society* 16 (1): 91–116.

Walkerdine, V. 2013. "Using the Work of Felix Guattari to Understand Space, Place, Social Justice and Education." *Qualitative Inquiry* 19 (10).

Walkerdine, V., A. Olsvold, and M. Rudberg. 2013. "Researching Embodiment and Intergenerational Trauma using the Work of Davoine and Gaudilliere: History Walked in the Door." *Subjectivity* 6 (3): 272–297.

Walkerdine, V., and J. Jimenez. 2011. *Gender, Work and Community after De-industrialisation: A Psychosocial Approach to Affect*. Basingstoke: Palgrave Macmillan.

Walkerdine, V., H. Lucy, and J. Melody. 2001. *Growing Up Girl: Psycho-social Explorations of Gender and Class*. Basingstoke: Palgrave Macmillan.

Wulf, C. 2013. "Mimesis in Early Childhood: Enculturation, Practical Knowledge and Performability." In *Children, Development and Education: Cultural, Historical and Anthropological Perspectives*, edited by M. Kontopodis, C. Wulf, and B. Fichtner, 89–103. New York: Springer.

Young, M. I. 2005. *On Female Body Experience: 'Throwing Like a Girl' and Other Essays*. Oxford: Oxford University Press.

The teacher–student writing conference reimaged: *entangled becoming-writingconferencing*

Donna Kalmbach Phillips[a] and Mindy Legard Larson[b]

[a]College of Education, Pacific University, Forest Grove, OR, USA; [b]Education Department, Linfield College, McMinnville, OR, USA

This analysis is experimental: we attempt to read data *with* the work of Karen Barad and in doing so 'see' teacher–student writing conferences (a common pedagogy of US elementary school writing) as *intra-activity*. Data were gathered during teacher–student writing conferences in a grade five US classroom over a six-week period. One conference between a researcher and a male Latino student, a Student of Labels, is diffracted. Reading and writing and thinking *with* Barad disrupt our habitual ways of privileging language as representational. Rather, we consider the material-discursive practices of schooling that produce what comes to *matter*, leading us to reimage the teacher–student writing conference as entangled becoming-writingconferencing, speaking to the multiplicity of participants, merging of bodies, continual movement, open-ended possibilities, and anticipated transformation of *intra-action*.

Barad (2008) asks us to stop: stop giving language so much power; stop with language as representational; stop the belief in the power of the Word to pre-exist and create; stop with our illusion of time as linear and always already cause-*then*-effect; stop placing our human selves in the centre of all things that *matter*. She asks us to see ourselves as *of* the world, part of the lively and ongoing production of possibilities and exclusions, as *entangled*, as *phenomena*: as *intra-action*. Materiality matters, Barad argues, not as an add-on to language, not as a matter of language, but because the material can never be separate from language. Expanding on the work of Foucault (1975/1979) and Butler (1993), Barad (2008) argues, for a post-humanist performativity of which 'All bodies, not merely 'human' bodies, come to matter through the world's iterative intra-activity – its performativity' (141).

Barad's (1998, 2007, 2008) thinking and reasoning stops us, leaves us gasping, working to reimage centuries of entrenched educational scientific 'objective' and representational ways of doing research, habitual ways of thinking, seeing and defining what *matters* in teaching and learning. We find ourselves diffracting the waves of Barad's theoretical concept of agential realism: shall we keep pretending we can stand aside? Shall we play when the tide is low in the tide pool? Shall we dive in? What are the implications of the latter? How shall we live as researchers and teachers and writers if we accept we are *of* the world? And a greater fear exists: so imprisoned are 'we', the collective subjectivity 'we' of schools and classroom practice, in the clutch of representationalism, can we begin to 'think a difference' (Deleuze 1968/1994) with agential realism?

Foucault (1984/1985) writes, 'There are times in life when the question of knowing if one can think differently than one thinks, and perceive differently than one sees, is absolutely necessary if one is to go on looking and reflecting at all' (8). And the laughing, crying, angry, happy voices of children with whom we work; teachers who bear the responsibilities of teaching in and through their bodies of a nation addicted to standardisation; families who wear the materiality of US norms through painful realities; move us to a deeper understanding of Foucault's words: *we have no other choice*. We attempt this project as our 'experiential and our experimental' (as cited in Semetsky 2006), as a way of 'seeing *with* data' (Hultman and Lenz Taguchi 2010, 536), to read the teacher–student writing conference as intra-activity, so as not to 'repeat the already formed and recognized' (Colebrook 2006, 15).

In this analysis, we reimage subjectivity as a collective of material-discursive practices, illustrating how students, teachers, and non-humans intra-act, collide as phenomenon in a grade five classroom. Specifically, we analyse the teacher–student writing conference, a one-on-one teaching strategy employed to meet the individual needs of student-writers. We disrupt our habitual reading of the teacher–student writing conference as a 'teacher' – 'student' – 'conference,' as a two-way street of clear communication, as 'teacher-directed' pedagogy; instead, reading for the 'material dynamics of intra-activity' (Barad 2007, 141). We honor the complexities of teaching and learning, the materialisation of bodies and practices, so that our collective 'we' as teachers, researchers, and writers might emerge differently, so that we might live more ethically in diffracting the waves of US educational norms. We embrace that, 'We are responsible for the world within which we live not because it is an arbitrary construction of our choosing, but because it is sedimented out of particular practices that we have a role in shaping' (Barad 1998, 102). In this analysis, we study such practices as they relate to the teacher–student writing conference in a diverse elementary classroom.

A theoretical mapping

Barad's (1998) *agential reality* recognises that the:

> political potential of deconstructive analysis lies not in the simple recognition of the inevitability of exclusions, but in insisting upon accountability for the particular exclusions that are enacted and in taking up the responsibility to perpetually contest and rework the boundaries ....it is an understanding of reality that takes account of both the exclusions upon which it depends and its openness to future reworkings. (103–104)

Agential realism is the ongoing reworking of boundaries that do 'not sit still' (Barad 2008, 135). It is a view of reality not 'composed of things-in-themselves or things-behind-phenomena, but of "things"-in-phenomena' (135). A teacher–student writing conference, then, is *movement*. It cannot be captured in a three-dimensional still snapshot: it is desire, discourse, power, identities of human, and non-human, *entangled*. Boundaries are blurred like a watercolour not yet dried, spilling, seeping over the perceived outlines of 'teacher', 'student', and 'writing'.

'The primary ontological units are not 'things' but phenomena – dynamic topological reconfigurings/entanglements/relationalities/(re)articulations' (Barad 2008, 135).

What is real exists out of phenomena or the 'inseparability of agentially intra-acting "components"' (133) materialised as particular practices that make real intelligible. Writing, itself, is reconfigured: a discursively materially moving collective where finding 'the' writer is enfolded in intra-activity. 'Manuscript' and 'author' no longer exist as a binary; there is no clear beginning or ending to the narrative. Material and the discursive, apparatuses, and phenomena are not and cannot be separate but are all a *matter* of intra-action: 'Material-discursive apparatuses are themselves phenomena made up of specific intra-actions of humans and nonhumans ... what gets defined as a "subject" (or "object") and what gets defined as an "apparatus" is intra-actively constituted within specific practices' (Barad 1998, 105). What is intelligible, what is 'real' in the teacher–student writing conference? We 'see' a teacher and student sitting close, blank paper between them, and we read the three as two separate humans and one object, following a writing conference protocol, towards the defined goal of improved writing. But see how the previous sentence is laden with the apparatuses of 'writing conference protocol' and school expectations. See how the phenomena of writing are entangled with the collective verb subjectivities of 'teacher' and 'student', and how the paper itself is heavy with school expectations and how all of 'these' are a collective, moving 'them' intra-acting even as 'they' become constituted within the practice of school and writing instruction.

Intra-activity is a 're(con)figuring' (Barad 2007, 179) of space, time, and matter. The beauty of intra-activity is how change and the possibility for change, for *becoming*, is the very dynamism of the world. Ironically speaking, this is 'foundational', in understanding intra-activity: this moving, becoming, changing, open-space, on-going (re)working of boundaries as enfolding, the 'sedimentation' of past and future as present, intra-playing subjects and objects as collective verbs diffracting, the 'iterative differentiatings of spacetimemattering' (179). It defies the linear nature of printed text and the confines of English grammar, the trajectory of reading and thinking in sequential units, such as left to right. It plays hide and seek with the concept of a teacher–student writing conference as a protocol, or a four-phase process proceeding towards an intended and known goal.

> Iterative intra-actions are the dynamics through which temporality and spatiality are produced and iteratively reconfigured in the materialization of phenomena and the (re)making of material-discursive boundaries and the constitutive exclusions. (179)

Each teacher–student writing conference is a moment of *becoming*, of possibilities. It is not just a teacher and student and blank paper performing writing nor is it a coming together of these individual entities to produce writing, rather it is 'reconfigurings/ entanglements/relationalities/(re)articulations' (Barad 2008, 135) of what is seen and unseen so we are left asking, "Who is the writer? Who is the teacher, the student? Who produced this writing? What and who is produced and what and who is excluded? And now do they work, here, at this moment of the writing conference?

Agential realism: how does it work?

Critical to this paper, then, are elementary students as writers, the act of writing, and the product of writing within the context of school. A humanist view would hold these as separate entities. A student-writer, given an assignment to write, initiates an idea from within himself, then, following a step-by-step process, applies pencil to blank page, forming words, then sentences, then paragraphs, and pages of text which is viewed as the product of the student-writer. In this way, the produced writing is representative of what the writer knows and the writer's abilities to communicate through writing. Rethink this as intra-activity. The 'student-writer' is a product of material-discursive practices, or practices that are 'boundary-making' that 'have no finality in the ongoing dynamics of agential intra-activity' (Barad 2008, 139). The student-writer is, then, a moving verb of iterative historical, cultural, political, gendered, and raced practices so who we see as the student-writer might be *He, Latino, and Labels of State* (*Talented and Gifted or Special Education*), and this defines and sets boundaries on the expectations of the *He/Latino/Student/Writer/Special Education* as different than the *She/White/Student/Talented* and *Gifted* 'writer'. The writers are simultaneously produced by the material configurations of what is intelligible as 'school': desks, chairs (engineered to scientific norms of physicality); the clock keeping and marking time; and, the untenable routines and materiality of schooling that marks He/Latino/ Student/Writer/Special Education and She/White/Talented and Gifted intelligible, different and real. The changing topology of subjectivity is always already diffracting the terms of boundaries imposed by the intra-actions of material-discursive practices. The 'student-writer' is 'not a preexisting subject with inherent properties' but 'a phenomenon that is constituted and reconstituted out of the historically and culturally situated iterative intra-actions of material-discursive apparatuses of bodily production' (Barad 1998, 115).

Apparatuses are also materially discursively produced. In this analysis, consider the poetry-writing-format as an apparatus, an instrument designed to engineer successful poetry writing. The poetry-writing-format is a published piece of pedagogy, a type of 'formula' used to prompt writers' ideas and guide them through a writing process. Materialised in print with cover, title page, and copyright, it is a material-discursive practice of 'evidence-based' pedagogy. It carries with it the weight of authority: if followed correctly, students should be able to write a poem, to be 'poets'. As an apparatus, it acts as discipline, as a

> specific technique of a power that regards individuals both as objects and as instruments of its exercise ... the technique that make it possible to see induce effects of power, and in which, conversely, the means of coercion make those on whom they are applied clearly visible. (Foucault 1975/1979, 170–171)

The poetry-writing-format acts as a boundary setting apparatus, excluding other possible poetry writing, authorising a particular kind of poetry, and this is further disciplined by what is deemed appropriate through scientific evidence establishing developmental writing benchmarks, along with trends for males and females student-writers, and, therefore, what is 'acceptable' writing completed in 'school.'

Yet, apparatuses are open-ended because they are *phenomena* and always in the process of intra-acting with other apparatuses (Barad 2008). School discourse or the discursive practice of school intra-acting with the poetry-writing-format defines what counts as meaningful poetry, but the outcome is not predetermined. Potentialities and agency always exist as apparatuses intra-act with other humans and non-humans. Likewise, objects are material-discursively produced. The blank page facing the student-writer is not a neutral object waiting for human action to give it form. Rather, as Semetsky (2006) writes, 'it is what is unseen ... that in the long run decides what is there to be seen' (111). The blank page, in the context of school, is always already infused with expectation. It is the apparatus of achievement, of evidence, of data that will be used for or against the student-writer; it has a history, culture, and political past and future enfolded in its material-discursive intelligibility to teachers. There is nothing blank about a blank page. The expectation for what is appropriate school writing is well established through authoritative and scientific educational research resulting in developmental rubrics and norms.

There are no objects that are neutral: the pencil, the chair, the clock, and the intercom, for example, are all material-discursively formed; all are recognisable as the particular tools of 'school.' Fifth-grade children do not use mechanical pencils associated by yet another material-discursive discourse as the tool of engineers; they use a sturdy yellow pencils, and this object, too, has a history, culture, and political past and future enfolded into the moment it intra-acts with male or female, Latino, or White hands. And it is this differing that 'cannot be taken for granted; it matters −indeed, it is what matters' (Barad 2007, 136).

These material-discursive practices 'produce, rather than merely describe, the subjects and objects of knowledge practices' (Barad 2007, 147); humans and non-humans are subjectivity and are identified as 'human' and 'non-human' by material-discursive practices making them intelligible as such. Literacy educational research informs us that males will most likely write action stories and females will write stories with dialogue and collaboration (Newkirk 2002) and this disciplines the body of male and female writers, influences the practice and expectations of teachers, the publication of certain texts 'better for boys' through an endless, authoritative, yet authorless practice and materiality that is discourse, the 'ongoing agential intra-actions of the world' (Barad 2007, 150).

It follows then that these moving and changing bodies *perform* writing not as separate activities, but as *entangled*.

> To be entangled is not simply to be intertwined with another, as in the joining of separate entitles, but to lack an independent, self-contained existence. Existence is not an individual affair. Individuals do not preexist their interactions; rather, individuals emerge through and as part of their entangled intra-relating . . . .time and space, like matter and meaning, come into existence, are iteratively reconfigured through each intra-action, thereby making it impossible to differentiate in any absolute sense between creation and renewal, beginning and returning, continuity and discontinuity, here and there, past and future. (Barad 2007, ix)

Writing entangled is intra-action. Despite common references to *the* writing process in writing pedagogy, writing is not a linear process, a trajectory moving from finding and idea to producing a final product. Writing as intra-action is not what happens between writer and blank page, but the entanglement of human and non-human subjectivity as phenomenon, open for the (re)configuring/(re)articulations, for agency and possibility, from which humans and non-humans emerge. As post-humanistic performativity, the focus shifts from how writing is a mirror of the writer 'to matters of practices, doings, and actions' (Barad 2007, 135).

Barad (2007) writes, 'There is a vitality to the liveliness of intra-activity, not in the sense of a new form of vitalism, but rather in terms of a new sense of aliveness' (177). It is this aliveness we seek in reading our data *with* Barad, changing the topography of ourselves as we write this research, emerging differently, so we might act more responsible as researchers and teachers of writing.

A 'methodology'
Context and data collected

Data were collected over a six-week period. During this time, we both conducted writing conferences with children in a fifth-grade classroom alongside the classroom teacher. Data included: audio recorded and transcribed writing conferences, field notes, written notes from on-going data analysis conversations, and written analytic memos. Children in this classroom are marked by labels of material-discursive power: *Male/Female; English Language Learners; Latino/a; White; Attention Deficient Hyperactivity Disorder; 504* (a category of students established by the Civil Rights amendment to the US Constitution). Additionally, children are marked by intervention programmes where students are physically called out of the classroom and given additional instruction.

The school, too, carries a label of the Federal Government: *Title One* (a school in the USA with over 40% of students receiving free or reduced lunches). Eighty per cent of the students receive free or reduced lunches; food is the material absent in their lives. The school is under constant surveillance (Foucault 1975/1979) and pressure by the State to ensure compliance with State and Federal standards for academic achievement.

Such labels have 'very real consequences for how those bodies [human and non human] inhabit cultural space' (Hekman 2008, 101). These consequences are explored in our analysis of the teacher–student writing conference.

'Participants'

We might say that the writing conference is between Donna, one of the two researchers/teachers of this study, and Esteban, a fifth-grade writer. We might report that the writing conference takes place during a poetry unit and that students on this day were writing 'six-room poems' (Heard 1998). But this would be a representational, one-dimensional account; an account that assumes Donna and Esteban are isolated identities in a world where communication is a 'two-way street;' a world without intra-activity; without entanglement; without a historical, cultural, and political past, present, and future, enfolded; without discourse and material practices of power. Yet for the purposes of the required research-writing norm (itself a material-discursive apparatus), we identify these two as participants in the featured writing conference.

There is also the participation of the classroom teacher as the Teacher with Authority, the six-room poetry-writing-format as a discursive-material apparatus of authoritative pedagogy, the Blank Paper, as School Expectation, and Esteban's friends who engage in the writing conference – all of which and whom are not isolated identities or separated by categories of human and non-human, but collectives intra-acting. And so we ask, 'Who and what comes to the writing conference highlighted in this paper and how do they emerge differently from the conference?' And – 'How does this *matter?*'

Data analysis

Barad (1998) writes, 'Producing a "good" ultrasound image is not as simple as snapping a picture; neither is reading one' (101). We might apply this to 'methodology', a material-discursive practice of the apparatus that is 'qualitative research'. Data move. Data intra-act. Data perform: we can produce an 'image' but it will appear static on the page, blurry at best, and difficult to read as it risks humanist reflections rather than post-humanist diffractions. What are data? The transcriptions and field notes taken by researchers in the 'field'? See how the sentencing produces separate entities outside of subjectivity and power, a researcher 'set aside'? Researcher, notes and instruments – all intra-act: all are data, and data and researcher emerge differently through the intra-action with the apparatus that is research.

To think a *difference* (Deleuze 1968/1994), we read our data *with* Barad, asking of our data these questions based upon her work to act as a provocation, to disturb our habitual thinking as researchers and teachers: (1) What apparatuses are in motion in these student-teaching writing conferences? (2) What are the discursive and material forces? (3) How is the past and present folded into this moment? (4) How do humans and non-humans emerge differently as we re-enact this experience through multiple readings and writings with the data? How do we as researchers and teachers of writing emerge differently? (5) What are the material consequences of our reading of the data? How will we live differently as researchers and teachers?

Writing, as intra-activity, is our mode of inquiry (Richardson and St Pierre 2005). If writing is intra-activity, a transformative process of which the writer emerges changed, then ought not the 'results' act as a provocation to the reader to emerge changed from the intra-activity of reading? We have embarked on a diffractive reading and writing of data. Hultman and Lenz Taguchi (2010) write,

> a diffractive 'seeing' or 'reading' the data activates you as being part of and activated by the waves of relational intra-actions between different bodies and concepts (meanings) in an event *with* the data. As you read, you *install* yourself in an event of 'becoming-with' the data. (537)

We are installed as researchers/writers/readers in this data. The question becomes, how shall research 'results' look, read on the paper to invite the reader to a diffractive and intra-active reading *with* the data as well?

We employ a form of narrative, a version of a memory story, not as representative of the writing conference, not as metaphor, but as a tool for unthinking teaching and learning through a disruptive writing. Our claim as authors is that the following (re)told story of a writing conference is intra-activity, a play *with* language and data, intended to evoke and provoke a *difference* (Deleuze 1968/1994). Using narrative risks, the illusion of a beginning, middle and end to the (re)told writing conference; but there is no beginning, middle, and end, only the ongoing intra-actions of *mattering* (Barad 2007). We use Capitals throughout our writing to indicate a material-discursive authority, not as an identifiable and static source, but as a naming of an authorless yet authoritative power that is discourse (Bakhtin 1981). We also use quotation marks to acknowledge the limitation of pronouns such as 'He', as if a singular, unified 'he' can exist. At times, we set aside conventions of syntax to disrupt the reader and the reading: for example, deliberately using a plural verb with a singular subject to denote the multiplicity of subjectivity. Doing so is one way of rejecting data as representational; it is a way of reimaging thinking and subverting traditional research writing. Playing with the narrative and the naming of the 'teacher-writing' conference through a disruptive writing is meant to keep the reader at edge and provoke a difference. Borrowing from Massumi (1992), the question of this writing is not 'Is it true? But, Does it work? What new thoughts does it make possible to think? What new emotions does it make possible to feel? What new sensations and perceptions does it open in the body?' (8).

Teaching and learning in the writing conference as intra-activity

In this analysis, a teacher–student writing conference is diffracted. Our responsibility in this undertaking is to 'perpetually contest and rework the boundaries' (Barad 1998, 104) of what 'we' see as teaching and learning through reading the data *with* Barad as intra-activity. And so the (re)telling continues (its beginning cannot be located nor will it end here) with the question: Who comes to the teacher–student writing conference? What agential cuts are made, what becomings made possible, when we describe Esteban, the fifth-grade writer, teachers, and the poetry-writing-format, and other unseen and unnamed beings and expectations come to the writing conference?

Who are 'Esteban' who come to the writing conference?

Esteban comes to the teacher-writer conference. Who are Esteban? 'He' are Male and Latino; English Language Learner; At Risk (of failure/passing tests/sitting properly/ dropping out of school prior to graduation); *in* Poverty (lacking 'food security'); Academically Below Grade Level (according to results on standardised exams); 504 plan recipient (displays impulsivity according to norms for gender and age group; therefore, qualifies for this US label). Esteban 'designates an element of agential reality, a phenomenon that is constituted and reconstituted out of the historically and culturally situated iterative intra-actions of material-discursive apparatus of bodily production' (Barad 1998, 115). Esteban as phenomena includes 'those apparatuses/phenomena out of which it [He] is constituted' (115): 'his' body as gendered male, raced as Latino; 'his' student subjectivity articulated by Labels of State and Science (labels such as 'At Risk'). 'He' are constructed 'through particular boundary articulations involving the particular discursive constraints in the construction of the apparatuses themselves' (115). Such boundary articulations/apparatuses 'include' the work of biology to construct gender (Barad 2007; Butler 1999; McWhorter 2004; Ruffolo 2007), developmental norms (McWhorter 2004) and the establishment of a 'deviant' population through these norms resulting in the production of race, racism, and acceptable gender practices (Foucault 1976/1990; McWhorter 2004). School contrived/constructed labels produced through science are entangled and enforced through state authority are 'Esteban', producing him as a Student of Labels – SOL: *shit out of luck*, as the slang term implies. Esteban as a trajectory into a dead end without appropriate State and School 'interventions'.

Yet the 'subject' of Esteban, according to agential realism is 'not a pre existing object of investigation with inherent properties' (Barad 1998, 115); is not a fixed being, not a trajectory with a predictable outcome,

> but rather a 'way of being' – a verb rather than a noun. The subject is an effect of multiple encounters that entails the history of the previous encounters, the present and the potentialities of the future encounters that might take place (Hultman and Lenz Taguchi 2010, 532)

the constituted and (re)constituted of iterative intra-actions: the body of boundaries, exclusions, and possibilities. 'Intra-actions always entail particular exclusions, and exclusion foreclose the possibility of determinism, providing the condition of an open future' (Barad 2007, 177). All that is excluded from the composite of the SOL is possibility as 'intra-actions iteratively reconfigure what is possible and what is impossible' (177). The subject is not static, predetermined, but alive and of 'the world's effervescence, its exuberant creativeness [which] can never be contained or suspended' (177). Esteban is possibility because 'agency never ends; it can never "run out"' (177).

Who are 'Teacher' and 'teacher' who come to the writing conference?

Teacher and teacher also come to this writing conference. And the same kind of partial description of the constituted and (re)constituted historically, culturally, and politically situated iterative intra-actions of material-discursive apparatuses producing their bodies might be made. 'Teacher' is not an individual; rather apparatuses of school make this label intelligible. Barad's (2007) description of a factory 'worker' can be applied to 'teacher.' A teacher 'is not a fixed and unitary property of individual human beings, but an actively contested and disunified – but nonetheless objective – category that refers to particular material-discursive phenomena (not individuals)' (243). The same can be said for labels of 'Woman' and 'White': the teachers of the writing conference are gendered and raced and positioned by material-discursive practices that make them intelligible, *real* teachers *of* society. They embody Caregiver/Mother/Savior/ Counselor and Guardian of Character/Disciplinarian/Authority: subjectivities that are *performed*, as a network of relations of human and non-human, as an effect of phenomena or the 'effects of power-knowledge systems, of boundary drawing projects that make some identities/attributes intelligible, to the exclusion of others' (Barad 1998, 106). Teacher is never singular but always already plural. This naming them as Teacher is 'at once the setting of a boundary, and also the repeated inculcation of a norm' (Butler 1993, 7–8). They are intelligible by objective referents 'constituted through the intra-action of multiple regularity apparatuses' (Barad 1998, 106) so the curves of their bodies and the unseen presence of wombs are pronounced and performed as the female and nurturing teacher (Grumet 1988; McWilliam 1994; Walkerdine 1992; Weber and Mitchel, 1995).

The Teacher is the 'real' teacher in the study analysed here. Ask any student in the fifth-grade class; the Teacher is known by her performance: the placement of her name above the door; the power she wields to pass or fail students; to withhold recess or require lunch-study time; her steadfastness and the routine of her being. She is *the* class-room teacher, the Authority, the Eye of Surveillance (Foucault 1975/1979), disciplining and acting as apparatus, even as she is collective, 'she' appears as the unitary identity of Teacher. At the end of the school year, the student tests scores will be tabulated and the results will be listed *under* Her name, and She will be 'held accountable' for the success and failure of students *under* 'Her' care and tutelage.

The lowercase 't' teacher are the visiting researcher. Ask any student in the fifth-grade class and they know she is not the 'real' teacher: Her name is 'Visitor' indicated by a plastic badge worn around her neck. She carries with her an iPod to record voices; she will not be here every day, or even for the entire year, yet she 'acts' like a teacher asking the students to get out their paper and pencils, to pay attention, to get busy with the task of writing. She is introduced as an 'a writing expert', and the fifth graders move their bodies in different ways when with her, hiding behind their papers in some cases, eager to share and receive a response in other instances – seeking affirmation of their subjectivities as 'writers.' She is , too, a multiple and changing topology.

Both Teacher and the teacher are intelligible by their performance of 'teacher.' It is not a new performance; it is the fact that it has been performed over and over again that gives it shape and substance. The apparatuses of School and Science and Culture produce this material-discursive Teacher and teacher who the children recognise. The apparatus, the discursive-material practices, mark the body and a way of seeing and perceiving classroom practice and thus what comes to matter as 'teaching' and 'learning', and yet, as with Esteban, these are not foreclosed subjects but subjects always already becoming; this is not a matter of cause and then effect, rather the mattering is 'the sedimenting historiality of practices/agencies *and* an agentive force in the world's differential becoming. Becoming is not an unfolding in time but the inexhaustible dynamism of the enfolding of mattering' (Barad 2007, 180). Within every intelligible practiced performance of School this dynamism of enfolding and thus of a different possibility, a different agential cut exists.

Who are the objects/apparatuses coming to the writing conference?

From an agential realist perspective, the six-room writing-poetry-format as 'proven pedagogy' comes to the writing conference as apparatus. The six-room writing-poetry-format is a material-discursive production, a published set of instructions to guide students in brainstorming and writing free-verse poetry, written by Heard (1998), a teacher-poet (herself discursively materially produced) who has 'evidence' of success. In this way, it disciplines the would-be poet to produce a 'poem', according to Heard's directions: Students begin by folding a blank piece of paper into six sections or 'rooms.' In each room, the as-yet-unnamed-poet is asked to recall sensory details to describe a memory-image (quality of light, sounds, feelings, and questions) to brainstorm ideas for free-verse poetry. The last room, room six, the writer is instructed to look over the details from the previous five rooms and write a word or phrase three times for emphasis. Then, the writer uses the words and phrases from the six rooms to create free-verse poetry. As an apparatus, the six-room writing-poetry-format enacts an agential cut – 'a resolution of the ontological indeterminacy' (Barad 2007, 175) of what is marked as 'poem'. Yet 'apparatuses are ... open-ended practices involving specific intra-actions of humans and nonhumans' (Barad 2007, 171) so while authoritative discourses of proven pedagogy and published expertise discipline the poet through these apparatuses there is no guarantee of a 'poem', according to the structure of 'proven pedagogy' since 'different agential cuts produce different phenomena' (Barad 2007, 175). Therefore, the six-room writing-poetry-format is (re)constituted and (re)configured, *entangled* (not just intertwined or integrated), through intra-actions with student-writers and teachers and other human and non-human beings.

In the same way, there is nothing 'blank' or 'neutral' about the blank page the poet is to fill with a poem; the blank page filled with the unseen discourse of School Expectation, Poetry, and Acceptable and Developmentally Appropriate fifth-grade writing. No writing produced on such a blank page stands alone, isolated, as a fixed moment in time. Barad (2007) notes of her own authoring,

> There is no singular point in time that marks the beginning of this book, nor is there an 'I' who saw the project through from beginning to end, nor is writing a process that any individual 'I' or even group of 'I's' can claim credit for ... the practice of writing is an iterative and mutually constitutive working out, and reworking, of "book" and 'author'. (x)

The poem a student writes has a collective past and a future entangled into its materialisation, the entanglement of human and non-human since all lack an 'independent, self-contained existence' (Barad 2007, ix).

If, 'agency is about changing possibilities of change' (Barad 2007, 178), then the future of a writing conference 'between' teacher, Esteban, the six-room writing-poetry-format, the blank page, and in relation to Teacher and other students, the physical classroom and still other unnamed and unseen material-discursive practices is assured only of unpredictability: who can know the outcome of such an entangled intra-action?

The 'teacher–student writing conference'

A 'teacher' employs a pedagogical practice such as a six-room writing-poetry-format, presenting it to a 'student' who 'produces' a 'piece of writing' but see how through an agential realist perspective, this cannot be a simple line of cause and effect, a sentence with repetitive clauses marching towards a declarative end. The singular nouns of this sentence are verbs-in-motion, 'matter-in-the-process-of-becoming ... iteratively enfolded into its ongoing differential materialization' (Barad 2007, 179). Possibilities exist 'at every moment [they] do not sit still' (Barad 2007, 181). Perhaps, this is the wonder, the beauty of what we might reimage as 'teaching' and 'learning', even as it renders the phrase 'teacher–student writing conference' an impossibility: there can be no meeting between a singular-teacher and singular-student and conference as a singular-pedagogical-structure. Teaching and learning as intra-activity reimages any given moment of this conferencing not as a point where 'time leaves its mark as it were and marches on, leaving a trail of sedimentation to witness the effects of the external forces of change ... rather the past and the future are enfolded participants in matter's iterative becoming' (Barad 2007, 181). Becoming ... that is to emerge *differently*, or in Deleuze and Guattari (1987), terms to *become-other*, or 'different than the present self' (Semetsky 2006, 3). 'Becoming must keep on becoming' (Massumi 1992, 102); therefore, each teacher–student writing conference as intra-activity is a *becoming*, an event of possibility and transformation. Although still imperfect, perhaps the teacher–student writing conference is better reimaged, *entangled becoming-writing-conferencing*. 'Entangled' speaks of intra-activity; the use of becoming combined with a hyphen, of transformation; merging writingconferencing and maintaining the use of gerunds, signals movement and the inseparability of objects. *Entangled becoming-writingconferencing* is an attempt to reimage, not represent, the 'conference' as a multiplicity of participants (human and otherwise): the merging of bodies, continual movement, open-ended possibilities, and anticipated transformation of intra-action.

Anything is possible: entangled becoming-writingconferencing

One entangled becoming-writingconferencing follows: typed in italicised font, indicating it as narrative data, as intra-activity. This (re)telling is at best a partial and temporal intra-action of (re)telling, in which the 'property [that] comes to matter is re(con)figured in the very making/marking of time' (Barad 2007, 180). The (re)telling is re(con)figured (yet again) through the intra-activity of 'reading' by the reader. As an event entangled becoming-writingconferencing, it is remade through the 'past and the future' of the 'enfolded participants' the conferencing in 'matter's iterative becoming' (Barad 2007, 181).

'Esteban' (the collective) fold 'his' Blank Page once horizontally, and now into thirds, marking boundaries for 'rooms,' six rooms, each with a writing prompt: Room one –

think of an image or memory associated with a strong emotion; Room two – look at the image and focus on the light; describe the colors; Room three- picture the same image and focus on the sounds; Room four – write down any questions about the image; Room five – how does the image make you feel?; Room six – look at the five rooms and select one word, a few words, a phrase, or a line that feels important and write it down three times (Heard, 1998). Now use these rooms to write a poem.

'Esteban' hesitate. 'He' shove his desk, making another student lurch forward, a pencil flies across the space, the impact of fist against flesh – laughter: Student of Labels fulfilling the Expectation of Misbehavior. The School Boards of State and Federal Oversight in the Best Interest of Student Learning and Development have engineered the room, the tables, and chairs to discipline just 'these' students so they will focus and write and learn except the students can squirm and wrap the tissues of their bodies around metal, wood, and plastic in ways The Engineers of Student Desks never imagined. The students are playing with the six-room poem paper, making it into new forms of air travel, even as the teacher (the one with the little 't') comes with Expectation, followed by the I's/Eyes of Surveillance of the Teacher.

[Identities here are inherently 'unstable, differentiated, dispersed, and yet strangely coherent,' (Kirby 2002 Personal communication, quoted in Barad 2007, 184). Which is to say, the classroom appears 'normal' through the discursive-material practices of traditional school perception, the habits of mind most known to elementary teachers.]

The 'teacher' (with the lowercase 't') knows the conference protocol, trusts the six-room poetry-writing-format: 'she' (all of them) have a history, a 'proven' track record (and this produces in 'her' an anticipated and predictable future).
Victor, Esteban's friend, who shares many of Esteban's labels, including Latino and Male, is writing a poem about soccer (not futbol; not golf, tennis, or lacrosse) and teacher prompts him according to conference protocol, 'Tell me more – what was it like moving that soccer ball down the field. Did the crowd cheer?' while teacher simultaneously pats the desk where Esteban squirms, 'ignoring the inappropriate behavior,' encouraging the 'model' that is Victor. (Behavior Management affirms teacher: excellent behavior modification.)
  'Esteban' (none of them) don't want to write a poem, 'It is boring.'
  'Then,' teacher says, 'write a poem about poetry being boring!'
  The Esteban who does not trust this every-now-and-then teacher eyes her: He (the one who is street-smart) knows a trick when he hears one. The Esteban who is labeled 504 'Impulsive' slams his desk again, simultaneously living labels and breaking codes of the 'normed' student. The teacher worries Teacher will notice: what will Teacher think?

[But look now, we have written this as if each body acts separately, on its own, independent, but this is the delusion of perception according to our Eyes Trained by Western Thought and Expectation – habitual ways of being. 'See' *intra-activity*.]

Esteban, eye the six-room poetry-writing-format. 'He' (all of the he/them), remodels this poetry house, collapsing a few stem walls, (re)configuring Room five (How does it make you feel?) and Room six, Write a line or phrase that feels important; write it three times:
  I am stupid.
  I am stupid.
  I am stupid.
  teacher (her little 't' shrinking even more, dissolving hopefully into a void), 'Esteban, You are not stupid!' As if these words were the Word, could interpolate, through the power of individual will and produce being. 'Saying something is so does not make it so'. (Barad 1998, 108)
  Esteban, (all over again simultaneously living labels and breaking codes of labels; making another agential cut, setting in motion a diffraction, yet, who's eyes will see

this differing?), continuing to rupture the pattern of imitation, employing Student of Labels to break the norm and the label, and find a place in-between, breaking binaries and Esteban writes again and again:

I am stupid

I am stupid

I am stupid

[The Blank Paper, Pencil, and Poem Room Five and Poem Room Six, have a body: 'meaning is materialized as performance [the performance of writing], and, at the same time, constructed through performance' (Lenz Taguchi 2010, 155): writing as a performative act of many, an intra-action, a flurry of motion.]

SHE, Teacher/Mother/Savior raises the I's/Eyes'-brow of surveillance and it is flung, dart-like across the room to teacher who feels deeply feels the impact, the smack of disapproval, violation of visiting expert's role. How can 'this' happen? Teacher puts a hand on Esteban's shoulder.

The teacher (the one with the shrinking lower-case 't') reads the paper, and the reading is intra-activity, and entangled subjectivities: she reads 'I am stupid,' and the words as waves, overwhelm her, name her: how will she diffract them?

['Diffraction pattern: marking differences from within and as part of an entangled state'. (Barad 2007, 89)]

A diffractive reading of an entangled becoming-writingconferencing

Intra-actively speaking: Who or what wrote, 'I am stupid'? (And who is reading it, anyway?)

And of course, these questions rest upon a faulty premise: the questions assume an independent entity, a person or thing responsible for the writing and the reading. But this is not the *mattering* that occurs in this moment of intra-action: the *mattering* here is not a 'linguist construction but a discursive production' (Barad 2007, 151). Like a wave, the materialisation of 'I am stupid', slams against teacher and Teacher and this reconfigures the boundaries: teacher and Teacher when reading the words, 'caught once again looking at mirrors' (Barad 2008, 145), find first an indictment of themselves, reading language as reflection, rather than diffraction. The indictment is the material-discursive force of 'teacher', the construction of who and what a teacher is.

Teacher or teacher would not feel the reflection of 'I am stupid', except they read the writing of 'I am stupid' as representational of Esteban; if teacher has made Esteban feel stupid and if Teacher has failed to protect and nurture Esteban, they are implicated as 'failures'. But such a reading ignores the multiplicity of subjectivities of 'Esteban', 'Teacher', and 'teacher'; it ignores the apparatuses of school and of the six-room poetry-writing-format, of materiality. It narrows a point of failure to 'a person' (whether Esteban, Teacher, or teacher) and it is this kind of discursive narrowing that leads educational policy to search for a 'fix' and a 'cause', a way to make a 'better teacher', and a 'smarter student' while ignoring issues of labelling, constructs of the physical school and classroom, nutrition (or lack thereof), apparatuses of sexism and racism. Lenz Taguchi (2010) writing about intra-action in her classroom says,

Every organism in the intra-activities taking place can be understood as acting from their own agency and responsibility ... Any evaluation must include identifying the intra-

activities taking place in-between other matter in the event including the physical environment and the questions and input of teachers. (175)

Who, then, writes, 'I am stupid'? *All of the above intra-acting.*

A representational interpretation of 'I am stupid' excludes possibilities. By reading the statement as declarative, as representative, Esteban remains snared in the grid of SOL: he fulfils the expectation of the 'At Risk Student', damaged property, in need of an school intervention that did not happen. He is SOL, *shit out of luck*. But read the statement through agential realism and it emerges as a 'sabotage of the existing order' (Massumi 1992), as a space in-between Esteban (not the SOL Esteban and not a normed student writing expected fifth-grade poetry, but as a different 'he' defying labels) playing the game of school in another way: 'he' follows directions (write how it makes you feel; write it three times) and he does this outside of the assumed abilities of fifth-grade poetry writing; Esteban's writing as an agential cut of differing.

It might have been a great poem.

If we cut agency 'loose from its traditional humanist orbit' (Barad 2007, 177), then Esteban's intra-action with the six-room poetry-writing-format holds the possibility of an authentic poem of suffering, anger; of humour and satire (far beyond presumed fifth-
grade writing abilities) – and is this not the stuff of poetry? Let the 'I am stupid' move, intra-act, and see where 'it' goes because 'agency never ends; it can never "run out"' (Barad 2007, 177).

We are not suggesting simply making another interpretation of data through an agential realism perspective, rather we are asking how we might re-live this event and understand it and ourselves differently. Lenz Taguchi (2010) advises,

> We should not think that we can know what is right and wrong *before* living and knowing about the complexities of life. Rather, the approach we need is an ethics that *derives from living and lived life in the process of living it.* (Smith 2003, 178)

In the process of living, in the enfolding of past and future into the moments of the entangled becoming-writingconferencing and the multiple intra-actions of writing this paper, how might we live more ethically as teachers and researchers? (Lenz Taguchi 2010).

An ending without finality

> ... since the possibilities for what the world may become call out in the pause that pre-
> cedes each breath before a moment comes into being and the world is remade again, because the becoming of the world is a deeply ethical matter. (Barad 2007, 185)

We emerge from this entangled as teachers and researchers more committed to living, to asking what can we do to 'affect something or someone in a different way in line with an affirmative thinking of unknown potentialities, rather than what we *should* do in line with the transcendent idea of a higher value to be strived for' (Lenz Taguchi 2010, 176). We can approach children during writing conferencing knowing the event will be entangled, and in doing so, approach with wonder, understanding our actions will cause a diffraction, perhaps visible (perhaps not), to humans and non-humans: we can ask, 'how can our actions begin a diffraction of affirmation?' We can look for the power of material-discursive practices, such as the labelling of children that have real material consequences limiting what children do and say and how teachers will understand their actions. We can train ourselves against these habits of thinking, seeking potentiality and possibility in our becoming-writingconferencing, listening for a *difference*. We can embrace writing as intra-activity, not as a product of an individual writer, not as representative of what is known, not simply as a tool for clear communication, but as a materialisation of meaning that sets yet other diffraction(s) in motion(s). Rather than being tied to our 'proven' conference pedagogy as step-by-step process, we can see pedagogy as relational with humans and non-humans, as historically, culturally, and politically constructed, as having a past and future enfolded into a present. We can be *of* the present when working with children, looking for 'what emerges, what *can* become' (Lenz Taguchi 2010, 177).

The US is now consumed with the standardisation of standards; of pedagogy; teaching and learning; teachers and children; and writing as a thing produced, as representational; we emerge from the intra-activity of writing this paper understanding how such standards might act as apparatus and materialise 'writers' and to better insist upon an accounting for the exclusions enacted by this practice, even as we perpetually contest and rework boundaries of it (Barad 1998).

While we have argued in this paper that 'teacher' is always already a plural and collective noun, it does not mean that living as *becoming*-teacher cannot at times be a lonely pursuit. The teacher wears the materiality of accountability on her body – exhaustion at the end of the day felt deeply in clinched and weary muscles and mind. Yet, we find agential realism to be hopeful, intra-vigorating, emerging through intra-action, anticipating diffraction, knowing the world is moment-by-moment remade, trusting the Verbs in-motion (human and non-human) in our classrooms, leaving off binaries of failure/success; mistakes/correctness for *transformation*. This allows us as teachers and researchers to think *differently*, gives possibilities to the SOL to break the code that binds, gives way to joy, to the evolution of us all, to the entanglement of *becoming*.

References

Bakhtin, Mikhail M. 1981. *The Dialogic Imagination: Four Essays*. Austin: University of Texas Press.

Barad, Karen. 1998. "Getting Real: Technoscientific Practices and the Materialization of Reality." *A Journal of Feminist Cultural Studies* 10 (2): 87–128.

Barad, Karen. 2007. *Meeting the Universe Halfway: Quantum Physics and the Entanglement of Matter and Meaning*. Durham, NC: Duke University Press.

Barad, Karen. 2008. "Posthumanist Performativity: Toward an Understanding of How Matter Comes to Matter." In *Material Feminisms*, edited by Stacy Alaimo and Susan Hekman, 120–154. Bloomington: Indiana University Press.

Butler, Judith. 1993. *Bodies that Matter: On the Discursive Limits of "Sex"*. New York: Routledge.

Butler, Judith. 1999. *Gender Trouble: Feminism and the Subversion of Gender*. New York: Routledge.

Colebrook, Claire. 2006. *Deleuze: A Guide for the Perplexed*. London: Continuum.

Deleuze, Gilles. 1968/1994. *Difference and Repetition*. Translated by Paul Patton. New York: Columbia University Press.

Deleuze, Gilles, and F. Guattari. 1987. *A Thousand Plateaus: Capitalism and Schizophrenia*. Translated by Brian Massumi. Minneapolis: University of Minnesota Press.

Foucault, Michel. 1975/1979. *Discipline and Punish: The Birth of the Prison*. Translated by Alan Sheridan. New York: Random House.

Foucault, Michel. 1976/1990. *History of Sexuality volume 1: An Introduction*. Translated by Robert Hurley. New York: Vintage Books.

Foucault, Michel. 1984/1985. *History of Sexuality volume 2: The Use of Pleasure*. Translated by Robert Hurley. New York: Vintage Books.

Grumet, Madeleine. 1988. *Bitter Milk: Women and Teaching*. Amherst: University of Massachusetts Press.

Heard, Georgia. 1998. *Awakening the Heart: Exploring Poetry in Elementary and Middle School*. Portsmouth: Heinemann.

Hekman, Susan. 2008. "Constructing the Ballast: An Ontology for Feminism." In *Material Feminisms*, edited by Stacy Alaimo and Susan Hekman, 85–119. Bloomington: Indiana University Press.

Hultman, Karin, and Hillevi Lenz Taguchi. 2010. "Challenging Anthropocentric Analysis of Visual Data: A Relational Materialist Methodological Approach to Educational Research." *International Journal of Qualitative Studies in Education* 23 (5): 525–542.

Lenz Taguchi, Hillevi. 2010. *Going Beyond the Theory/Practice Divide in Early Childhood Education: Introducing an Intra-active Pedagogy*. New York: Routledge.

Massumi, Brian. 1992. *A User's Guide to Capitalism and Schizophrenia: Deviations from Deleuze and Guattari*. Cambridge: The MIT Press.

McWhorter, Ladelle. 2004. "Sex, Race, and Biopower: A Foucauldian Genealogy." *Hypatia* 19 (3): 38–62.

McWilliam, Erica. 1994. *In Broken Images: Feminist Tales for a Different Teacher Education*. New York: Teachers College Press.

Newkirk, Thomas. 2002. *Misreading Masculinity: Boys, Literacy and Pop Culture*. Portsmouth: Heinemann.

Richardson, Laurel, and Elizabeth St. Pierre. 2005. "Writing: A Method of Inquiry." In *The Sage Handbook of Qualitative Research*, edited by Norman Denzin and Yvonne Lincoln, 959–978. Thousand Oaks, CA: Sage Publications.

Ruffolo, David V. 2007. "Giving an Account of Queer: Why Straight Teachers can Become Queerly Intelligible." *Queering Straight Teachers: Discourse and Identity in Education*, edited by N. M. Rodriguez and W. F. Pinar, 255–270. New York: Peter Lang Publishing.

Semetsky, Inna. 2006. *Deleuze, Education and Becoming*. Rotterdam: Sense Publishers.

Walkerdine, Valerie. 1992. "Progressive Pedagogy and Political Struggle." In *Feminisms and Critical Pedagogy*, edited by Carmen Luke and Jennifer Gore, 15–24. New York: Routledge.

Weber, Sandra, and Claudia Mitchell. 1995. *That's Funny you don't Look Like a Teacher! Interrogating Images, Identity and Popular Culture*. London: Falmer Press.

Theorising learning and nature: post-human possibilities and problems

Jocey Quinn

Institute of Education, Plymouth University, Drake Circus, Plymouth, UK

In their predominantly theoretical turn to the material, post-humanist feminists often focus on 'nature', arguing that the nature/culture binary has collapsed and that fixed distinctions between human and non-human spheres no longer hold. Conversely, outdoor learning sees nature as a space where humans act and has been more concerned with empirically based studies of practice than with theory. The purpose of this paper is twofold: to use post-human ideas to advance theoretical understanding of outdoor learning and to evaluate post-humanism's analytic capacity by putting it to work with empirical data on outdoor learning. Drawing on two studies, one on young people in jobs without training and one on young people living in an area designated as one 'of outstanding natural beauty', the paper explores young people and their everyday outdoor learning: engaging with animals landscape and elements. Post-human perspectives help to uncover the vibrancy and power of this learning, but they are less useful in exposing the ways it is shaped by social inequalities. Whilst post-humanism reveals that inequalities are not fixities and cannot themselves totally suppress the vital materiality of these young people, these social inequalities remain a challenge to the affirmative aspirations of post-humanism.

Introduction

The purpose of this paper is twofold: to use post-human ideas to advance theoretical understanding of outdoor learning and to evaluate post-humanism's analytic capacity by putting it to work with empirical data from research studies on young people's outdoor learning. In doing so, the focus on 'nature' immediately throws up conceptual problems. The Western romantic view of Nature as a special, even sacred, space set apart from mundane human lives is so pervasive (particularly amongst urbanites who have had a liberal education) that slippage into this way of thinking is very easy. However, through a post-human lens, there is no separate sphere of nature; nature and culture are 'mangled' together at every point, from the kitchen to the mountain top, as 'the agency of matter is intertwined with human agency' (Hekman 2010, 24). How then to write about young people engaging in just such 'sacred spaces', like woods and moorlands, without resorting to reified notions of nature? This is all the more important because the young people in the research studies I am discussing do not romanticise nature at all. Alaimo and Hekman (2008) use the term 'bodily nature' to express the materiality of nature post Nature. However, this is problematic, as some of the experiences I shall discuss seem to exceed the bodily frame and be both material and ineffable. I have considered coining the term 'open nature', which could be helpful in conveying a sense of forests and moorlands, but negatively would serve to sub-divide nature in a binary way. Ultimately, finding a solution to this philosophical problem of naming is not within the scope of this article. Therefore, I have attempted to work with the term 'nature' in ways which do not lapse into humanism and do not position it in opposition to culture. If this is not always successful, this is because romantic views of nature are mangled up in my materially and culturally constituted subjectivity.

In the context of education, there is a wealth of research on nature. Most of the work in this field concentrates on 'outdoor education' where activities are organised in which forests, plants, marine environments and so on are explicitly used as a focus for educational ends, either by schools or by organisations in the voluntary sector (see, for example, O'Brien 2009; Harrison 2010; Waite 2011). There is also a genre which can be termed 'outdoor learning' in which learning takes place informally and incidentally as a by product of outdoor engagement, during such activities as environmental activism (Hsu 2009) and leisure pursuits (Pike and Beames 2013). Or as a part of everyday life. The focus of this paper is on young people and their everyday outdoor learning engaging with animals, landscape and elements.

In the outdoor literature, there is an emphasis on practice, and theoretical debates are not very well developed. Conversely, in post-humanist feminist literature, there is much theoretical discussion about 'nature'. The 'nature' of outdoor learning and the 'nature' of post-humanism are not co-terminous. Whilst outdoor learning sees nature as a space within which humans act (recognising that pockets of such spaces also exist in cities and towns), post-humanists argue that the nature/culture binary has collapsed and that fixed distinctions between human and non-human spheres no longer hold. It is, therefore, wrong to assume that outdoor learning is inevitably an obvious focus for post-humanist enquiry. However, since post-humanism is a philosophical approach to the world and all its manifestations, there is no reason to suggest that it cannot be used to interrogate and problematise outdoor learning. Moreover, as Braidotti suggests, post-human thought is 'very much a philosophy of the outside, of open spaces and embodied enactments' (2013, 194). To bring outdoor learning and post-humanism together in order to cast light upon each other thus seems like a potentially fruitful move. The purpose of this paper is twofold: to use post-human ideas to advance theoretical understanding of outdoor learning and to put post-human theory to work with empirical data from outdoor learning, in order to demonstrate post-humanism's analytic capacity. This is helpful because, whilst educational research that took the linguistic turn has prioritised language and human relations, post-humanism brings matter to the forefront, in a move that could deepen understanding of outdoor learning. The paper also offers an opportunity to explore post-humanism's utility in the analysis of research data.

In an earlier paper (Quinn 2012), I began a process of demonstrating that nature offers opportunities for learning for marginalised young people and using Barad to unpack this process. In this current paper, I will further extend the discussion to a broader group of young people and to the work of Bennett. Barad and Bennett have been characterised as 'material feminists' or 'new materialists' (Jackson and Mazzei 2012, 9), but they can also be termed 'post-humanist feminists' and in the context of this paper this term seems the most apposite to use. In this paper, the nature of outdoor learning provides a bounded geographical locus for the research studies I am discussing and encapsulates a range of manifestations located in what we might call the countryside in England: in this case moorlands, woods, water, fields and animals. However, these studies are then viewed through a post-humanist lens, whereby nature exists everywhere:

> What I am calling vital materiality or vibrant matter is akin to what is expressed in one of the many historical senses of the word *nature*. Though nature can refer to stable substrata of brute matter, the term has also signalled generativity, fecundity, Isis or Aphrodite. (Bennett 2010, 117)

In the paper nature is something that can be seen and touched, but is also the force that generates those material forms and as such suffuses all matter, including human bodies.

From a cultural perspective there is no singular 'Nature', rather 'multiple natures' embedded in and produced by different socio-cultural practices and processes (Macnaghten and Urry 1998). These natures serve different human interests and are often in opposition and struggle with each other. Opportunities to engage with forests, moorlands and woodlands are constrained by gender and 'race' (Travlou 2006, 24) and humans respond differently to them, with pleasure, fear, awe or indifference (Milligan and Bingley 2007). In some cultures, nature is perceived as important and in others as of little significance (Travlou 2006). However, vital materialists like Bennett point out that a purely cultural approach to nature is not adequate: 'culture is not of our own making, infused as it is by biological, geological and climatic forces ... it is futile to seek a pure nature unpolluted by humanity, and it is foolish to define the self as something purely human' (2010, 115–116). Barad has also challenged the dominance of the cultural perspective and argued that the 'matter' of nature, rather than the representation of it, must be grappled with if we are to understand the meanings generated by human/nature intra-actions: 'Nature is neither a passive surface awaiting the mark of culture, nor the end product of cultural performances' (Barad 2003, 827). This intellectual shift towards matter is potentially illuminating when it comes to understanding how far and in what ways nature facilitates learning.

The opportunities that this turn presents for educational research have already been highlighted by writers such as Hultman and Taguchi (2010) and Jackson and Mazzei (2012). Hultman and Taguchi argue that a move from theories that 'take humans or human meaning-making as the sole constitutive force' to 'a turn to relational materialism, where things and matter, usually perceived as passive and immutable, are instead granted agency' creates a more ethical research practice (2010, 539–540). In particular, they suggest that it might 'increase our attentiveness to things, artefacts and spaces in pre-schools and schools that are often overlooked in favour of the social or interpersonal relations' (2010, 540). In this paper, I shall expand this focus and attentiveness to young people engaged in informal learning outdoors.

Researching nature and learning: two studies

I first became interested in young people and outdoor learning through a study I conducted with colleagues on young people in jobs without training in South West England (Quinn, Lawy, and Diment 2008) and in post-humanism through work with feminist colleagues (Hughes, Quinn, and Tamboukou 2011). Although nature was not a focus of the first empirical study, it emerged as an enough of an issue to make it worthy of consideration. With other colleagues, I have since been involved in a further study looking at young people living on and around Exmoor, an area designated as one of 'outstanding natural beauty' in England (Merchant, Quinn, and Waite 2013), and this study included a more specific focus on engagement with such factors as animals and landscapes. Within this paper, I will employ data drawn from both of these research projects.

The jobs without training study, funded by the European Social Fund, the Learning and Skills Council and Connexions involved 114 young people aged 16–21 working in jobs without training in South West England. These are the kinds of essential but invisible jobs, such as working in shops, hotels, building sites and farms that keep societies functioning, but are afforded low status and low wages. These young people are seen as a problem group with few positive attributes and low prospects. The study mainly consisted of qualitative data comprising 182 interviews plus a small focus group; 114 young people were interviewed once and of these 68 interviewed again over the space of a year.

The study also involved a participative seminar, where interim data were presented to stakeholders, such as youth workers, education and training providers and employers. By no means all of the young people interviewed in this project had anything to say about nature, but there were enough accounts, including amongst those interviewed twice in depth, to allow learning in nature to emerge as a distinct and significant issue. These young people did not pause to discourse on their love of nature; rather they dropped it in the conversation as an integral part of every life which played an important part in shaping learning, work and behaviour. The study itself had many interesting findings and has been widely consulted in policy and academic circles (Quinn 2010). However, in this paper, the specific focus is on what it shows about young people and nature.

The second study (Merchant, Quinn, and Waite 2013) was funded by Exmoor National Park Authority (one of a number of bodies charged with conserving 'areas of outstanding natural beauty' across England) and by the Institute of Health and Community, Plymouth University. It is built on the earlier study, in that it continued the focus on informal learning, but also explicitly sought to explore young people's engagement with animals and landscapes. It had as its focus, Exmoor National Park, and sought to explore the lives of young people living on or near the park.

109 qualitative questionnaires were collected either on-line or in paper format from 16- to 24-year-olds who lived and/or grew up in or near to Exmoor National Park. The questionnaire was circulated via community groups, local employers and facilities such as sports clubs, shops, schools and libraries. Five focus groups consisted of 5–10 participants in each, they were held in cafes and pubs that were local to the participants' homes. To gain a broad cross section, we aimed to gather responses from both those who were active in the community, such as Young Farmers, and those who may have been more isolated/insular. Whilst we did achieve this via the questionnaire, the majority of the focus group participants were active in a variety of social and community groups, and despite being contacted, those approached via Youth Offenders Teams and Child Services declined to participate.

An interesting aspect of the research was that whilst participants seemed to actively and fully engage with the questionnaires and focus groups, attempts to use visual prompts and techniques did not prove successful. Two focus groups were presented with a set of photographs depicting 'traditional' rural life in the 1960s. These photographs were taken from the James Ravilious online archive featuring images of 'the hunt', fencing making, cattle showing, lamb delivery and 'baling'. The participants were asked to reflect on what the images meant to them. Responses to the Ravilious photographs were negative, they were felt to be stereotypical and the focus groups preferred to continue without reference to them. As I shall discuss, this resistance to photographic images may be connected to the ways in which participants eschewed one-dimensional and anthropomorphic visions of nature.

Nature was not the only focus of this Exmoor project, although it was explicitly fore-grounded in contrast to the jobs without training study. The study also explored educational and employment experiences, the social and economic issues faced by young people, peer group activities and future expectations. In this paper, I will focus particularly on the data concerning nature, but, as I shall explain, this is inextricably linked to other factors.

Post-human positions

In this paper, I want to discuss the post-human ideas of Barad and Bennet and how they might help explore the data from these two studies. There are many forms of post-humanism (see Pederson 2010, 242–243, for discussion), but they share a perspective that that the human is not inviolable or distinct but co-exists in multiple forms with the non-human, such as machines and animals, and that humanism, with its assumptions of a sovereign, essential, individualised human nature is not only deluded but politically and environmentally disastrous.

Is a post-human perspective inherently inimical to the project of education as we have known it? 'Western pedagogy is firmly rooted in a 'humanist' tradition where the human subject is considered both the instrument and the end product of education' (Pederson 2010, 241) and the educated human is to have certain 'cognitive, social and moral abilities' (237). This ideal human subject of course was always assumed to be male, white and upper/middle class and overthrowing this subject has always been a core task of feminism. As Braidotti says: 'becoming post-human speaks to my feminist self, partly because my sex, historically speaking, never quite made it into full humanity' (2013, 81).

Pederson asks 'Is the post-human educable?' The answer must be no, not educable in any traditional sense, with human-centred practices which are not only inadequate but even antithetical to post-humanism. However, the post-human is certainly capable of learning in a different way. One of the strengths of a post-human perspective is that it reveals the interconnectedness of all matter, so that the project of learning becomes not what distinguishes me from all that is around me and makes me superior to it, but what makes me part of it. Post-humanism is also clearly indebted to decades of feminist thought on what constitutes valid knowledge (see, for example, Code 1991; Haraway 2004). It also has debts, possibly unacknowledged, to works such as Mary Daly's *Gyn/Ecology* (1970) which in decentring the male subject offers up a more than human vision of the world. It also has limits which I have argued lie in lack of acknowledgement of the social (Quinn 2012) as I shall further explore.

Turning specifically to Barad and Bennett, in what ways might their ideas help to generate new ways of understanding learning in nature? Barad (2003, 2007) argues that both humanist approaches, which are predicated on a unified subject with agency and choice, and anti-humanist approaches which assume that 'human bodies and subjectivities are the effects of human-based discursive practices' privilege the human and 're-inscribe the nature-culture, human-non-human, animate-inanimate binaries' (2007, 171). Instead, her theories of agential realism bring matter and the non-human to the centre of the discussion:

> Matter is agentive and intra-active ... generative not merely in the sense of bringing new things into the world but in the sense of bringing forth new worlds .... Bodies do not simply take their place in the world. They are not simply situated in, or located in particular environments. Rather 'environments' and 'bodies' are intra-actively constituted. (2007, 170)

Taking this approach, neither young people nor nature are to be understood as fixed pre-existing entities that then interact. Rather, meaning and reality lie in the phenomena constituted by their intra-activity: the 'new world' and the new bodies that emerge.

Whilst Barad is scientific in her approach, inspired by quantum physics, Bennett, a political theorist, is rather more poetic. Her essential argument of 'vital materiality' is that the matter of human and non-human is intermingled so that the distinction between the human and non-human cannot be sustained, neither is it desirable to do so: 'If envir-onmentalists are selves who live on earth, vital materialists are selves who live as earth' (2010, 111). The stories that she tells

> highlight the extent to which human being and thinghood overlap, the extent to which the us and the it slip-slide into each other. One moral of the story is that we are also non-human and that things too, are vital players in the world. (4)

Such vitalism does not come from God, neither is it a form of creativity that only belongs to humans; it can be exhibited by things, even those things seen as rubbish and detritus.

In *Vibrant Matter* (2010), Bennett reflects on finding an array of discarded objects:

> On a sunny Tuesday morning on 4 June in the grate over the storm drain ... there was
>
> One large men's plastic work glove
>
> One dense mat of oak pollen
>
> One unblemished dead rat
>
> One white plastic bottle cap
>
> One smooth stick of wood
>
> ... the items on the ground that day were vibratory-at one moment disclosing themselves as dead stuff and at the next as live presence: junk, then claimant: inert matter then live wire. (2010, 5)

This pulsating image immediately recalled to me Ginsberg's poem 'In back of the real' (2006) where the vitality that runs through industry and nature is synthesised in an unlikely object, an ugly weed lying on the road. In turn it also evoked the ways in which the young people in the jobs without training study presented them-selves as both waste and as vibrant matter. They were cast out and discarded: 'I'm rubbish' (Carl), but also humming with possibility: 'I want to pass on thoughts of college, I just want to float' (Abigail). The key point here is that the young people in jobs without training see themselves through the eyes of society, but also feel within themselves the pulse of matter that cannot be contained by culture. They are 'dead-end kids in dead-end jobs' but also very much alive and kicking. So the fact that most of them have done very badly at school, have few qualifications and seem destined for low paid work, positions them as 'failed', but their everyday experiences move them into a world of things not words, where the matter of their bodies has vibrancy and potential. In the words of Braidotti 'Life ... expresses itself in a multiplicity of empirical acts: there is nothing to say, but everything to do' (2013, 189–190). The unresolved tension here is between deep rooted social inequalities which tend to fix such young people in place and the young people's vital materiality which can never be totally suppressed. Whilst a socio-cultural perspective alerts us to barriers and boundaries, post-humanism offers a way of understanding that these boundaries are not immutable.

In 2010, I discussed the many ways in which people located on the margins are cast as waste in our society. I argued that the challenge was to 'work so that others can see the value of those they overlook, the dirty dusty flowers of the world' (Quinn 2010, 122). Bennett offers a fresh perspective: if the distinction between waste and valuable object is broken down and we acknowledge that waste is a vibrant part of everything including ourselves, then there is nothing that can be repudiated or dismissed. This is very helpful in understanding the terms on which young people in both the studies considered here engaged with nature. Every 'thing', be it grotesque, or prey, had a vitality that they acknowledged and with which they exhibited a form of kinship. Their capacity to learn from things rather than words is, therefore, both illuminated and validated by Bennett's post-human theories, in contradiction to the humanist tradition where words are given primacy.

In the following section, I will look more closely at the ways in which Barad and Bennett present both possibilities and problems in generating understandings of young people, learning and nature.

Post-human possibilities

Animal magic

Although the research literature on outdoor learning pays little attention to animals, animals constitute a vital element for the learning of young people outdoors. It can be argued that post-humanism offers a chance to relearn what we have unlearnt, for example, our identification with animals. In an interesting discussion, I had recently with PhD students about post-humanism, we reflected on the ways in which small children take on the identity of animals, running around like a dog, preferring to communicate by barking. I remembered how my own daughter used a small toy zebra as her transitional object when entering primary school, clutching it and sucking it and refusing to answer to her human name. Since noting this I have of course seen it everywhere, most recently a small child on the bus who would not speak but only 'miaow' like a cat all the way into town. These behaviours are usually very soon regimented out of existence by formal schooling, and even embarrassed parenting, but perhaps post-humanism makes these affinities respectable and opportunities to learn.

Pederson asks 'what happens to education and learning when the human subject is decentred and nonhuman animals are allowed to emerge as subjects, rather than objects, tropes or species representatives?' (2011, 3). Post-humanism works to decentre the human subject and so, as previously discussed; the implications for learning are profound. If we can develop:

> a posthumanist understanding of what it means to learn *with* and *from* rather than *about* nonhuman animals. What kind of learning experience do they set in motion? 'Learning' in this context may be perceived as essentially a convergence of energies. (Pederson 2011, 7)

Pederson herself has made moves to develop a methodology where animals themselves are agents within the research process, for example, in her study of avian education where hens, by their own actions, interrupt and problematise the terms of the quantitative study in which they are involved (2011). My research does not offer this direct engagement with non-human subjects, but it does give a sense of the 'convergence of energies' between young people and animals, albeit through the eyes of the young people themselves. My initial study of young people in jobs without training indicated that animals played a surprisingly large role in the lives of some young people. Training dogs and being with dogs as sole companions, working with animals like pigs and horses and hunting and shooting animals all were sources of affect. In some cases, the emotional attachment to animals was far greater than that to humans and ease and comfort with animals contrasted to estrangement from family or peers. The second study, by making this relationship a direct subject of enquiry, gives a greater sense of what that role might be.

For the young people living on Exmoor animals are a familiar part of daily life and not to be reduced to a one-dimensional anthropomorphic flatness. Animals are constantly in the line of sight or popping up to give surprise and pleasure. There is an interesting mix of the ineffable and the pragmatic in their accounts. Animals are 'in life' not on a screen or a page. It is about 'seeing' but also 'knowing' how they are:

Joe: And what you see as well, like I saw an adder in the summer, and see deer at least 2 or 3 times a month. It's just, that wildlife is just brilliant, you know, you don't know, wherever I've been it's just there, on your doorstep, just keep seeing it. Oh, and lizards.

Laura: I think, living here, when I did my Countryside Management degree I did get frustrated with some people on my course who were very much about loving all the cute and fluffy animals, and it's just like, it's not like that in life.

Laura: It's about knowing.

In Barad's terms, the intra-activity that happens when the adder is seen by the young man is the phenomenon that matters and is the meaningful unit of enquiry, not the human or the animal. The characteristic of that phenomenon is joy and delight in otherness. By means of the young people's emphasis on knowing, the non-human is not simply subjected to the human gaze which takes away its life and replaces it with a cuddly simulacrum, If, in Bennett's terms, the animal is suffused with the same vital materiality as the young people are, then it is capable of having an impact on the world around it and therefore is also also open to moral judgements.

Joe: You understand that an animal can be good or bad and not just 'Oh there's a little rabbit!'

They differentiated between where animals belonged and where they did not, seeing them in some ways as an intrinsic, even historic, part of the landscape.

Andy: I don't mind the ponies up there, the ponies are fine, they're part of the landscape, they've been here for millennia. Cows, no. Keep them in the fields.

Whilst Pederson (2011, 2012) is very much concerned with the rights of animals as autonomous subjects, but in doing so seems to suggest that they are beyond human judgement, for these young people the animal matters and is good or bad in so far as it either promotes or inhibits 'livelihoods'. There is an inter-dependence between non-human animals and human animals on the moor, in farming, tourism and leisure pursuits.

> Tom: But there's also preservation of the healthy animals. Nobody wants to see all the badgers wiped – of course you want to see badgers, you want to see the healthy ones and then you will have healthy livestock and healthy cattle herds, but it's really, really heart-breaking for a farmer to lose, to cull from his herd, just for the sake of some infected badgers.

Animals teach the young people about the continuum of culture/nature and the necessity of balance and equilibrium. Of course this is very far from being an equal relationship; whilst Bennett might argue that animals have power and agency they do not have guns and traps with which to kill humans. Nevertheless, once the animal is given its due, a different form of knowledge emerges about factors which are key to the survival of humans, such as the chain of production and where our food comes from.

> Tina: We know where milk comes from! Like, a lot of people wouldn't know how to turn a sheep up.

> Lucy: Yes, whereas other people just take it for granted 'cause they don't understand, they just buy it from the supermarket

In some respects, these young people possibly knew more than they wanted to know. They engaged with mortality on a daily basis and this kind of knowledge they gained from animals. Animals therefore, were dark agents of knowledge production.

> Joe: I think, coming from here you sort of think, it's not so, you know, black and white, you can't save every little creature in the world, it's a bit more – I don't know – it's just not so clear cut …

> Laura: Like hitting a bird on the road, they're going 'oh, let's pet it better' it's like, no, let's wring its neck and get on with it

Both Barad and Bennett posit a world in which human and more than human exist in perpetual and meaningful exchange. Animals are not backdrops or toys or things that exist simply to be picturesquely represented and thus possessed. Taking this perspective, the data from the Exmoor study demonstrates the agency of animals and the learning that is generated by human/animal intra-activity.

Landwise youth

Young people in the Exmoor study freely admitted that they were not 'streetwise' and might struggle in an urban environment. They were however 'landwise', knowing things in and through the landscape. In response to the questionnaire, 50% of the young people claimed to be on the moor 'all the time'. Geographers such as Edensor (2000) have pointed to the ways in which rural youth felt physically close to the land and connected to plants and animals. Wylie (2005) entitles this 'landscaping', the shaping of self, body and landscape, through performance in the landscape.

However, from Bennett's point of view this does not take the connection far enough. Her argument is that land and human body are made of the same vital materiality. This means perhaps that the oneness with the land that exists in their accounts is simply a heightened example of a condition that exists for us all, whether on Exmoor or on an urban rubbish dump. The question then is what do we do with this, what do we learn? In our Exmoor study, we explicitly focused on the kinds of skills this particular fused body/landscape could generate.

James: There are a lot of 'outdoor' skills that you learn because you are naturally in the environment all the time – general life skills as well like – how to find your way

… Kate: But like, people in towns wouldn't know how to like, survive for themselves whereas probably like we would be able to survive for ourselves like with his pheasant shooting, he would be able to shoot a pheasant and prepare it for himself. That type of thing

Here there is a continuum and crossover between body and land: the land teaches the body how to move over it and how to survive on it, the body shapes the land by its movements. The two become indivisible, a skill of living, a 'life skill'. Other skills then extrude from this synthesis:

Hannah: So things like (fencing) and just sort of like general, practical, manual kind of – just knowing how to do things a bit better, I guess. And like handling livestock and working with livestock and things like that

Ineffable elements

One of the struggles researchers face in exploring people's engagement with nature is finding words to express what are ineffable and also paradoxical encounters. Exmoor is officially designated an area of 'outstanding natural beauty' yet in trying to describe their responses to it young people also evoked images that were backward and threatening.

Researcher: How would you describe the area to someone who isn't from round here?

Finn: Deliverance Country

In drawing on this image from the film *Deliverance,* which famously depicts rurality as depraved and barbaric, Finn plays with cultural images of nature. Here in counter to the tenets of post-humanism, nature is placed in opposition to the civilising power of human society. In trying to describe the Exmoor area to 'outsiders', he can only fall back on cultural stereotypes. Others evoked the area by summoning what Barad would term the 'new bodies' created by the intra-activity of Exmoor and those who live on it

Lizzie: You wouldn't want to really be anywhere else. It's beautiful

Sarah: You can breathe. You can't do that in a city

For post-humanists like Barad and Bennett, the seasons and the elements are not backdrops across which humans move. Instead they act as agents shaping human opportunities and capabilities.

Lizzie: Yeah, it's a seasonal thing again, with like, job opportunities, isn't it? Like, very much like, the pubs as well, when they have the school holidays that is basically their biggest time in snowdrop valley, if we don't have that, like, and it's a really bad year, you've really got to start questioning whether you've got job security or not, or whether they can afford to keep you on. And then if you've got that worry, and then you've got your parents worrying because they don't know if they've got a job, because it's like, seasonal, especially with the economy ...

In the Exmoor study, the passage of time and the transmission of opportunities and anxieties across generations are very much present in the minds of young people. The seasons come and go and with them chances to work and make a living. The seasons teach young people about time and inter-generational vulnerability. Whilst post-humanism is seen as a future-oriented philosophy it also helps illuminate age-old patterns of living.

Post-human problems

As I have suggested, post-human thinkers help to gain a new purchase on the power of the material in human lives: of the agency of animals, land and elements in producing forms of knowing. However, as I have previously argued (Quinn 2012), taking post-humanism on wholesale may lead one to ignore social inequalities. In my earlier article, I discussed how, in Barad's terms, intra-activity with nature amongst some of those young people in the jobs without training study, created new bodies and worlds for them which were qualitatively different from the unhappy deficit learning experiences they had had at school. However, I also demonstrated how inequality still filtered through and shaped this materiality. So for Jane, Gary and John from that study their active engagement with nature was still shaped by social inequalities. Jane's activities doing beating on shoots served the needs of an upper class family, the family who also owned the house she lived in; Gary only had access to sailing through a regimented organisation, the Sea Cadets, and John fled to the woods to get away from the poverty and dangers of his family life.

In the Exmoor study, there was a clear division between those young people who lived on the moor, whom we accessed via social groups such as the Young Farmers, and those who lived on the margins and were accessed through a Youth Group. Whilst the activities of the young farmers were socially, bodily and emotionally tied to the moor, engagement was not the same for their counterparts:

What do you do in your spare time?

Matt: Eat chips!

Emma: Survive!

Do you spend a lot of time on the moors or do you really, kind of, mainly stay in the village?

Matt: Mainly stay in the village. It's just easier to get about than by travelling by bus and stuff.

Whilst those active in the young farmers either wanted to stay and work on the land in a family tradition or had opportunities to move away gained from going to university, options seemed restricted for the others:

> So you don't really spend much time on there. Do you guys know what you want to do?

> Chelsea: We're going to (FE college) to the hairdressing course

> You're doing the same thing. Do you reckon living here has influenced the career choices you've made?

> Emma: No. Definitely not

> Do you reckon it's kind of, almost made you want to go away?

> Holly: Sometimes it gets really boring. There's nothing to do. Well, that's mostly all the time

> Sam: There's never anything to do

So the almost rapturous intra-activity with nature that Barad would see as producing new bodies and Bennett as vital materiality did not exist for these young people. Nature constituted absence: nothing to do, nothing to want from it. Whilst young people on the moor and beyond the edges of the moor all experienced the same kinds of problems: housing, transport, restricted school and college curricula, the moor was only really a resource when it was embedded in daily and family life and traditions. Whilst Barad provides a perspective which allows the foregrounding of the non-human and the potential for liberation, going too far down that road hides the fact that the intra-activity of human and nature is still shaped by social positions.

Bennett too poses certain problems. She argues that 'the category of "structure" is ultimately unable to give the force of things its due' (2010, 29). However, conversely, does a focus on things neglect the power of social inequalities? We are all composed of matter shared with the non-human, but we are not all equally well placed to deal with any potential problems this may cause. Bennett discusses how our bodies are home to tribes of bacteria: 'My flesh is populated and constituted by different swarms of foreigners' (112). Nevertheless, social inequalities determine whether the bacterial balance will be disrupted and what happens next. A good example would be Jane from the jobs without training study. Over the period of interviews, Jane worked in a large fish farm. This was a dirty and unpleasant job but one of the few open to her in her area. Whilst doing so, she caught Lime's disease because of unhygienic conditions on the farm. She was unable to work and so lost her job and she was also unable to claim the back pay owed to her. Embedded inequalities of poverty, class, locality and work enabled her employer to exploit her with impunity. So the romance of matter that Bennett conjures so well is still profoundly culturally produced and eminently social.

Bennett is particularly good at evoking what she calls 'thing power', both the material and the symbolic power of the non-human. Her vision is that things have agency and make actions happen in the world, both for good and ill. This stance challenges a human-centred way of seeing where it is humans who determine what happens both to them and to the environment around them. In focusing on the potential of symbolic connections with and among things, she pays less attention to the ways in which humans imagine and symbolise their own connections with other humans. Thus, although learning with and through things is valid and important, as previously discussed, the young people in both studies know enough about the dominant symbolic order to understand that this has little currency in our society. They may be able to learn successfully with things in nature, but if they fail to get to grips with words in school they will always be positioned by others, and even by themselves, as 'the thick bunch'. As previously discussed, post-humanism helps to undermine the static nature of this positioning, the body (and society) is always open to change and in a future world a shift from word to thing may characterise educational practice. Nevertheless, as a starting point, failure with words puts young people at a serious disadvantage in Western society as it is currently constituted.

Both Barad and Bennett draw attention to matter in ways which are productive and useful. However, in terms of these empirical studies, to privilege the material in the generation of learning and knowledge would be a mistake. One of the important factors emerging in the Exmoor study is that for the young people living on the moor, the land and the social are indivisible. Often when asked to talk about the space around them, they evoke the people who make the space.

> Mick: Things like, you know, the moors, or just the landscaping, they (the National Park Authority) do a good job of keeping that from being spoilt and maintaining it but I think that, you know, for that to be worthwhile then you need to encourage people to stay, or to, people to live here, it's like a lot of it's the farmers and things that keep the countryside the way it is. You know, a lot of the farmers on Exmoor would be going on a bit, to encourage the next phase of farmers to come through they need to be able to build a house or to have somewhere to live, to be able to afford to live here and to stay otherwise it's going to kill Exmoor.

Friedel (2011), in discussing urban Native youths' responses to their involvement in outdoor learning projects in Canada, suggests that they are much less interested in engaging with nature than they are in making connections with each other and with their common cultural heritage: 'Learning about nature as taught by outdoor and environmental educators proved far less captivating than the opportunity the program gave youth to relate to one another in kinship and community' (2011, 533). Friedel is talking about indigenous youth who have historically had their land stolen from them and now live in cities. Their situation is patently different from the white English youth who still have the privilege of living on the land their families come from. Nevertheless, Friedel's analysis is illuminating. Whilst the National Park Authority on Exmoor and ourselves as researchers prioritise the material space, the young people focus on families, heritage and threats to continuity. It is not nature itself which is the conduit of learning but the kinds of practices it historically fosters. Mirroring my earlier comments about everyday learning, Friedel argues: 'The notion of learning as embedded in everyday life and Indigenous values and practices as to some extent dynamic provides a context in which to regard youth as co-constructors of culture' (2011, 536). Moreover, her emphasis on looking through the lens of orality: 'a merging of the past with the present (and by extension, the future)' (2011, 537) is also evocative of the Exmoor study where everyone knows each other and their family history. Here communication and circulation of stories occurs as if by magic so that: 'if a farmer sees you stop to have a pee behind a hedge everyone knows about it'. This sense of past, present and future as always held in fragile tension pervaded the Exmoor focus group discussions:

> Sophie: I think its really, really sad, that there will, there will be loads of farms up for sale and they just get broken up, And I don't think they are very good at keeping farms together, to keep farms in families, because that's where the knowledge is, that's where it lies
>
> Anna: Yes you just end up with a few big landowners who've got the money and fewer small producing farms, which actually hog the knowledge, I think, and are better at looking after that landscape.

The land is actually teaching them a vivid social lesson about economics and class and so, in many ways, they are far more preoccupied with society than with vital materiality.

Conclusion: forms of learning in/with nature

Learning takes place in and through nature for the young people in both of these studies. One of the most important aspects which differentiates this from the activities of 'outdoor education' is the daily nature of this process, part of work or leisure: it is not something set up formally for them as a form of environmental consciousness or pedagogic activity. If education developed in the enlightenment tradition is redundant in the era of the post-human, then perhaps such different forms of informal learning are more fruitful.

A post-humanist approach to both research studies reveals some vital materialists learning lessons with nature. These lessons are not about stepping back from nature and reflecting and categorising it, they are about immersion. Instead of the mind/body human/non-human dichotomy on which the enlightenment tradition relies, such boundaries tend to slip away; although we should note that subjugation of the non-human is still very much in evidence, whether it be in dog training or hunting and shooting. This immersion produces tangible skills which become refined with practice and can also be taught to others. It also produces a disposition that is amenable to learning: a sense of openness rather than closure. There is also a paradoxical note of comfort: in situations that might to some seem dangerous, dirty, exhausting, these young people could finally relax. Post-human perspectives help to uncover the vibrancy and power of this learning, but, as I have demonstrated, they are less useful in exposing its limitations. Although learning in nature offers comparative freedom, these experiences are very much shaped by social inequalities.

Braidotti argues that post-humanism is an affirmative approach to the world: and who could deny that this is needed amongst the wreckage caused by humans who considered themselves inviolable:

> A post-human ethics for a non-unitary subject proposes an enlarged sense of inter-connection between self and others, including the non-human or 'earth' others, by removing the obstacle of self-centred individualism ... an affirmative bond that locates the subject in the flow of relations with multiple others. (Braidotti 2013, 29–30)

In this sense, post-humanism is dedicated to equality. However, as an analytic tool, as in the work of Barad and Bennett, it tends to foreground material possibilities and pay less attention to social problems. 'Self-centred individualism' is not the only, or even the main 'obstacle' to interconnections between self and others. These selves are too often limited by poverty, by unequal access to education, housing, land to be able to make positive bonds with either humans or non-humans. While post-humanism helps us to understand that these inequalities are not fixities and cannot totally suppress the vital materiality of young people, the problems and their consequences still do not disappear.

Perhaps post-human theory presents an ideal, which a socio-cultural perspective can then start to trouble. By operating with this dual perspective, we can identify both what is possible and what is yet to be done. However, taking the argument a step further, if we accept the validity of post-humanism then we have to question any notion of society and culture as separate from nature, and therefore the reliability and the terms of any socio-cultural perspective also need problematising. What role does nature play in structuring poverty, class, gender or ethnicity, for example? How is nature in the classroom as well as outdoors? Here the image of endless spiral presents itself but this need not be as frustrating as it seems. As MacClure (2010, 284) suggests, one of the joys of theory may be the 'gift of a *headache*'. In attempting to theorise nature and learning my thoughts spiral out of control, but this is energising and productive, leading me on to new and tantalising questions.

Acknowledgements

The jobs without training study was funded by the European Social Fund, Learning and Skills Council and Connexions. The Exmoor study was funded by The Exmoor National Park Authority and the Institute for Health and Community, Plymouth University. Thanks to the anonymous reviewers for their useful comments.

References

Alaimo, S., and S. Hekman, eds. 2008. *Material Feminisms*. Bloomington: Indiana University Press.

Barad, K. 2003. "Posthumanist Performativity: Toward an Understanding of How Matter Comes to Matter." *Signs* 28 (3): 801–831.

Barad, K. 2007. *Meeting the Universe Half Way: Quantum Physics and the Entanglements of Matter and Meaning*. London: Duke University Press.

Bennett, J. 2010. *Vibrant Matter*. London: Duke University Press.

Braidotti, R. 2013. *The Posthuman*. Cambridge: Polity Press.

Code, L. 1991. *What Can She Know: Feminist Theory and the Construction of Knowledge?* Ithaca, NY: Cornell University Press.

Daly, M. 1970. *Gyn/Ecology: The Metaethics of Radical Feminism*. Boston: Beacon Press.

Edensor, T. 2000. "Walking in the British Countryside: Reflexivity, Embodied Practice and Ways to Escape." *Body and Society* 6 (3–4): 81–106.

Friedel, T. L. 2011. "Looking for Learning in All the Wrong Places: Urban Native Youths' 'Cultured Response to Western-oriented Place-based Learning." *International Journal of Qualitative Studies in Education* 24 (5): 531–546.

Ginsberg, A. 2006. *Collected Poems 1947–1997*. New York: HarperCollins.

Haraway, D. 2004. *The Haraway Reader*. London: Routledge.

Harrison, S. 2010. "'Why Are We Here?' Taking 'Place' into Account in UK Outdoor Environmental Education." *Journal of Adventure Education & Outdoor Learning* 10 (1): 3–18.

Hekman, S. 2010. *The Material of Knowledge: Feminist Disclosures*. Bloomington: Indiana University Press.

Hsu, S. J. 2009. "Significant Life Experiences Affect Environmental Action: A Confirmation Study in Eastern Taiwan." *Environmental Education Research* 15 (4): 497–517.

Hughes, C., J. Quinn, and M. Tamboukou. 2011. Symposium on Barad, International Gender and Education Conference, University of Exeter.

Hultman, K., and H. L. Taguchi. 2010. "Challenging Anthropocentric Analysis of Visual Data: A Relational Materialist Methodological Approach in Educational Research." *International Journal of Qualitative Studies in Education* 23 (5): 525–542.

Jackson, A. Y., and L. Mazzei. 2012. *Thinking with Theory in Qualitative Research.* Abingdon: Routledge.

MacClure, M. 2010. "The Offense of Theory." *Journal of Education Policy* 25 (2): 277–286.

MacNaghten, P., and J. Urry. 1998. *Contested Natures.* London: Sage.

Merchant, S., J. Quinn, and S. Waite. 2013. Social and Economic Aspirations of Young People Living on and around Exmoor National Park, Exmoor National Park Authority/Institute for Health and Community, Plymouth University.

Milligan, C., and A. Bingley. 2007. "Restorative Places or Scary Spaces? The Impact of Woodland on the Mental Well-being of Young Adults." *Health & Place* 13 (4): 799–811.

O'Brien, Liz. 2009. "Learning Outdoors: The Forest School Approach." *Education 3-13* 37 (1): 45–60.

Pederson, H. 2010. "Is 'the Posthuman' Educable? On the Convergence of Educational Philosophy, Animal Studies and Posthumanist Theory." *Discourse: Studies in the Cultural Politics of Education* 31 (2): 237–250.

Pederson, H. 2011. "Counting Affects: Mo(ve)ments of Intensity in Critical Aviation Education." *Canadian Journal of Environmental Education* 16: 14–28.

Pederson, H. 2012. "Undercover Education: Mice, Mimesis and Parasites in the Teaching Machine." *Studies in the Philosophy of Education* 31 (4): 365–386.

Pike, E. C. J., and S. Beames, eds. 2013. *Outdoor Adventure and Social Theory.* Abingdon: Routledge.

Quinn, J. 2012. "New Learning Worlds: The Significance of Nature in the Lives of Marginalised Young People." *Discourse: Studies in the Cultural Politics of Education, iFirst* 1–15.

Quinn, J. 2010. *Learning Communities and Imagined Social Capital: learning to Belong.* London: Continuum.

Quinn, J., R. Lawy, and K. Diment. 2008. *Not Just Dead-End Kids in Dead-End Jobs: Young People in Jobs Without Training in South West England.* Marchmont Observatory, University of Exeter.

Travlou, P. 2006. *Wild Adventure Space: Literature Review.* OPENspace – Research Centre for Inclusive Access to Outdoor Environments.

Waite, S., ed. 2011. *Children Learning Outside the Classroom: From Birth to Eleven.* London: Sage.

Wylie, J. 2005. "A Single Day's Walking: Narrative, Self and Landscape on the South West Coastal Path." *Transactions of the Institute of British Geographers* 30 (2): 234–247.

Gendered subjectivities of spacetimematter

Malou Juelskjaer

Department of Education, University of Aarhus, Copenhagen, Denmark

This paper investigates enactments of human subjectivities with a focus on how subjectivities may be studied if spatiality and temporality are taken up as constituting forces in the production of subjectivities. By reading poststructuralist feminist theorising, agential realism and empirical material diffractively through each other I re-situate gendered subjectivity to be *of* spacetimemattering [Barad, K. 2007. *Meeting the Universe Half Way – Quantum Physics and the Entanglement of Matter and Meaning*. Durham: Duke University Press] rather than something occurring *in* space and time. From a study of students who changed schools in order to experience 'new beginnings' the paper presents an in-depth case study of Mary. By following Mary's transition and how she is complexly enacted through her past and present school lives, it becomes possible to investigate how spatiality and temporality co-existed as forces in her becoming. I argue that this perspective opens up alternative possibilities for understanding the constitution of subjectivity.

Opening

How do forces of space, time, materialities and bodies co-constitute the on-going shaping of human subjectivities? This article explores how we might consider this theoretically and engage with it empirically. The empirical material with which to think *from and with* this question was drawn from a study of 13-year-old students who changed schools to experience 'new beginnings'. No one in the new school knew them and so they could start afresh as students and as classmates (Juelskjaer 2009). The research was designed initially as a social psychological, poststructuralist, feminist study of the multiple subjectivities that are associated with school transitions and what might be opened and closed down in terms of the constitution of subjectivities inspired by Butler, Davies, Phoenix, Staunæs, Søndergaard, Wetherell and others. The research was furthermore designed so that components such as time, space, bodies and (other) materialities could 'surface' as constitutive forces in the production of subjec-tivities. As the study progressed, additional theorising was needed. In the work of Barad (2007), space, time and mattering are the constituting forces in the production of natural–cultural worlds. Barad's (2007) theorising is achieved by queering quantum physics by diffractively reading Niels Bohr's work with feminist science studies, notably Haraway's, Foucault's and Butler's poststructuralist work. However, we need to acknowledge that there is a problem of 'scale' in considering Barad's insights from quantum physics, in relation to processes of subjectivication that take place within everyday human and nonhuman life. I am aware that the shift in scale may be viewed as highly problematic, no matter what form it takes (Sokal and Bricmont 1998), and that translations need to be undertaken carefully. Yet, the new thinking this translation makes possible warrants the effort (cf. Childers 2013; Højgaard and Søndergaard 2011; Juelskjaer et al. 2013; Lenz Taguchi 2010, 2013; Palmer 2011; Plauborg forthcoming; Schrader 2010; Søndergaard 2013).

According to quantum physics in contradistinction to classical physics, time and space cease to be external units of measurement. In a Baradian re-working, the implications of this are that time and space are produced through iterative intra-actions that materialise specific phenomena, where phenomena are not 'things' but relations. Mattering and materialising are dynamic processes through which temporality and spatiality are produced as something specific. Barad names this process spacetimemattering (Barad 2007) to emphasise the way components are produced together in one ongoing movement. This is a profound re-framing, or one might say, 'queering' of time and space (Barad 2010) which has significant consequences for what we know about time and space in specific historical material–discursive practices. Barad notes:

> Why should we find the metaphysical individualism of classical physics so 'natural' in its obvious applicability to human phenomena, while refusing to consider the possibility that the relational ontology of quantum physics might yield a different set of insights worth considering about human and nonhuman worlds, and the ways that boundary gets made and enforced? Notice that what I'm suggesting here is a shift in the ontological and epistemological underpinnings of our theories, not an insistence that quantum physics can provide an explanation for everything under the sun. (Barad in interview: Juelskjær and Schwennesen 2012, 18)

What if, then, in some form or the other, insights from quantum physics can throw a different light on conceptions of time and space in the realm of human everyday existence? How does the troubling of pre-fixed spatial scales and conceptions of past/present change the analytical practice and what we might be able to 'see' analytically? How might these new concepts of spacetimemattering make us think otherwise about subjectivities, particularly gendered subjectivities? The case study presented below is guided by this line of questioning.

I first explain the central concepts of Barad's agential realism and relate this to poststructuralist feminist thinking. Next, the research apparatus and the possibilities of how to consider interviews within an agential realist framing are elaborated. The rest of the article is dedicated to empirical analysis, and it concludes with a consideration of where all of this may take feminist agential realist work on subjectivities.

Intra-actions and a move to onto-epistemology

In her theorising, Barad moves from epistemology to onto-epistemology (Barad 2007), a reworking which is of great importance when considering space and time as active components. Barad enacts this shift through the work of Niels Bohr. First and foremost, she considers Bohr's resolution of the wave–particle discussion which may be summed up as follows: depending on the measuring device, light can behave as either a wave or a particle. Different interpretations of this phenomenon have been debated. Bohr's resolution was of *indeterminacy* (whereas Heisenberg's was *uncertainty*): implying that light does not have an inherent nature; instead, the form that light takes is the effect of the measuring apparatus. Light, therefore, and other forms of matter, must be recognised as phenomena that are always relational and specific to the apparatuses through which they emerge. In other words, before measuring takes place, the phenomenon is indeterminate. Barad (2007) argues that Bohr's acknowledgement that the researcher is part of the apparatus remains at an epistemological level of argumentation, while Barad herself takes it to an ontological level. She argues, following Bohr, that concepts are material and have material effects. She suggests that 'intra-actions' among components such as experimental apparatus, light and the researcher, and the 'agential cuts' in the intra-actions, produce 'phenomena' and that phenomena are thus always already inherently relational. Both the phenomena of the laboratory and phenomena of the world are enacted through specific apparatuses and their agential cuts. Thus, the material and the discursive are produced through each other as 'intra-activity'. This further means that when Barad 'pushes' Bohr's work there are various consequences, such as, for example, that apparatuses are *not* new conceptual containers or place-holders; they are transformative arrangements, enacting what comes to matter. There is a double reference in Barad's theorising: mattering as the cuts produced by the research and mattering in an ontological sense, as that which goes on regardless of the research (Juelskjær 2009). The apparatus is both a technical means (or method) of tackling a philosophy of science premise *and* a conceptualisation of a fundamental condition of this premise; the world is in constant, unpredictable, transformative movement. Conducting science in/by/with this world entails setting up apparatuses through which something can matter and thereby be studied. In a way, one could say that it is about setting up fruitful experiments (i.e. research) in which the researcher is part of that very apparatus. At the same time, apparatuses are also central to Barad's conceptualisation of the fundamental conditions of social/ world processes of becoming *as such*, since what is enacted *at all and anywhere*, is enacted through agential cuts in apparatuses of material–discursive production (Juelskjær 2009). This move to onto-epistemology, where practices of knowing and being are mutually implicated, posits knowing as a direct material engagement and concepts as 'material articulations of the world' (Barad 2007, 139). Agential cuts open up and rework the conditions of possibility. *Prior* to the intra-action and the agential cut, words and things are indeterminate and consequently there is no such thing as 'knowing from a distance', only knowing from within various and specific intra-actions. Instead of there being a separation of subject and object, there is an entanglement of subject and object (Dolphijn and van der Tuin 2012, 53). This makes Barad's onto-epistemology a form of performative thinking in which not only the social but also the natural and the material are iteratively and processually enacted. Matter is a doing; it is co-productive of possibilities and constraints. Furthermore, gender, as a nature–culture/material–discursive phenomenon, is productive in and of those processes. With Barad, then, it is not so much an issue of how bodies are positioned and situated in the world, rather, it is a matter of how bodies are constituted along with the world, or rather, as 'part' of the world; 'being-of-the-world' not 'being-in-the-world' (Barad 2007, 160). Embodiment, we see from this, is material–discursive and is the provisional effect of agential cuts that constitute material configurations of bodies and boundaries. Here, we may begin to see elements of what kind of feminist thinking Barad offers as she shifts Judith Butler's concept of gender performativity (as iterative citationality, a 'doing' instead of being), altering it through quantum physics. Later, the article illuminates some of the consequences of this shift. Next, the research apparatus required for this endeavour is described.

Research apparatus

According to a Baradian approach, the apparatus used in quantum physics experiments has to be included in the description of the research design. As already mentioned, apparatuses are 'specific material reconfigurings of the world' (Barad 2007, 142) and designate a form of boundary-making, or temporary definition that establishes specific demarcations of processes and their effects. Furthermore, along with apparatus, researchers are implicated in research practices enabling some things to matter more than others. As specific material–discursive practices, apparatuses enact agential cuts; cuts that constitute boundaries, categories and 'properties' of phenomena, cuts through which specific concepts and specific material–discursive reconfigurations of the world become meaningful (Højgaard, Juelskjær, and Søndergaard 2012).

Later, I discuss how a 'new beginning' was productive of specific subjectivities of the school change analysed in the study. Before this, I present the research design, the empirical matter and the theorising. As mentioned above, my aim is to draw on Barad's theory to think through an empirical study that explored how 13-year-old students experienced 'new beginnings' as they changed to another school where they could start afresh as students and classmates. Some of the students had been bullied in their previous school, some had conflicts with teachers and some were simply bored and curious about what another school would be like. The study was longitudinal and involved observing and interviewing students over a year with a focus on the constitution of 'new' gendered subjectivities, considering time, space and materialities as constitutive forces. The case study presented below involved one of the students from the study, referred to as Mary.

The research design set time and space and the researcher in motion by following the students across time and space. Students were interviewed before they left one school and several times after changing to a new school. Students were asked to reflect in interviews on their movements and on processes through which they became a student in their new school. The research was initially conceived theoretically according to a poststructuralist approach that viewed subjectivities as contextual achievements made possible through interaction, negotiation of social categories, such as whiteness, gender, age, sexuality and within discursive practices (Davies 2000; Petersen 2004; Søndergaard 1996; Staunæs 2005; Walkerdine 1990; Youdell 2006). In addition, the design was informed by empirical studies on intersectionalities including gender-youth-ethnicity-school (Frosh, Phoenix, and Pattman 2002; Staunæs 2005), race-class-gender (Knapp 2005; Skeggs 2004), racialisation-whiteness (Kofoed 2005; Myong 2009; Ratschack 1998), as well as by theoretical and methodological discussions around intersectionality (Brah and Phoenix 2004; Crenshaw 1994; Lykke 2010; McCall 2005; Phoenix 2006; Staunæs and Søndergaard 2006). However, empirical studies of subjectification within this poststructuralist field often do not include space and time as explicit dimensions; these are merely implied through associated concepts such as 'context' and 'position'.

Useful as a poststructuralist analytic is in offering a study of the positioning or renegotiation of, for example, 'disobedient boy/student' or 'the quiet girl in the class', and in providing analyses which are highly sensitive to the complexities of these relational positionings in the 'here and now', I was left with a sense of there being 'more', or something 'else' to account for. There seemed to be a force in students' becomings that I could not 'access'. When diffractively reading social categorisation through the concept of spacetimemattering/agential realism, it seemed that social categories and positioning put space and time 'to rest'; treating these as naturalised givens (as in a Newtonian universe). It could even be argued, as does Massumi (2002), that this theorising produces a social coordinate system rather like a stable grid. However, we might pay closer attention to the theories instead of dismissing them as Massumi suggests. Foucault's notion of spatiality as relational seen in the mutual constitution of space–power relations in the Panopticon and heterotopias (Foucault 1976, 1984, 1986) seemed to be relevant. Likewise, Foucault's genealogical thinking challenges the concept of linear time and the modern idea of 'progress'. Judith Butler also notes that subjectification is 'a temporal process which operates through the reiteration of norms' (Butler 1993, 10) and that this process is not linear, stable or predictable. What comes to be naturalised is:

> a sedimented effect of a reiterative or ritual practice [...] yet, it is also by virtue of this reiteration that gaps and fissures are opened up as the constitutive instabilities in such constructions, as that which escapes or exceeds the norm. (Butler 1993, 10)

Butler theorises how the dynamics of sedimentation and change have to do with the instability of the effects of the materialisation of the norm/alising and how subjectivication is inherently temporal, producing (through citing, performing and reiterating) what may 'be' and what may be abjected, that is, placed 'outside' time. Butler's notions of time are thus not those of linear time imagined as evenly spaced out moments. However, neither Butler's nor Foucault's thinking allowed me to study the 'thickness' of the students' subjectivities. I was searching for the possibilities of thinking about multiple temporalities working in the same moment as echoes or presences of other spaces. I wanted a different 'worlding' or epistemology and ontology of being. To find this, I turned to Barad and her reading of quantum physics. The consequences of her reading are both a queering of quantum physics and a re-formulation of how to conceptualise discourse and matter when time and space are reconsidered from the perspective of quantum physics. Barad suggests 'a shift in the ontological and epistemological underpinnings of our theories, not an insistence that quantum physics can provide an explanation for everything under the sun' (Barad in interview: Juelskjær and Schwennesen 2012, 18). I cannot elaborate on quantum physics within this article, but central to her theorising is the idea of entanglement, leading her to conclude that 'phenomenon are material entanglements enfolded and threaded through the spacetimemattering of the universe' (Barad 2012, 44). The 'past' and the 'future' are implicated in what makes a phenomenon. Space, time – past/future – matter do not 'stay put' they are 'iteratively reconfigured and enfolded through the world's ongoing intra-activity' (Barad 2012, 44). So we get entanglement and specific agential cuts (agential separability), as a 'cutting-together-apart', of specific enactments of matter and meaning (world and worlding). This is not the creation of 'the new', nor a sedimentation/change, but rather a form of dis/continuity. Dis/continuity is a concept designed to avoid the dichotomies of past/present and stasis/change. She suggests instead that 'dynamic relationality between continuity and discontinuity is crucial to the open ended becoming of the world' (Barad 2010, 244). Thus, according to Barad's deconstructive, queer enactment of quantum physics, time, space and matter may be understood as iterative, intra-active performativity, thereby becoming active components in the iterative and specific formations of subjectivities. I drew on these insights from Barad in my study to think more radically about time and space and how these matter while studying the gendered subjectivities of students' new beginnings.

Re-thinking interviews

In light of this Baradian recasting of space and time, it is important to re-address the status of the narratives produced in interview situations and what they may say about, for example, a student's 'past school life'. Jackson and Mazzei (2012, 127) argue that:

> Narration [as] a performative practice requires a re-interpretation of the material, or a re-thinking of the relationship between the material and the discursive. Such re-positioning demands that we re-think voice, and data, and the subject, not as a separation of the theoretical from the material, but as an enactment, as a performative practice, one that asks 'how matter and embodiment come to matter in the process of research itself, and in the process of how participants account for what they tell us and how we view their tellings as enactments rather than descriptions.

So narration as a performative practice is not about representations of 'reality' or linguistic turn-taking; it is a material articulation of the world (Barad 2007, 139). It is useful to consider how time and space are implicated as part of those material articulations and what 'consequences' this may have for the enacted performative practice that we term 'an interview'. An example from the data can help in considering this problem. Mary and the other students were mobilised within an apparatus of 'new beginnings' with the idea of 'the willful subject' central in that apparatus of new beginnings as they change school. Students were interviewed before enrolling in the new school and as part of this, were asked to reflect on their desire to, and possibilities of, leaving specific social positions, attitudes and 'shortcomings' behind. A student had to choose to become someone else, someone 'improved', and the desire to do so was a mobilising component in daring to change schools. This involved moving from, for example, being recognised/positioned as a disobedient student who hates school to becoming a different sort of student. The fact that the new classmates did not know each other, that they were all 'new', was also an important mobilising factor. Changing school in this manner, where everybody was new to each other, was possible but not mandatory as there are some schools in Denmark that only begin at eighth grade.

By observing, talking with and interviewing students, I took part in how they worked on mastering versions of their pasts in order to position themselves in a desired present/future. Mary was an ethnic white girl and had moved from a multicultural school landscape in which she was perhaps the only girl who had managed to be part of the group of Muslim girls, girls who were descendants from the Middle East and brought up as Muslims. Mary had Danish roots and was brought up with a Christian/Protestant background. In other words, in 'doing Muslim with the Muslim girls', Mary was perhaps looking at the white ethnic majority from the in/outside of the minority category of Muslim: she was enacted through a 'hybrid identity' (Bhaba 1994; Staunæs 2005). The new school landscape, though, was an almost all-white landscape and her move was recognised/understood by herself and her peers as a transformation from being 'one of the Muslim girls' to becoming a 'white young girl'. With regard to time and space, Mary reflected during an interview:

... I viewed myself as one of them [Muslim girls]. I acted exactly like them and I really liked it back then. ... when I think about it now, then, I think, I don't think I would ever be able to think like that again, although I was fine about it then [...]. Thinking back, now, then I think, that I would think – that it was not really good back then, but I liked it – I didn't feel bad about it or anything.

First, let us follow a 'conventional' social constructionist/poststructuralist notion of what is going on and in the next move rethink it differently. A well-known analysis of this telling would be that the student 'sits' in a *time–space 1* (the interview context, a here and now) and tells about a *time–space 2* (producing a past school life through a narrative of the ways she behaved, the friends she had, etc.) and thereby produces a present school life, a *time–space 3* (manifesting the new beginning, the other place, positioning herself within that discourse). The process furthermore involves a *time–space 4*, in which the researcher conducts the analysis, while gathering the narratives of 'past school life' and 'present school life' from different parts of the interview. This approach neatly separates the data into four disconnected spatio-temporal orders loosely linked by a narrative. But what if we tried to think differently about what unfolds in interviews by viewing 'tellings as enactments rather than descriptions'? (Jackson and Mazzei 2012, 127). And what if we untidy the tidy order (of time–space 1–4) through the notion of multiple apparatuses producing specific spacetime-mattering instead of simply seeing the interview as a production of a specific 'present' in which Mary is positioned and positions herself within available discursive practices? If we do so, we may see more than how the pull of a linear narrative of a new beginning enacts Mary and come to see how the here-and-now shapes her. Then, we may see that beginnings are complex and already 'haunted' (Barad 2010, 253) by multiple apparatuses. If spacetimemattering is what also gets produced in the agential cuts of the apparatuses of the new beginning, then we will be able to conceive of multiple space–times as co-present and co-producing 'Mary-the-white-girl'. Thus, we can focus on the 'thickness' of subjectivities. In the following sections, I will trouble the spatio-temporal ordering of the new school beginning apparatus.

Analysing timespacemattering: subjectivities

In the area where Mary lived and went to school, ethnic Danish was not in any simple sense the majority group. Noerrebro is an area of Copenhagen with a diverse ethnic population. At a school that practices multiculturalism, it is possible and sometimes high status to 'cross' from 'doing white' to 'doing black'. Thereby the subject may become a sign of the success of a multicultural society; she becomes culturally avant-garde (Staunæs 2005). Perhaps this was the case with Mary, who said, 'Not many Danes at my school get to be with them [the Muslims], but I did', 'I saw myself as one of them. I talked like them. I acted totally like them'. Mary recounts from within an agential cut where she is cut off from that very being; it is a past doing. We see instead how she is enacted in that cut as somebody recasting herself being recast, as her whiteness was shaped by the material–discursive practice of 'doing Muslim girl'.

In the spatio-temporalities of the new school life, every morning Mary boarded a bus that transported her out of her neighbourhood into the suburbs, out of the landscape of high-rise blocks and into the landscape of detached houses and into the new school. When she entered the school, there were no sounds of 'broken Danish', no veiled girlfriends giving Mary a hug, saying good morning and inviting her to join their activities. Instead, she was met by white girls and boys talking and giggling sometimes about the party last Saturday and who kissed whom, etc. These comments were part of conversations that I often overheard as I passed by when doing observations. Mary was now *of* another landscape that was continuously shaped by and shaping her. She registered how even her tone of voice and pronunciation became different. She also told me that her sense of amusement (what sort of things did/not make her burst into laughter) and what did/not make her uncomfortable were changing. A new material–discursive–affective shaping was going on. After a while, Mary stopped associating with the girls from her old school. By the end of the new school year she said, 'I never see them anymore. It just stopped. I have changed too much, it just wouldn't, it couldn't'. There is a violent cut here. Ways of living had become impossible and hardly bearable. At the same time, what may be termed 'the past' reappeared and was continuously reordered in multiple and contradictory ways. Time, space, mattering and subjectivity threaded through each other. Mary seemed to have a sense of herself within an apparatus of her 'past life' while simultaneously trying to honour what she had been and being entangled within an apparatus of leaving the past behind, changing and becoming someone else. Sensing from within these apparatuses it became simultaneously very difficult to honour her past being. Her disjointed 'reasoning' was evident:

> … when I think about it now, then, I think, I don't think I would ever be able to think like that again, although I was fine about it then […]. Thinking back, now, then I think, that I would think – that it was not really good back then but I liked it – I didn't feel bad about it or anything.

The contradictory subjectivities of different spatio-temporalities are enacted and productive of how Mary seemed to sense her being. In this example, I have indicated how the spacetimemattering-subjectivities enact the sense of belonging in the new by sensing the 'difference'. Mary's past school life was not in a simple sense 'over'; it did not simply 'live' as a discourse of the past, but indicates the ways in which the ongoing re-configuration of spacetimematter-subjectivity is a matter of the specificity of these complex intra-actions. Another specificity concerns how Mary is enacted by the cuts of landscape where her old school is situated. Mary was told by an old classmate that she was now viewed as a traitor by her old friends. Mary said:

> When I am with the girls from my class, we take a detour [to get to Mary's home]. I know it is stupid, but I don't like meeting people [from her 'old life', her old school – who all lives in her neighbourhood].

In a crowd of ethnic-racialised Muslim girls, Mary could blend in as one of them and more recently, in a crowd of ethnic-racialised white girls she blended in as one of them. Yet she did not only blend in; the blending also made her 'stand out' in her home landscape as exactly that, a re-appropriated Dane. Mary commented further on her unease with moving about in her home landscape:

> I hate it when I have to go down to the supermarket. It is ridiculous. I have told my mother, because one day I got really upset about it, because I just didn't want to go down there, and then I told my mother why. On the block where we live there is a large yard, but they are going to build a sports centre there instead, and my mother doesn't want to live here then, so perhaps we will move. I hope that soooo much. I really want to move.

Trying to 'hold it together', while simultaneously being part of these mutually exclusionary landscapes or topologies made living quite unbearable. The schools extended into the landscape. They were not inherently bounded entities, they were an intra-active phenomenon which Mary was also specifically enacted within. Mary's entangled becomings were of these two specific geo-political topologies. In Noerrebro, a multi-ethnic area, often portrayed in the news as a problem area in relation to integration and with gang problems, Mary learned to live and think from within the material–discursive practices and categories of 'Muslim' and 'girl'. Her body was shaped through practices of covering ('you could never see my belly or my legs or anything'). She was actively engaged in particular processes of othering. When she talked about this from within her new school life she said, 'I had a lot of prejudices against "real" Danes'. On entering the new school, Mary described how her accent changed, she started wearing other sorts of clothes that revealed parts of her body that had formerly been hidden and how she started smoking, drinking and associating with boys. She had formerly understood all of these practices as practices that not she, but 'the Danes'/'the (then) local Others', did. The new gendered and ethnic-racialised material–discursive practices opened up new and various conditions of becoming while closing down others. At the new school, there was an absence of elements to co-materialise practices of 'doing Muslim'. Mary would have had to do it 'on her own', but stakes were high. Doing Muslim as an ethnic-racialised Dane would have had substantially different connotations within the all-white school. In this geo-political topology of white youth and its material–discursive setting where signs and practices of Muslimness were absent and Muslimness as 'the Other' was present, Mary had re-entered the material–discursive practices of white, even while being complexly entangled with the topology of Noerrebro. Perhaps this offers one way of grasping how material–discursive practices of whiteness work (Frankenberg 1993, 1997; Twine and Gallagher 2008) through entangled geo-politicised topologies.

This analysis of Mary's case study helps to suggest how subjectivities may be *of* (not in) such topologies – so let us try to go a step further. Imagine for a moment, Mary walking in her home landscape alone or in the company of her new friends. We can imagine: feet and pavement that 'know each other' through so many encounters and movements; her body sensing the surroundings – so well-known and yet not 'known' in any simple sense. Whether she takes the exact same route or a detour, Mary's movements and the being of the landscape are something else; the movements are perhaps hesitant, watchful, alert or uncomfortable. The landscape has become something else as have the subjectivities, bodies and senses that are of this landscape. This could be thought of like this: space is not just a simple and given container or context and time is not simply evenly (spaced out) moments that mark separations and the ('natural') order of events (where natural indicates linear, evolutionary time). Instead, we could imagine that something else is going on, that timespacemattering are active and transformative agents that simultaneously come to matter in specific ways that affect specific bodies and qualities of subjectivities. There are no fixed and given time and space. Time and space are 'thick' with multiple and shifting times, spaces and subjectivities. The analysis I offer here enacts such 'thickness' – a thickness that resonates with Barad's concept of dis/continuity instead of that of sedimentation/change:

> This 'beginning', like all beginnings, is always already threaded through with anticipation
> of where it is going but will never simply reach and of a past that has yet to come. It is not

merely that the future and the past are not 'there' and never sit still, but that the present is not simply here-now. [...] Quantum dis/continuity troubles the very notion of dicho-tomy – the cutting into two – itself (including the notion of 'itself'!). All this 'quantum weird-ness' (the display of an increasing array of uncanny phenomena) is actually 'quantum queerness' [...] the un/doing of identity. Quantum dis/continuity is at the crux of this im/possible, im/passible, trans/formation. [...] here-now, there-then have become unmoored – there's no given place or time for them to be [...] dynamic relationality between continuity and discontinuity is crucial to the open ended becoming of the world. (Barad 2010, 244)

So let us think with a sense of thickness and dis/continuity – engaging both concepts of change and stasis.

'Spacetimemattering with a touch of affectivity'

At the new school, there were two dominant stories that I came to know about Mary. The first was about her as 'the expert' on 'the others'. Several classmates said that through Mary they had come to know much more about Muslims, what they are like, about their lifestyle, etc. They said it was cool that she hung out with them. More-over, Mary's political (left-wing) engagement had made them much more interested in politics. The second story was told with some anxiety by others: they said that before changing schools Mary had actually considering starting to wear a headscarf and con-verting to Islam. Within the new school setting, to convert to Islam was viewed by white students as turning your back on the exciting youth culture that they had just embarked upon, which included experimenting, dancing, drinking, smoking and (con-sidering) having sexual relations. They suggested that to consider converting to Islam was to submit to something 'very un-Danish', and they thought that this was a radical choice at this age. So we see various kinds of intensity mobilised or running through the entangled spacetimematter. See Andreassen (2013) for an analysis of the Danish debates on Muslim head and body covering, Duits and Van Zoonen (2006) for a Euro-pean perspective and Staunæs (2005) who provides an analysis of an ethnic Danish girl caught between Danish and Muslim youth culture. On another occasion, when con-fronted with the active sex lives of some of her new friends, Mary said, 'this is too much [...] this could never have happened at Noerrebro'. We can see in Mary's comment, from the way Noerrebro is re-enacted or folded to create a moral, a perhaps somewhat superior judgement in which resentment also becomes possible. Her comment would not have had the same emotional quality and strength of resent-ment/resistance without the 'presence' of Noerrebro. This opens other possibilities of what kind of white girl Mary has the possibility to become as the boundaries of her gen-dered subjectivity are continuously reconfigured by multiple and non-linear spacetimematterings.

Agential cuts are made and subjectivities are made and unmade through these cuts. Mary and the other students live through the existence of multiple apparatuses of space-timemattering while negotiating hopes and practices of their version of a 'new begin-ning'. There involves an ongoing storying of oneself and each other brought about by the apparatus of 'new beginning' (in which the research apparatus was also implicated). Students lived the 'change' of the apparatus, talked about the 'change' (including talk about the 'past', the 'future', the 'now') and about social categories while at the same time reflexively maneuvering and mastering them. They were simultaneously con-ditioned and dependent on the specific conditions of possibilities of their new beginnings, and part of this involved the need to display reflexivity and social mobility. Thus, Mary had to work on keeping 'the past' a past. It was in no simple way a past by itself. She tried to control it while simultaneously being of these spacetimematterings; they do and undo her in ways that are out of her control. Past and present are troubled, and her sense of subjectivity, sometimes as a gendered specificity and sometimes not, is troubled as it is threaded through these multiple spacetimematterings.

I have tried to indicate some of the affective qualities of how the apparatuses are entangled and how the subjectivities of the cuts are lived such as: the sensation of attraction and perhaps repulsion when confronted with the sexual practices of her class-mates; the feeling of confidence when being the one who knows something about 'the other', or the anxieties about treading the pavement of her home landscape. As Massumi (2002) notes, affectivity flows 'pre-personally'; it is virtual. We can consider affect as 'virtual stuff' that flows among the multiple apparatuses of spacetimematter. Perhaps affect is the 'stuff' that connects and enacts these multiple apparatuses and so determines what elements of past–present–future-spaces are actualised in a specific cut and with what kind of qualities and sentiments. Affective flows enter the substance of the body and make something of that body that is of that apparatus.

And so ...

My argument in this article so far has been that past, present, future and beginning are re-done through affects flowing through and among specific apparatuses. The past, par-ticularly, gets made in ever more specific, different and shifting cuts of neighbourhood-landscapes-bodies-belonging. Inspired by the queering of quantum physics, we are confronted with dis/continuity (Barad) instead of 'movement' and 'change' (Butler) when considering Mary's the new beginning. When spatio-temporal locations become 'unmoored' (Barad 2010, 248) the complexities of the constitution of gendered subjectivities and the analysis hereof are multiplied and refocused. In paying close attention to these multiple apparatuses, time, space and subjectivities appear altered analytically and onto-epistemologically. With these suggested new lenses, banal, everyday activities seem to be implicated within more radical forms of creation. Subjectivities are of and part of the spacetimemattering, not contained as positions within them. When the point of view is no longer the social category, Mary ceases to be in a special position in time and space, and becomes emergent within specific material–discursive apparatuses, which themselves are created along with her.

As Mary moves about in her home landscape, her body, tinged with hesitancy, is cautious and the intra-actions produce a sensuous and material–discursive experience of her exclusion. It is a stifling existence of non-belonging, of physically being cast out, of having the pavements and the roads show her, her inappropriatedness, her other-ness, that produce the desire and hope to get out of the landscape all together (although she is completely dependent on her mother's decisions). These new movements reinforce the feeling that there is 'no way back', that there is only a new beginning, that she cannot 'do both/and'. She cannot both practise being one of the Danes and one of the Muslims –it is a geo-political, spatio-temporal im/possibility. The situation simultaneously stresses the impossibility and the possibility, the ambiguity, of the cut; it is a 'cutting-together-apart' (Barad 2010, 247). Mary is an iterative production of mul-tiple space–times and subjectivities, just as her material body is in no simple sense a bounded entity, it is iteratively and specifically materialised and shaped and makes itself felt. Furthermore, note that it is not just 'Mary' who is reconfigured but also 'the landscape'; as her body is no longer an unproblematised part thereof. The landscape has become something else; it has become an apparatus that segregates whites from the Muslims, it materialises as something slightly different.

Working with spacetimemattering involves setting time and space in analytical motion. To consider the subject analytically, then, is to see a temporary localisation of specific subjectivities, as when 'Mary' is actualised in specific agential cuts entangled with apparatuses in unforeseen ways. Subjectivity is therefore of spacetimemattering, not something occurring in space and time.

The question is not whether Mary and the rest of the students get a new beginning; actually it is an undoing of the question of 'the new' and of the willful subject of the new. The question, then, is how they are done and undone in complex ways – and how spacetimemattering is simultaneously done and undone – while living this new beginning. The question is also how material–discursive practices constitute moral obligations and responsibilities of success vis à vis 'the change', as the students are continuously hailed into enacting themselves as either successful or blamed as failed subjects of change. As Deleuze writes,

> ... the individualized subject-of-will is both an idea and an accomplishment that we each labor over, attempting to make real an idealized image of ourselves-as rational, as responsible-in relation to which we are always judged and found wanting, and against which we judge others and find them wanting. (Deleuze 1980 in Davies 2010, 55)

The point is that we do not get to re-set time and self; this is a fantasy about the subject as master of time–space–subjectivity, just as we see Mary trying to produce a narrative of a past that is linear, a past that she has left behind, and social categories that have been 'exchanged'.

When read diffractively with feminist poststructuralist thinking and on the basis of specific empirical material, agential realism can be enacted in ways that are productive for thinking about the constitution of gendered subjectivities. I have shown how subjectivity is of spacetimemattering where the agential cut takes place, not something occurring in space and time. The research task then becomes a matter of producing apparatuses that allow for possible multiple spatio-temporalities to intra-act in the analysis, thereby opening the concept of subjectivity/subject formation. As Barad asks:

> If the nature of causality is troubled to such a degree that effect does not simply follow cause end over end in an unfolding of existence through time, how is it possible to orient oneself in space or in time? Can we even continue to presume that space and time are still 'there'? (Barad 2012, 40)

A weird human

In this article, I have offered a diffractive reading of Mary's space–times, through poststructuralist feminist work and the work of Karen Barad, with the intent of coming to know something different about the gendered subjectivities of a new beginning. I have shown how a queered quantum physics works within a research apparatus in ways that bring the 'empirical material' into being by specific methods. I have argued that this makes possible a universe that gets to some of the 'thickness' of subjectivities. My diffractive reading is an offer of an altered way of explaining the constitution of subjectivities in gendered and ethnic-racialised specificities. In taking Barad's post-humanist performativity into the realm of the human, by attending to the everyday life of students at school and in home landscapes, I offer a notion of a 'slightly weird' human, one always already haunted; one not just placed in time and space, but a 'thickened human' who is not a bounded entity, but a human where boundaries of what that human might, and might not, be are set in motion in so many different and specific ways, places and temporalities. The skin is no longer the boundary which holds together the entities we have come to know as humans. I offer the 'weird human' as an effective move out of the realm of The Willful Subject, mastering space, time, and matter. Rather, I offer a way of getting to know something else about the struggles of subjectivity. This slightly re-configured human has the post-human folded within but does not quite 'turn out' as the same. It is perhaps something a bit different just as the research agenda is also a bit different. However, both are still concerned with processes concerning (weird) subjectivities, therefore, contributing to thinking of the human within 'post-psychology' (Staunæs and Juelskjær 2013). The weird human, in which poststructuralist and agential realist thinking is put to work, reframes the subject-matter of psychology, so that subjectivities, self and identity can then be rethought as psychological phenomena, which are also performative and phenomenal entanglements of spacetimemattering where socio-material–discursive–affective processes are at work.

Acknowledgements

I thank the editors Gabrielle Ivinson and Carol Taylor for their careful language revisions.

References

Andreassen, R. 2013. "Take Off that Veil and Give Me Access to Your Body: An Analysis of Danish Debates about Muslim Women's Head and Body Covering." In *I Shifting Control: Gender and Migration Policy, 1917–2010*, edited by Schrover and Moloney. Amsterdam: University Press B.V.

Barad, K. 2007. *Meeting the Universe Half Way – Quantum Physics and the Entanglement of Matter and Meaning.* Durham: Duke University Press.

Barad, K. 2010. "Quantum Entanglements and Hauntological Relations of Inheritance: Dis/Continuities, SpaceTime Enfoldings, and Justice-to-Come." *Derrida Today* 3 (2): 240–268.

Barad, K. 2012. "Nature's Queer Performativity." *Kvinder, Koen og Forskning* 21 (1–2): 25–54.

Bhabha, H. K. 1994. *The Location of Culture.* London: Routledge.

Brah, A., and A. Phoenix. 2004. "Ain't I a Woman. Intersectionality Revisited." *Journal of International Women Studies* 5 (3): 75–86.

Butler, J. 1993. *Bodies that Matter. On the Discursive Limits of "Sex".* London: Routledge.

Childers, S. M. 2013. "The Materiality of Fieldwork: An Ontology of Feminist Becoming." *International Journal of Qualitative Studies in Education* 26 (5): 599–609.

Crenshaw, K. W. 1994. "Mapping the Margins: Intersectionality, Identity Politics, and Violence Against Women of Colour." In *The Public Nature of Private Violence*, edited by M. Fineman and R. Mykitiuk, 93–118. New York: Routledge.

Davies, B. 2000. *A Body of Writing.* Walnuc Creek, CA: Alta Mira Press.

Davies, B. 2010. "The Struggle Between the Individualised Subject of Phenomenology and the Multiplicities of the Poststructuralist Subject: The Problem of Agency." *Reconceptualizing Educational Research Methodology* 1 (1): 54–68.

Dolphijn, R., and I. van der Tuin. 2012. *New Materialism: Interviews & Cartographies.* Ann Arbor: Open Humanities Press.

Duits, L., and L. Van Zoonen. 2006. "Headscarves and Porno-Chic: Disciplining Girl's Bodies in the European Multicultural Society." *European Journal of Women's Studies* 13 (2): 103–117.

Foucault, M. 1976. *Discipline and Punish: The Birth of the Prison.* Harmondsworth: Penguin.

Foucault, M. 1984. *Of Other Spaces: Utopias and Heterotopias Diakritics*, 22–27, Baltimore: Johns Hopkins University Press.

Foucault, M. 1986. "Space, Knowledge and Power." In *The Foucault Reader*, edited by P. Rabinow, 239–254. London: Penguin.

Frankenberg, R. 1993. *White Women, Race Matters. The Social Construction of Whiteness*. Minneapolis: University of Minnesota Press.

Frankenberg, R. 1997. *Displacing Whiteness. Essays in Social and Cultural Criticism*. Durham: Duke University Press.

Frosh, S., A. Phoenix, and R. Pattman. 2002. *Young Masculinities*. London: Palgrave.

Højgaard, L., M. Juelskjær, and D. Søndergaard. 2012. "The What of and the What If of Agential Realism – In Search of the Gendered Subject." *Kvinder, Koen og Forskning* 21 (1–2): 10–23.

Højgaard, L., and D. M. Søndergaard. 2011. "Theorizing the Complexities of Discursive and Material Subjectivity: Agential Realism and Poststructural Analysis." *Theory & Psychology* 3 (3): 338–354.

Jackson, A., and L. Mazzei. 2012. *Thinking with Theory in Qualitative Research: Viewing Data among Multiple Perspectives*. London: Routledge.

Juelskjaer, M. 2009. *En ny start – bevægelser i/gennem tid, rum, krop og sociale kategorier* [A new beginning – movement through time, space, bodies and social categories]. Aarhus: University of Aarhus.

Juelskjær, M., and N. Schwennesen. 2012. "Intra-active Entanglements: An Interview with Karen Barad." *Kvinder, Koen og Forskning* 21 (1–2): 10–23.

Juelskjær, M., D. Staunæs, and H. Ratner. 2013. "The Return of the Freudian Couch." *International Journal of Qualitative studies in Education* 26 (9): 1132–1152.

Knapp, G. 2005. "Race, Class, Gender: Reclaming Baggage in Fast Travelling Theories." *European Journal of Women's Studies* 12: 249–265.

Kofoed, J. 2005. "Holddeling: Når der gøres maskulinitet og hvidhed." *Kvinder, Køn og Forskning* 3: 42–52 (eng.: Selecting the team: doing masculinity and whiteness).

Lenz Taguchi, H. 2010. *Going Beyond the Theory/Practice Divide in Early Childhood Education: Introducing an Intra-active Pedagogy*. London: Routledge.

Lenz Taguchi, H. 2013. "Images of Thinking in Feminist Materialisms: Ontological Divergences and the Production of Researcher Subjectivities." *International Journal of Qualitative Studies in Education* 26 (6): 706–716.

Lykke, N. 2010. *Feminist Studies. A Guide to Intersectional Theory, Methodology and Writing*. New York: Routledge.

Massumi, B. 2002. *Parables for the Virtual. Movement, Affect, Sensation*. Durham: Duke University Press.

McCall, L. 2005. "The Complexity of Intersectionality." *Signs* 30 (3): 1771–1800.

Myong, L. 2009. *Adopteret: Fortællinger om transnational og racialiseret tilblivelse*. Copenhagen: Danmarks Pædagogiske Universitetsskole, Aarhus Universitet. (eng: "Adopted: stories on transnational and racialized becoming").

Palmer, A. 2011. "'How Many Sums Can I Do'? Performative Strategies and Diffractive Thinking as Methodological Tools for Rethinking Mathematical Subjectivity." *Reconceptualizing Educational Research Methodology* 1 (1): 3–18.

Petersen, E. B. 2004. *Academic Boundary Work: The Discursive Constitution of 'Scientificity' Amongst Researchers Within the Social Sciences and Humanities*. Copenhagen: University of Copenhagen.

Phoenix, A. 2006. "Interrogating Intersectionality: Productive Ways of Theorizing Multiple Positioning." *Kvinder, Køn og Forskning* 2–3: 21–31.

Plauborg, H. Forthcoming. *Intra-actions: Didactics, Sociality, Subject Matter and Learning (Working Title)*. Aarhus: Aarhus University.

Ratschack, S. H. 1998. *Looking White People in the Eyes. Gender, Race and Culture in Courtrooms and Classrooms*. Toronto: University of Toronto Press.

Schrader, A. 2010. "20 Responding to *Pfiesteria piscicida* (the Fish Killer): Phantomatic Ontologies, Indeterminacy, and Responsibility in Toxic Microbiology." *Social Studies of Science* 40: 275–306.

Skeggs, B. 2004. *Class, Self, Culture*. London: Routledge.

Sokal, A., and J. Bricmont. 1998. *Intellectual Impostures*. London: Profile Books Limited.

Søndergaard, D. M. 1996. *Tegnet på Kroppen. Køn: Koder og Konstruktioner blandt unge Voksne i Akademia*. København: Museum Tusculanums Forlag.

Søndergaard, D. M. 2002. "Poststructuralist Approaches to Empirical Analysis." *International Journal of Qualitative Studies in Education* 15 (2): 187–204.

Søndergaard, D. M. 2005. "Making Sense of Gender, Age, Power and Disciplinary Position: Intersecting Discourses in the Academy." *Feminism & Psychology* 15 (2): 189–208.

Søndergaard, D. M. 2013. "Virtual Materiality, Potentiality and Subjectivity: How Do We Conceptualize Real-Virtual Interaction Embodied and Enacted in Computer Gaming, Imagination and Night Dreams?" *Subjectivity* 6 (1): 55–78.

Staunæs, D. 2005. "From Culturally Avant-garde to Sexually Promiscuous: Troubling Subjectivities and Intersections in the Social Transition from Childhood into Youth." *Feminism and Psychology* 15 (2): 149–167.

Staunæs, D., and M. Juelskjær. Accepted for publication. "Post-psykologisk subjektivering-steori og 'problemet med personlighed' version 2.0 [Post-psychological theory of subjectification and 'the problem about personality' version 2.0]." In *Personlighedspsykologi*, edited by J. Dammeyer and S. Køppe. Hans Reitzel.

Staunæs, D., and D. M. Søndergaard. 2006. "Intersektionalitet – udsat for teoretisk justering." *Kvinder, Køn og Forskning* 2–3: 43–56.

Twine, W. F., and C. Gallagher. 2008. "The Future of Whiteness: A Map of the 'Third Wave'." *Ethnic and Racial Studies* 31 (1): 4–24.

Walkerdine, V. 1990. *Schoolgirl Fictions*. New York: Verso.

Youdell, D. 2006. "Subjectivation and Performative Politics – Butler Thinking Althusser and Foucault: Intelligibility, Agency and the Raced-Nation-Religioned Subjects of Education." *British Journal of Sociology of Education* 27 (4): 511–528.

Making matter making us: thinking with Grosz to find freedom in new feminist materialisms

Alecia Youngblood Jackson

Department of Leadership and Educational Studies, Appalachian State University, Boone, NC, USA

In this paper, I offer a very close reading of Grosz [2010. "Feminism, Materialism, and Freedom." In *New Materialisms: Ontology, Agency, and Politics*, edited by Diana Coole and Samantha Frost, 139–157. Durham, NC: Duke University Press] thinking with Bergson in order to re-conceptualise freedom, matter, and the subject in new feminist materialisms. My central argument is that these free acts are mutually constituted in the intra-action [Barad 2007. *Meeting the Universe Halfway: Quantum Physics and the Entanglement of Matter and Meaning*. Durham, NC: Duke University Press] between human and non-human forces. The guiding questions for this paper are, 'What if we locate freedom in doing, rather than being? How does associating freedom with acts, rather than attaching it to the subject, change how we think about ontology and agency?' I use interview data from a research study with first-generation academic women in order to explore these concepts and put them to work.

How do we make matter (matter), and how does matter make us (matter)? This question is the guiding force of this paper, and the question is not to be read as a practice with a linear function of production but an entangled process that occurs spatially, temporally, and simultaneously. Therefore, it is difficult to capture this entanglement, much less *untangle* the elements in the making. However, one entrée into such an analysis would be to examine what is mutually constituted in the intra-action among matter, including the human and the non-human – not the inter-action (or dynamic between the separable things) but the *intra-action*, the ways in which all matter makes other matter, or how they produce each other in a mutual process of becoming (Barad 2007; Deleuze and Guattari 1987). To venture into this new material feminist of matter 'as indeterminate, constantly forming and reforming in unexpected ways' (Coole and Frost 2010, 10) – or matter 'becoming' rather than merely 'being' – requires a reconsideration of the concept of *freedom*. Grosz's (2010) provocative essay, 'Feminism, Materialism, and Freedom' centers on her reading of Bergson; she 'explores the subject's freedom through its immersion in materiality' (141). Grosz pushes aside conventional, subject-oriented concepts of freedom ('freedom from' and/or 'freedom to') to focus on *free acts*: 'those which both express us and transform us, which express our transformation' (146). In this paper, I offer a very close reading of Grosz thinking with Bergson in order to reconceptualise freedom, matter, and the subject in new feminist materialisms. My central argument is that these free acts are mutually constituted in the intra-action (Barad 2007) between human and non-human forces.

Free acts

The guiding questions for this paper are, 'What if we locate freedom in doing, rather than being? How does associating freedom with acts, rather than attaching it to the subject, change how we think about ontology and agency?' Grosz prompts such questions in her reading of Bergson. First, it is important to consider how *free acts* are a different conception of freedom. In both structuralist and post-structuralist theories, freedom is attached to the subject. That is, in structuralist theories (e.g. Marxism), freedom is external; it is a right, a commodity, and a possession; that is, you either have freedom, or you do not. The problem with this view of freedom-as-a-possession is an assumption that those who 'have' or are naturally endowed with freedoms intentionally decide and act on their own free will. By contrast, in post-structural theories, freedom remains situated within a model of constraint; however, freedom is not endowed but becomes possible through a range of choices that are produced through historical, linguistic, and discursive forces. That is, subjects become free only on the conditions within which they are produced by discourse. Their expressions of subjectivity – their freedoms – are always constituted (paradoxically) by that which seeks to contain. In post-structural theories of freedom, there is neither a prior intention nor a 'doer *behind* the deed' (Butler 1995, 134) – yet the attention remains on the positionality of the subject. The free will and determinism opposition with regard to a subject's freedom has been taken up and critiqued by many post-structural thinkers – namely in Foucault's (1979, 1980a, 1980b, 2000) power/knowledge and Butler's performativity (1990, 1993, 1995, 2004). Particularly for Foucault and Butler, freedom is a paradox, in that it is at once produced and constrained by conditions outside of (but not transcendent to) the subject – conditions such as power relations and normative and governing discursive grids of intelligibility. For Foucault and Butler, the subject is produced as an *effect* of freedom and agency.

Grosz's (2010) reading and application of Bergson's free acts depart from each of these deterministic and anti-deterministic positions; she explains:

> If this subject from which acts spring is never the same, never self-identical, always and imperceptibly becoming other than what it once was and is now, then free acts, having been undertaken, are those which transform us, which we can incorporate into our becomings in the very process of changing us. (146)

I find Grosz's application of Bergson's free acts both relevant and provocative for use in material feminisms. Grosz (2010) wrote, 'Bergson might help to rethink how subjectivity and freedom are always and only enacted within and through the materiality that life and the nonliving share' (142). Bergson's freedom is not one of choice, intentionality, alternatives, options, or selections. However, Bergson departed from Foucault and Butler in that he is not concerned about to what extent subjects are free, but rather it is *acts* that are free. By *free acts*, Grosz explained that Bergson referred to those which 'not only originate in or through a subject, they express *all* of that subject' (Grosz 2010, 144). Here it seems that Bergson is gesturing towards freedom as immanent, in a Deleuzian sense – not that we inherently possess freedom or are produced by constraints but that *free acts* must somehow cohere to that which made the free act possible. Free acts emerge in the middle of things, in the in-between space in which humans and non-humans intra-act.

To further explore, experiment with, explicate 'free acts' and engagement with matter, I use some interview data from a qualitative study of first-generation women academics, a collaborative book project (Jackson and Mazzei 2012). Applying Grosz's interpretation of Bergson reveals how one woman academic – whom I refer to as Cassandra – *makes matter* in her academic life. In turn, the *matter makes her* in that the materiality with which she works transforms her academic life into something more viable. I illustrate how these acts were not determined in advance but, following Grosz (2010), 'contracts matter into what is useful for future action and to make matter function differently in the future than in the past' (153). Such a view of freedom is linked to invention, transformation, and innovation – and opens up new ways of becoming and *doing* in the world.

Eruptions

As Grosz (2010) contends, 'Free acts erupt from the subject insofar as they express the whole of that subject even when they are unexpected and unprepared for' (145). In this section, I move to an example to experiment with how free acts might work. This example is a data excerpt from an interview with Cassandra, a first-generation African-American woman academic who at the time of the research study (Jackson and Mazzei 2012) lived and taught in southern USA. Cassandra was aggressively recruited to her current institution, Regional State University (RSU), in 1992. Cassandra said that the university needed someone to

> teach and enhance diversity, and they had gotten a very large grant that allowed them to bring in minority, primarily African-American students, to get their master's degree in [my area of academic specialty] and they wanted someone to serve as their mentor and also to develop a course and some programs that would promote diversity within the profession, so that's what I came here to do.

Therefore, in 1992, Cassandra was hired into RSU as an African-American woman academic at the level of associate professor to recruit and mentor African-American students in her area of specialty – a role that she had filled for 15 years at Southern State University, a smaller, historically black university. Cassandra, then, entered RSU, a university that was predominately white in terms of faculty and students, a mid-sized comprehensive university that, as of 1992, had never promoted to full professor an African-American woman. Cassandra herself had been educated, as an undergraduate student in the late 1960s, at Southern State University, and she had returned to that same state university to teach while completing her master's and doctoral degrees. Cassandra explained that she took seriously her role as a mentor and used similar practices with minority students (e.g. open-door policies that welcomed students into her office for 'hanging out time') that she had been using for many years before at Southern State, where she had begun her academic pursuits and firmly established herself as an effective teacher. She described her mentoring practices in this way:

> I had been brought here to be a mentor to the African American students and to create courses and programs and so forth to talk about diversity, and so some of the white students felt that I was paying too much attention to the black students and so they wrote these long, very critical letters of me that accused me of reverse discrimination and that

I was showing favoritism to the black students because they would come in to my office. My office is small now, but it was even smaller then and they [the black students] would be sitting all on the floor and everything and we just hung out together. I was a mother figure. That was pretty much the same thing that I did at [Southern State University], so I knew how to work with those students and I knew that they needed a lot of personal attention. Now there was never a time when I didn't give the same amount of attention to any white student who wanted it. But it became so huge that it went all the way up through the provost's office, and I found myself spending a lot of time writing letters of rebuttal and that kind of thing.

In this data excerpt here, there is a lot of matter that matters. Cassandra harnesses the potentiality of her office as a material space to express her free act of mentoring minority students. Other materialities come into play as well: black bodies positioning themselves in her office in casual, homely, nurturing ways. The materiality of her office as well as the presence of black bodies comes through Cassandra's expressions of herself – or free acts – as a 'mother figure'. In this example, we can perhaps come to realise Grosz's (2010) interpretation of Bergson's assertion that free acts come from somewhere, 'come from or even through us – the origination of the act does not matter … what matters is how it is retroactively integrated into the subject's history and continuity' (Grosz 2010, 146). Grosz explained that Bergson's freedom is not one of choice, intentionality, alternatives, options, or selections; Cassandra's autonomy was not something that was given to her. Her freedom was the connection to her actions 'as an embodied being who is acting in a world of other beings and objects' (Grosz 2010, 147).

The capacity to act and the effectiveness of action, then, depends on the ability to use matter – not necessarily with intent, but with *purpose*. Cassandra's free acts can be characterised as purposeful, in that they are expressions of her certain 'doing' that are important to how she sees herself and that which sustains her life. Her mentoring practices of black students were taken from her past experience, but are both materially and discursively expressed in her office at a predominately white institution. I return to this point more fully in the next section, but at this juncture it may be useful to distinguish between what makes Cassandra's freedom *purposeful*, rather than *intentional*. The difference between intent and purpose is an important distinction, and for Grosz's reading of Bergson, purpose lies in consciousness. Grosz (2010) clarified that Bergson framed consciousness not as self-presence, or tied to reason, or linked to the capacity for reflection; rather, consciousness is life and is activated via materiality. That is, *consciousness is expressed through how we intra-act with the material world*. Grosz (2010) interpreted it this way: 'People act not through deliberation or conscious decision but through indetermination, through the capacity they bring to the material world and objects to make them useful for life in ways that cannot be specified in advance' (150). *Useful* is the operative word here, as it implies the intra-action between things (human and non-human) – not what the things mean, but what they are doing, what they make, what they unmake. Purpose and consciousness are not located in the mind but become processes of viability and livability, the pulling together of material and discursive practices that make freedom.

The link between consciousness, purpose, materiality, and freedom can be further illustrated in the data example. Black bodies use the materiality of the office – and other black bodies – for expressions of free acts. As Jackson and Mazzei (2012) wrote in our book,

This office, as a force producing a materialization of bodies, creates an intimate (cramped) space that welcomes (deters) students and that invites a closeness (repulsion) of bodies 'sitting on the floor' and hanging out together. This material of the office produces a social environment of refuge and intimacy for the black students who are in the minority at Regional State University. It creates a belonging space where for a brief moment, they are on the inside looking out, rather than vice versa. These black students, 'sitting on the floor' are able to refuse constraining norms about power and prestige and in turn produce Cassandra differently as a mentor. (126)

If we follow Grosz's interpretation of Bergson in that free acts are always characterised by indeterminacy rather than intentionality, then we must also accept that matter is also indeterminate – that the material does not always exist as stable through time and space and place. The material tends towards determination, but when it is taken up and used in free acts, the material has the capacity to yield. Grosz (2010) wrote, 'Immersed in matter and erupting from it, life is the continuous negotiation with matter that creates the conditions for its own expansion and the opening up of matter to its own virtualities' (151). Therefore, if Cassandra's office is an instrument of freedom, then how does it also give way to a future that it cannot contain?

When white students complain that Cassandra is acting out of the so-called reverse discrimination, free acts are indeed indeterminate, in that the office becomes a projection of consciousness and purpose, depending on the bodies that desire that materiality, bodies that are also laden with politics, culture, and history. Cassandra's office as a material force is never neutral or stable but experiences its own becoming as both Cassandra and white and black students enact freedom. The office furniture in its becoming is arranged in a material way as intimate and welcoming for black bodies, while the intra-action of white bodies with the office shifts its use to a source of deterrence and even repulsion. The office expands to propel white students to write letters of complaint and Cassandra to write letters of rebuttal. The work of the office was not the same for white students as it was for black students. In this instance, *the agency of the office – constituted by both material and discursive forces – pushed back against Cassandra's practices*, and she then accommodated by writing 'letter after letter of rebuttal,' free acts that shifted her ways of being through encounters with both the non-human, material-discursive agency of her office and with the human, material-discursive agency of her Others.

The sorts of objects used to write these back-and-forth letters (be it handwritten, typewriters, or computers) is unknown, but in any case, letter-writing is another free act endowed with materiality. I have no data regarding the students' free acts, but in this next section, I consider Cassandra's writing as a free act.

During Cassandra's first few years at RSU, students wrote letters of complaint about not only her mentoring practices, but also her academic competence. In the interview, Cassandra explained that a group of white students accused her of incompetence. The students wrote long letters to her Dean, and again, she had to write a rebuttal and the case was dismissed. She recounted many events during which students challenged her knowledge base during class by asking her 'simple,' 'obvious,' and 'factual' questions. These instances of students challenging Cassandra (with her in turn having to justify her teaching) became more elaborated by students when they involved colleagues. She explained that some students had 'actually gone to my colleagues and told them what I said [in class] and asked them what they thought about it.'

Cassandra took matters into her own hands and continued to express her acts of freedom by writing letters of rebuttal and standing her ground by not leaving RSU, despite the material, cultural, and racial relations and forces with which she intra-acted.

Both the indeterminacy of her free acts as well as the indeterminacy of material objects used in academia were apparent in her story:

> One of the good things that came out of my coming here to [Regional State University] is that I was very content at [Southern State University] with just being a teacher, playing the teacher/mentor role, but there wasn't really much of an emphasis on research. I was told that that would not be the case when I came here, but I found out after I got here that there was, in fact, an unwritten expectation that you would do certain kinds of things. I wrote a textbook, which I would never do if I had stayed [at Southern State University], which has been very well received. The book is ten years old and, but I still keep getting these checks and so that has opened up all kinds of doors for me in terms of name recognition and in terms of offers to do conferences and things and I've become, in some circles, the go-to person for an answer to that kind of thing. So when people ask certain kinds of questions they either email me or they will call me to do conferences … It has just really made me feel good about carving out my little niche and doing well in that professional endeavor. So even if someone challenges me, I'm not at all affected the way that I would've been prior to having done these kinds of things … I'm not afraid to say, 'I don't know the answer to that.' And then I will either say, 'I will try to find out for you' or 'Perhaps you could go to this' particular source.' … I've come to the point that I can say, 'I don't know' and not feel bad about not knowing because I always felt, for many, many years, for most of my life, actually, that I just couldn't say that.

Cassandra could not have known in advance that her mentoring practices with minority students would be criticised; i.e. she had no control over the effects of her intentions. Cassandra confronting accusations about what her office *is doing, or failing to do, or is criticised for doing* is an act of freedom infused with purpose that erupts immanently and expresses the entanglement of *all* of the forces at work – material, discursive, social, historical, and so on. Thus, Cassandra's office is also transformed in what it *does*: it becomes a material-discursive place-of-practice that holds black bodies together in both real and symbolic ways, *and* it becomes a material-discursive place-of-practice that incites Cassandra to advocate for herself. For example, the desk chair that she inhabits as she 'mothers' black students with confidence is, physically, the same desk chair that she inhabited as she composed letters in her own defense and wrote a book. Yet the chair has no inherent meaning. There is no 'chairness' to the chair. Instead, it is *becoming-chair* as it intra-acts with material-discursive elements in the expansive yet immanent realm of free acts. It 'supports' her – or functions – in a myriad of unpredictable ways.

Finally, the academic book that she wrote became not simply a semiotic and material mark of success in the academy, but the writing that produced it was a free act that erupted from and through Cassandra to open her to new possibilities. There is no simple origin of her book-writing, no clear intention outside herself, no conscious decision from a selection of options outside Cassandra. Rebuttal-letter writing and book writing sprung from discursive-material forces. Book-writing as a free act occurred in various intra-actions with chairs/computers/desks, the same physical matter that functioned to contain her as a black woman academic immanent to free acts of teacher and mentoring, yet were also the same material elements that took on different functions and forces in the discursive and material practice of book writing. Writing-as-free-act produced a book that also expressed Cassandra's becoming, her transformation into someone else. Cassandra grew up as a black girl who picked cotton in the US Deep South during the time of political, cultural, legal, and social segregation.

Her freedom was located in acts of writing – rebuttal letters and then years later a book – that is linked to the ability to make and unmake. Cassandra made a book, and a book made Cassandra; freedom is located in that very intra-action. Cassandra's free act of writing, then, expressed all of her becomings, opened her to new possibilities for living, making her into whom she could have never imagined. As Barad (2007) wrote, 'Possibilities do not sit still' (234).

Last remarks

Grosz (2010) insisted that Bergson's concept of freedom links actions to a process of self-making, to that which emerges and even surprises: 'Freedom is thus not primarily a capacity of mind but of body – it is attained only through the struggle with matter, the struggle of bodies to become more than they are' (152). Cassandra, in a struggle with matter, expressed acts of freedom. She was not liberated, nor empowered, nor finally accepted and recognised for her difference, nor did she transcend her situations. The point in analysing free acts is not what they *are* – or their inherent meaning – but what they *do*: their ontological effects. What is vital to an analysis of free acts in a new material feminisms frame is how both the non-human and human are simultaneously and continually configured and reconfigured in a process of living life.

If freedom is located in acts rather than subjects, then freedom is not attached to any inherent quality of the subject but 'immanent in the relations that the living has with the material world' (Grosz 2010, 148). In this way, freedom is tied to the subject's ability to use *matter* in a way that transforms living: we make matter, and matter makes us. This concept of freedom points to a feminist material notion of 'freedom to create, to make, to produce' – it is an act of innovation, not reaction.

References

Barad, Karen. 2007. *Meeting the Universe Halfway: Quantum Physics and the Entanglement of Matter and Meaning*. Durham, NC: Duke University Press.

Butler, J. 1990. *Gender Trouble: Feminism and the Subversion of Identity*. New York: Routledge.

Butler, J. 1993. *Bodies That Matter: On the Discursive Limits of 'Sex'*. New York: Routledge.

Butler, J. 1995. "For a Careful Reading." In *Feminist Contentions: A Philosophical Exchange*, edited by Seyla Benhabib, Judith Butler, Drucilla Cornell, and Nancy Fraser, 127–144. New York: Routledge.

Butler, J. 2004. *Undoing Gender*. New York: Routledge.

Coole, Diana and Samantha Frost. 2010. "Introducing the New Materialisms." In *New Materialsims: Ontology, Agency and Politics*, edited by Diana Coole and Samantha Frost, 1–43. Durham: Duke University Press.

Deleuze, G., and F. Guattari. 1987. *A Thousand Plateaus: Capitalism and Schizophrenia*. Translated by Brian Massumi. Minneapolis: University of Minnesota Press [Originally published as Mille Plateaux. Vol. 2 of Capitalisme et Schitzophrénie. Paris: Les Editions de Minuit, 1980].

Foucault, M. 1979. *Discipline and Punish: The Birth of a Prison*. Translated by Alan Sheridan. New York: Vintage Books.

Foucault, M. 1980a. *The History of Sexuality. Volume 1: An Introduction*. Translated by Robert Hurley. New York: Vintage Books.

Foucault, M. 1980b. *Power/Knowledge: Selected Interviews and Other Writings: 1972–1977*. Translated by Leo Marshall, Colin Gordon, John Mepham, and Kate Soper. Edited by Colin Gordon. New York: Pantheon Books.

Foucault, M. 2000. *Power*. Translated by Robert Hurley et al. Edited by Paul Rabinow. Vol. 3 of *Essential Works of Foucault 1954–1984*. New York: The New Press.

Grosz, E. 2010. "Feminism, Materialism, and Freedom." In *New Materialisms: Ontology, Agency, and Politics*, edited by Diana Coole and Samantha Frost, 139–157. Durham, NC: Duke University Press.

Jackson, A. Y., and L. A. Mazzei. 2012. *Thinking with Theory in Qualitative Research: Viewing Data Across Multiple Perspectives*. London: Routledge.

Materialist mappings of knowing in being: researchers constituted in the production of knowledge

Lisa A. Mazzei

Education Studies, University of Oregon, OR, USA

In keeping with the editor's call for this special issue, this paper demonstrates how reading data *with* and *through* a new materialist lens opens up different ways of seeing and thinking. Drawing on material feminist theory, the author presents an illustration of how such practices produce a different encounter with data, research settings, and participants as she is made and unmade in intra-actions with matter, both material and discursive.

The purpose of this paper is to demonstrate how reading data *with* and *through* a feminist materialist lens opens up new ways of seeing and thinking, as well as to present an illustration of how such practices produce a different encounter with data, research settings, and participants. It is the project of material feminists or new materialists to explore how we are constituted by both the material and the discursive without privileging one over the other. Hird (2009) made an important distinction between the *emerging* fields of material feminism from what she described as the more familiar 'material feminism':

> This latter field is concerned with women's material living conditions – labor, reproduction, ... and so on. ... What distinguishes emerging analyses of material feminism – alternatively called 'new materialism,' 'neo-materialism,' and 'new sciences' – is a keen interest in *engagements* with matter. (pp. 329–330)

It is the work of Karen Barad and others named as 'new materialists' or 'material feminists' to ask how our intra-action with other bodies (both human and non-human) produce subjectivities and performative enactments enabling an approach that reinserts the material into the process of analysis.

In writing of what she terms a '(post)critical feminist methodology', Lather (2007) urged an interrogation of the enabling limits of research practices in order 'to grasp what is on the horizon in terms of new analytics and practices of inquiry' (p. 1). I take up Lather's call by demonstrating how material feminist readings can produce methodological practices that take into account the ways in which the discursive and material intra-act, to consider how discourse and matter are understood to be mutually constituted in the production of knowing. My aim is not merely to propose how methodological practices of reading data *with* and *through* a materialist lens open up new ways of seeing and thinking, but how they in fact produce a different encounter with data, research settings, and participants as we interrogate our own positioning and intra-actions as researchers.

Rethinking the material ←→ discursive

While all of the papers in this special issue address how agency, analysis, and the relationship between language and matter are fundamentally changed in a new materialist approach, this paper considers how researchers are constituted *and* constituting in the process of intra-action in ways that produce different knowledge.

This reinstallment of the material is being taken up by critical and post-structural feminists alike along with a conviction articulated by Diana Coole and Samantha Frost (2010) that 'materialism is once more on the move after several decades in abeyance' (p. 2). Coole and Frost continued by writing that 'Theorists such as Gilles Deleuze and Michel Foucault do, in fact, accommodate the material in their work' (p. 3), and yet, I find in the work of material feminists, a fruitful theorising of the relationship between discursive practices and the material world. As Rosi Braidotti wrote, I want to 'think through the body, not in a flight away from it' (p. 5). It is not enough to just think through the body, but also to articulate how my thinking and sense making put me into a different relationship with my body, my data, my participants, and my becoming.

In a recently published book with Alecia Jackson, we wrote, 'It is not that the material hasn't been present, it is that it hasn't been accorded its due in the discursive laden writings of poststructural theorists and methodologists' (Jackson and Mazzei 2012, 110). Maggie MacLure wrote also of the promise of a more 'materially engaged research practice,' an infra-empiricism as named by Patricia Clough, because as MacLure further explained, 'it attends to sensations, forces and movements beneath the skin, in matter, in cells and in the gut … ' (2010, 2). I have been thinking/feeling/sensing this beneath the skin and in the gut as I have attempted to both write and sense a different engagement with research, with data, with participants, and with analysis in writing – not of practices of reflexivity, nor of how participants are differently constituted in the context of an onto-epistemology, but how as a researcher, I become something else in the process. I constitute and am being constituted in the process of a more materially engaged research practice. I am constituted by and constituting data, my selves, my participants, and my mis-understandings. I am both made and unmade in such a process. While my project with Alecia Jackson involved thinking with different theorists and concepts,[1] we were aware of how we began to think and enact data analysis differently in this process of becoming unmade or undone. Through our engagement with material feminist theory and Barad's concept of intra-action, we began to produce thought about what was happening rather than to try to construct meaning.

In a qualitative study of first-generation women academics, we engaged in a process of reading the data *with* and *through* a materialist lens to open up new ways of producing thought. Such thinking requires a methodology that does not centre on our research subjects as the site of agency and therefore the focus of our inquiry, but rather, to consider the enactment of agency and the co-production of these enactments (Barad 2007; Tuana 2008). Such an approach relies on a process as described by Hultman and Lenz Taguchi (2010) as a 'flattening', whereby data and theory and researchers and participants are folded into a process that produces a flattened relationship with data. While qualitative researchers are beginning to account for the ways in which ontology, epistemology, and practices are fundamentally altered, what has not been adequately considered in my view is how as researchers we are constituted differently in these entanglements. While I have previously considered how the subjectivity of participants is constituted in the intra-actions with the materiality of their worlds or how it produces a different reading or analysis, what I have not addressed is how researchers are *also* entangled and becoming in the intra-actions with participants, data, and the materiality of *doing* research in ways that are both unsettling and productive.

Mapping a diffractive methodological approach

Barad (2007) wrote of what she named a 'diffractive methodological approach' in *Meeting the Universe Halfway*, one described as 'reading insights through one another' (25). In her project, she situated herself thus: 'I draw on the insights of some of our best scientific and social theories including quantum physics, science studies, the philosophy of physics, feminist theory, critical race theory, postcolonial theory, (post) Marxist theory, and poststructuralist theory' (p. 25). Such an approach provided Barad with important theoretical tools that acknowledge the roles of both the material and the discursive in knowledge production. In keeping with the practice of reading insights through one another, I draw on Barad's (2007) concept of intra-action, Grosz's (2010) concept of freedom, and Kirby's (2011) concept of the earth's grammar to enact a methodological approach in which I am both producing an analysis while at the same time being produced as a researcher.

Barad makes a distinction between diffraction and reflection, a practice viewed as sound methodology for many qualitative researchers. She takes the metaphor from the notion of diffraction as a physical phenomenon, for instance, when ocean waves pass through an opening or obstruction and are spread differently than they would be other-wise. She stated that, 'whereas the metaphor of reflection reflects the themes of mirror-ing and sameness, diffraction is marked by patterns of difference' (Barad 2007, 71–72). As a consequence of this, a diffractive strategy takes into account that knowing is never done in isolation but is always effected by different forces coming together, or in Barad's words; 'knowing is a matter of part of the world making itself intelligible to another part of the world' (p. 185). This means that in a diffractive process of data analysis, a reading of data *with* theoretical concepts (and/or multiple theoretical con-cepts) produces an emergent and unpredictable series of readings as data and theory make themselves intelligible to one another. Such knowing on the part of the researcher and her world requires a rethinking of agency as distributed between and among the human and non-human.

From a post-humanist perspective, agency is distributed in a way that avoids hanging on to the vestiges of a knowing humanist subject that lingers in some post-structuralist analysis. For example, Haraway (cited in Barad 2007) wrote, 'Reflexivity has been recommended as a critical practice, but my suspicion is that reflexivity, like reflection, only displaces the same elsewhere, setting up worries about . . . the search for the authentic and really real' (p. 71). According to Barad, 'Haraway focuses our attention on this figurative distinction to highlight important difficulties with the notion of reflection as a pervasive trope for knowing' (pp. 71–72), one that would con-tinue to produce the researcher as an 'intentional and conscious "I/eye"' (Lenz Taguchi 2013, 711). In a shift to post-humanist agency, intentionality is not attributable to humans but, for example, is, 'understood as attributable to a complex network of human and nonhuman agents, including historically specific sets of material conditions that exceed the traditional notion of the individual' (p. 23). Agency then, is an enactment of an entanglement of researcher–data–participants–theory–analysis, as opposed to an innate attribute of an individual human being. In other words, our agency to change the world and be changed by the world emerges within the intra-actions (pp. 139–141) of multiple people and things and does not pre-exist those encounters. In the post-human, 'material and human agencies are mutually and emergently productive [or constitutive] of one another' (Pickering 1999, 373).

Materialising myself into this paper

A few years ago I wrote a paper in which I talked about having been seduced by theory. I worked the metaphor to great effect linguistically but did not fully acknowledge (or want to acknowledge) the material product of my choice of metaphor and the bodily surrender of seduction. As I worked the metaphor, I began to consider how I was embracing my theoretical lovers intellectually by thinking *with* particular concepts in an intentional and deliberate tussle. I have written about thinking *with* Derrida, thinking data *with* Deleuze, Thinking *with* Theory,[2] and now am recognising that it is not 'thinking with' that is the apt description, for such description continues to emphasise the discursive end of the binary.

I often start the process of a new project by what I term 'writing myself into the paper' as prompted by Laurel Richardson and Elizabeth St. Pierre's (2005) positing of *Writing as a Method of Inquiry*. As I tried to write myself unsuccessfully into this particular paper, I realised that I was merely reproducing previous thought. What I needed was a movement of the body, or more specifically my body and that of my participants into the work – or as Braidotti wrote, thinking my body as 'an interface, a threshold, a field of intersecting material and symbolic forces' (2002, 25). Actually, it is not a movement of the body into the work, it is an attempt to account for the body that is *always already* in the work. It is a shift from a focus on epistemology to one of ontology, or onto-epistemology as named by Barad (2007).

Braidotti (2002) wrote that 'For Irigaray, as for Deleuze, the subject is not a substance, but rather a process of negotiation between material and semiotic conditions that affect one's embodied, situated self' (p. 94). My thinking and writing my body into this work is not an exercise in semantics, but it is what Braidotti described as 'distinct interventions aimed at throwing the reader out of the text and back into his or her embodied location. The aim is to trigger processes of transformation, or of becoming' (p. 96). What I will explore then is not only how I might throw the reader out of the text and back into his or her embodied location, but how I as researcher am thrown out and back into an embodied location that is a threshold of intersecting material and symbolic forces that I inhabit with my data, and with my research participants, in a process of knowing in being. Such a throwing out and throwing back produces a thinking of researchers constituted and constituting in a material $<->$ discursive intra-action with data. And while what I will present as data is a text in the form of a transcript, what I focus on for purposes of analysis is the way in which Sera and I are constituted in our continuous negotiation with matter that posits texts as ontoepistemological entanglements (Kirby 2011), 'by means of the activities that life performs on matter' (Grosz 2010, 153).

Viscous porosity and mutual productions of agency

In the intersection of the material and symbolic forces of thinking/doing/writing research texts, there is a loss of clear boundaries. Nancy Tuana named this blurring as a 'viscous porosity' to describe the interaction of phenomena between humans and the environment and social practices and natural phenomena.

> There is a viscous porosity of flesh – my flesh and the flesh of the world. This porosity is a hinge through which we are of and in the world. I refer to it as viscous, for there are membranes that effect the interactions. These membranes are of various types – skin and flesh, prejudgments and symbolic imaginaries, habits and embodiments. They serve as the mediators of interaction. (Tuana 2008, 199–200)

Such a loss of boundaries and certainty is fraught with much risk but also with the potential of producing new knowledge and new becoming selves. I go now to a data excerpt from a research project with first-generation women faculty and administrators, one of whom was Sera, in order to learn about their educational, sociocultural, and professional experiences. I go to this conversation with Sera to first illustrate how a blurring of the boundary between the material and discursive is mutually shared and produced. In this excerpt, this porosity is exhibited in the intra-action between Sera and the suit – a viscous porosity that acts as a hinge if you will between Sera and the suit. The following response by Sera was in reference to a question about things that she remembers from her undergraduate education that prompted her to consider the possibility of graduate education:

> I was in one of these classes where you have undergraduates and graduates take the classes together. So I had a sense of this one person who everybody just thought was this total nerd. You know, every time she had to teach, people were like whatever. But I thought she was like the coolest thing. She was really funny if you listened to her. And she was really nerdy, but in a great way. And so she and I were always pleasant to each other.

> And then she said, oh, hey, I'm doing the Regional Communication Association. I'm the vice president and I need somebody to man this registration table. Would you do that? And I said well, sure . . . . And I bought a suit, and I manned this registration table. And I remember putting on the suit feeling like I am so powerful. I couldn't get over how different I felt in the suit about answering questions and talking with people at the registration table. She didn't say wear a suit, but I figured I should. And so I bought one. And then I experienced that.

The above is a performative dimension of Sera's subjectivity and a process of taking up certain subject positions in response to discursive constraints. These constructions ask of her to dress, speak, and act according to professional norms that dictate what is acceptable and unacceptable in a business environment. And certainly, normative constraints offer a range of subject positions – 'suit-wearing' being one of many. Yet what is of interest from a post-humanist or new materialist perspective is to consider how the suit and Sera intra-act in a mutual production of agency. Suits are constructed to render an image on the part of wearer as conferring status, conformity, and confidence. In Sera's wearing of the suit, she not only wears a suit because it is what she 'figured she should do' but also the suit produces this in/with her. An agential realist elaboration of performativity allows matter its due (in this case, the suit) 'as an active participant in . . . ongoing intra-activity' (Barad 2007, 136). In this case, it also helps to provide an understanding of *how* discursive practices matter in our notions of what the suit should produce.

In the above data excerpt, the suit seems to have a life of its own and certainly intra-acts with Sera's body to produce a subject who is confident. It is not just that Sera appears to know what she is doing and that she belongs as viewed/experienced by conference participants, it is that she intra-acts with the suit in a way that exudes confidence and those who are helped by Sera at the registration table intra-act with the suit as well. While the suit conveys a particular image, the wearer of the suit (in this case, Sera) is produced in a mutual becoming with the suit. The suit molds Sera's body, producing a different carriage and a sense on the part of her and the others that she is in her place, she belongs, and is no longer an imposter. Similarly, I can talk about Sera's intra-action and positioning in relation to the registration table. She is positioned behind the table as this is how the table is intended to function and to position her. This placement of Sera behind a registration table is also an element of this intra-action that distances her from the participants in a way that places her in a position of authority. The table produces a response, not just in Sera, but in how those who approach Sera do so differently, again, because of this placement. The forces then of Sera, the suit, and the table act in a material $<$ - $>$ discursive production of one another.

And while I could go on and talk more about the viscous nature of the relationship between Sera and the Suit or Sera and the table, I wish to reorient and consider the viscous nature of the relationship between me and Sera, or me and the Suit, or Sera and the suit, or any of the intra-actions in which we might venture ourselves with the data. In this particular example, it is my and Sera's relationship with the sometimes restrictive nature of the suit or the power producing potential of the suit. While I am focusing on the suit as an agential force, it could also be an office space, a conference room, or other institutional markers, etc. that restrict us and with which we intra-act. To read diffractively (rather than reflectively) is to try to reposition ourselves as researchers otherwise than merely always already subject and our participants and their material conditions as always already object. Reading diffractively means that we try to fold these texts into one another in a move that 'flattens out' (Hultman and Lenz Taguchi 2010) our relationship to the material. In so doing, we install ourselves in the event that emerges in our reading and we ask ourselves how we are affected in our encounter with it (Lenz Taguchi 2012).

Reading Sera's description of what we name as her intra-action with the suit in a process of becoming is not just about what she says, what she experiences, and how we describe the phenomena of her relationship to/with/in the material. It is also very much about our own material $<$ - $>$ discursive reconfiguring that is occurring as we reinsert ourselves into the event. In other words, how we are becoming as researchers as we read and engage with Sera's account diffractively. How we seek what is produced in our own intra-action with Sera and with the intra-action of our own material engagements towards an understanding of the relationship between the material and discursive dimensions of power relations.

Returning to the data, it is not just about what Sera says, but how I imagine myself as intra-actively produced in tandem with Sera and how I reimagine her. How am I produced – or rather, how are Sera and I produced together in this analysis? When first reading the data, I encounter Sera's narrative in part as a product of a discursive construction left over from the 1980s that indicated how one must dress to be successful. I return to the constraints that such discursive constructions produced in my own resistance to and intra-action with clothing that 'said' something about who we were as women. Suits with big shoulder pads, wide lapels, and 'ties' that said, the more you can look like a man while still presenting a feminine image, the greater chance you will have for advancement. I could feel the affect, what it produced in us as women trying to assert ourselves and to be taken seriously and our compliance to norms and resistance in ways that brought the material back into my reading and knowledge making – both intellectually and physically. The suit intra-acted with my discursive constructions to produce a different subjectivity, both then and now. I therefore, at some level, can continue to read this intra-action as a result of a discursive construction that prescribes a specific list of do's and don'ts in order for women (and men) to be taken seriously in the work place.[3]

Or, in becoming-with-Sera in this event,[4] I can reinsert myself in ways not already coded with discursive readings and materialist intra-actions. I can try to take part in the phenomena that produces this as such an important example of difference. For Sera who grew up 'sitting next to the juke box in bars' while her parents were drinking, and without material things (necessities) that I take for granted, this event is not about success, but about *becoming*. I am brought back to my own need to conform and fit in, and the suit becomes a symbol through which I insert myself into the text, not in a reflexive or autoethnographic sense, but in keeping with Braidotti's 'thinking through the body'.

While I can continue to focus on the ways in which the suit produces conformity, I can also use the materiality of the suit (both Sera's suit and my memories of the over-coded ways in which suits restrict a thinking through the body) to a different analysis. Such an analysis does not remained trapped in a 'traditional focus on women's attainment of a freedom from patriarchal … constraint' (Grosz 2010, 141). Rather, it is invigorated by Grosz's feminist materialist rethinking of autonomy, agency, and freedom in ontological terms.

Making and being made

In the essay, 'Feminism, Materialism, and Freedom', Grosz (2010) wishes to emancipate the question of freedom from the 'concept of "freedom from," where freedom is conceived negatively, … [to] a "freedom to," a positive understanding of freedom as the capacity for action' (p. 140). Such a positive conception of freedom, posits 'freedom as the ability to act and in acting to make oneself even as one is made by external forces' (p. 142). Freedom for Grosz lies in the capacity for action in life, an action by agents, both human and non-human.

In a return to the agency of the suit and its ability to produce both conformity and restriction, I also wish to consider how the suit and also mine and Sera's becoming in the production of a telling 'liberates life from the constraints of the present' (Grosz 2010, 153). To reiterate, while this account relies on a textual artefact in the form of a transcript, the act of telling according to Grosz, produces a material reality.

> Life is the protraction of the past into the present, the suffusing of matter with memory, which is the capacity to contract matter into what is useful for future action and to make matter function differently in the future than in the past. (p. 153)

Kirby (2011) further elaborates the 'textual' nature of the world in a reading of Derrida's assertion against himself that there is 'no outside of text' (p. 36). In so doing, she divorces language from discourse and disavows a separation of Nature from Culture in positing an ontology of language that I equate to one of Being. If there is 'no outside of text' then the suit is a text that contributes to a narration of Sera that was already present, but not yet actualised – i.e. Grosz's 'freedom to'.

When Sera described her decision to buy a suit, or perhaps we might say her description of how she was being interpellated – or hailed – by the grammar of the suit and that which a suit affords, she is made or written by the suit – as powerful, knowledgeable, and credible. She is also, in Grosz's words, 'acting to make oneself [in a conferring of status afforded by the suit] even as one is made by external forces' (2010, 142). She does so as she is made/encountered differently by those who not only address 'her', but also address the 'suit' as well, and are addressed by the suit in return. Sera undertook the act of suit-wearing and having thus taken this act or made this cut is transformed by way of this process. The suit makes Sera and Sera makes the suit, not in a predictable way, nor with outcomes that can be known in advance, but in ways that are 'immanent in the relations that the living [in this case Sera] has with the material world [in this case the suit], including other forms of life' (p. 148). In other words, the multiple intra-actions with the suit produce a freedom that is not a 'quality or property of the human subject' (147) as in a humanist tradition, but can only be characterised as 'a process, an action, a movement' (p. 147).

Similarly, my analysis of the shared agency between Sera and the suit produces in me a relation with the material world as I recall my own intra-actions with garments that both made and unmade me. Just as Sera is becoming in the act of telling, I too am becoming in the act of suffusing her matter and memory with my own in the act of analysis. I can be bound by my own restrictive intra-actions with suits, or, I can be made and unmade by what Grosz, drawing on Bergson, makes known as the *possible*. 'It is only after a work of art, a concept, formula, or act exists, is real, and has had some actuality that we can say that it must have been possible, that it was one of the available options' (p. 146). If, as Grosz wrote, freedom is the capacity to make matter function differently in the future than in the past, then my own freedom, my own becoming is tied to 'that which is bestowed on us by others', in this case, that which is bestowed on me as I intra-act with Sera's matter, her memory, my matter, my memory, and our mutual becoming. 'As a result, the world itself comes to vibrate with its possibilities for being otherwise' (p. 153).

Such possibilities for being and knowing otherwise are possible in a return to Kirby. In her discussion, she reopens for consideration that the text or langue of the Earth authors us, thereby challenging the idea of humanity as the origin of re-presentation (41). Language then is not merely a question of epistemology, but of ontology. The langue of Sera, the suit, discursive constructions, textual practices, and becoming selves are mutually implicated in a production of possibilities both thought and unthought, actualised and unactualised. What matters is not the origin, but an opening of a different type of 'knowing produced in a co-constitutive relation between matter and discourse where it is impossible to pull apart the knower from the known' (Lenz Taguchi 2013, 715).

Being written by material texts

As I have tried to illustrate in this paper, my concern is not simply with a different type of knowing, but of a different type of being as I am constituted in this process of knowing and intra-action with the material force of research texts that I produce and which produce me. I hail Sera and ask her to give an account of herself (Butler 2005). At the same time, I am hailed by her, by the data, by the suits that we have worn and discarded, and by the other matterings that world us. In the telling that Sera provides and the tellings that I produce as I go back to the data again and again, these tellings are also 'doing something to me, acting on me, in ways that I may well not understand as I go' (p. 51).

As a researcher, I produce and am produced by texts in the form of data, theory, and analysis that act with a material force. I am not the sole author of such material texts, nor are they the sole authors of me. We (me, Sera, clothing, relationships, theories, memories, and our wording of our worlds) are transformed in an act of mutual becoming. We act on each other in ways not always discernible or predictable, thereby producing possibilities for becoming otherwise as we rethink practices of knowing and being known.

Notes

1. This work comes from my and Alecia Jackson's recent book, *Thinking with Theory in Qualitative Research: Viewing Data Across Multiple Perspectives* (Jackson and Mazzei 2012). Our purpose in the book is to challenge qualitative researchers to use theory to think with their data (or use data to think with theory) in order to accomplish a reading of data that is both within and against humanistic practices of analysis and interpretation.
2. See Mazzei (2004, 2010) and Jackson and Mazzei (2012) for illustrative examples.
3. I refer here to John T. Malloy's, *Dress for Success*, first published in 1975 and updated to also include a *New Women's Dress for Success*, described by some in the 1980s as required reading for those in the business professions.
4. For a lovely discussion of this, see, Lenz Taguchi (2012).

References

Barad, Karen. 2007. *Meeting the Universe Halfway: Quantum Physics and the Entanglement of Matter and Meaning*. Durham: Duke University Press.

Braidotti, Rosi. 2002. *Metamorphoses: Towards a Materialist Theory of Becoming*. Malden, MA: Polity Press.

Butler, Judith. 2005. *Giving an Account of Oneself*. New York: Fordham University Press.

Coole, Diana, and Samantha Frost. 2010. "Introducing the New Materialisms." In *New Materialsims: Ontology, Agency and Politics*, edited by Diana Coole and Samantha Frost, 1–43. Durham: Duke University Press.

Grosz, Elizabeth. 2010. "Feminism, Materialism, and Freedom." In *New Materialsims: Ontology, Agency and Politics*, edited by Diana Coole and Samantha Frost, 139–157. Durham: Duke University Press.

Hird, Myra J. 2009. "Feminist Engagements with Matter." *Feminist Studies* 35 (2): 329–346.

Hultman, Karin, and Hillevi, Lenz Taguchi. 2010. "Challenging Anthropocentric Analysis of Visual Data: A Relational Materialist Methodological Approach to Educational Research." *International Journal of Qualitative Studies in Education* 23 (5): 525–542.

Jackson, Alecia Y., and Lisa A. Mazzei. 2012. *Thinking with Theory in Qualitative Research: Viewing Data Across Multiple Perspectives*. London: Routledge.

Kirby, Vicky. 2011. *Quantum Anthropologies: Life at Large*. Durham, NC: Duke University Press.

Lather, Patti. 2007. *Getting Lost: Feminist Efforts Toward a Double(d) Science*. Albany, NY: SUNY Press.

Lenz Taguchi, Hillevi. 2012. "A Diffractive and Deleuzian Approach to Analyzing Interview Data." *Feminist Theory* 13 (3): 265–281.

Lenz Taguchi, Hillevi. 2013. "Images of Thinking in Feminist Materialisms: Ontological Divergences and the Production of Researcher Subjectivities." *International Journal of Qualitative Studies in Education* 26 (6): 706–716.

MacLure, Maggie. 2010. "Qualitative Inquiry: Where are the Ruins?" Keynote speech presented at the New Zealand Association for Research in Education Conference, Auckland, New Zealand, December 6–9, 2010.

Mazzei, Lisa A. 2004. "Silent Listenings: Deconstructive Practices in Discourse-Based Research." *Educational Researcher* 33 (2): 26–34.

Mazzei, Lisa A. 2010. "Thinking Data *with* Deleuze." *International Journal of Qualitative Studies in Education* 23 (5): 511–523.

Pickering, Andrew. 1999. "The Mangle of Practice: Agency and Emergence in the Sociology of Science." In *The Science Studies Reader*, edited by M. Biagioli, 372–393. New York: Routledge.

Richardson, Laurel, and Elizabeth A. St. Pierre. 2005. "Writing: A Method of Inquiry." In *Handbook of Qualitative Research*. 3rd ed., edited by N. K. Denzin and Y. S. Lincoln, 959–978. Thousand Oaks, CA: Sage.

Tuana, Nancy. 2008. "Viscous Porosity: Witnessing Katrina." In *Material Feminisms*, edited by Stacy Alaimo and Susan Hekman, 188–213. Bloomington: Indiana University Press.

Re-turning feminist methodologies: from a social to an ecological epistemology

Christina Hughes[a] and Celia Lury[b]

[a]Department of Sociology, University of Warwick, Coventry, UK; [b]Centre for Interdisciplinary Methodologies, University of Warwick, Coventry, UK

This paper proposes an ecological methodology in order to re-think the concept of situatedness in ways that can take into account that we live in relation to, and are of, a more-and-other-than-human world. In doing so, the paper proposes that situatedness should be understood in terms of processes of co-invention that, fractally and recursively, open onto other co-inventions that include the non-human. The paper illustrates this through the concept of patterning. It advances a number of terms – cutting, knotting, contrasting, figuring – as potential practices that can be drawn on to provide analyses of dynamic and multiple relations that cross the boundaries between human and non-human forces.

Introduction

How does accepting that we live in, and are of, a more-and-other-than-human world[1] reconfigure the concept of being 'situated' as a core element of feminist epistemology? This paper re-turns to the significance of situated knowledge in respect of debates that are now challenging the lexicon of concepts within which it has been conventionally understood. In setting out the expanded habitats within which situated knowledge must be considered, this paper advances an ecological epistemology that argues for the methodological necessity of articulating dynamic intra-actions between human and non-human forces.

In doing so, the suggestion is that situated knowledge is to be found in the moments of difference between gathering/grasping together and dispersal/letting go that emerge in processes of *patterning*. We use the term patterning here because it draws attention to the importance of processes of repetition and differentiation that are at issue in the cre-ation of situated knowledge, and to the dynamic and multiple relations between figure and ground that are at the heart of what we describe as an ecological epistemology. As part of such an ecology, the paper advances a set of terms – cutting, knotting, contrast-ing, figuring – that are designed to illustrate potential practices for developing situated knowledge.

The past 30 years have seen feminist methodology emerge as a recognised field across disciplines in the social sciences and humanities. This has involved the develop-ment of a number of core concepts such as 'standpoint' 'situated knowledge', 'feminist empiricism', 'strong objectivity', 'intersectionality' and 'reflexivity' (see, inter alia, Crenshaw 1989; Haraway 1988; Harding 1993; Harstock 1983; Hill-Collins 1986; Hughes 2013; Smith 1997; Stanley and Wise 1993). More recently, other terms have come to prominence such as 'cut', 'intra-action' and 'diffraction' (see, for example, Barad 2007) to the extent that there appears to be a significant shift in methodological thinking. The epistemological and ontological underpinnings of these more recent terms draw on a critical rejection of the unity and linearity of Euclidean models of social life in favour of complex, quantum and ecological thinking. These terms rework the opposition between the social and the natural in feminist debate and push us towards analysing the material world as an actant or as vibrant (Bennett 2010). They presume that phenomena are always in relations of entanglement and that boundaries, while sometimes open and sometimes closed, are always productive. In doing so, they challenge any essentialism of identity while yet providing terms to explore how persons and things may become.

Indeed, in many ways we might consider that feminist methodology is undergoing a turn or paradigmatic shift similar to the significant redirection of methodological development consequent upon theorisations of standpoint epistemologies (Hekman 1997). However, we suggest that this is not so much a turn as a *re*turn in the sense that Whatmore (2006) describes. Rather than the currently ubiquitous narratives of 'turns' with their endless twists, ruptures and sudden encounters, such *re*turns are products of repetition, of coming back to persistent troublings; they are turnings over. In such re-turnings, there is no singular or unified progressive history or approach to discover. Rather, there is the intensity of multi-dimensional trajectories, as concepts are de- and re-contextualised. Within this intensity the long-standing feminist concerns with positionality, relationality and interdisciplinarity remain, with what can be known and who can be a knower, and with the centrality of ethical, transformative practices within relations of power, as well as a sometimes forgotten but nonetheless sustained acknowledgement that we live in, and are of, a more-and-other-than-human world. Such a re-turning allows us to re-think one of the most significant concepts in feminist epistemology, that of situated knowledge or situatedness in a way that takes account of how '"the human" is no less a subject of ongoing co-fabrication than any other socio-material assemblage' (Whatmore 2006, 603).

Such a return keys into other recent concerns for methodological innovation or inventiveness (Lury and Wakeford 2012). Yet while inventiveness certainly calls on creativity, imagination and ingenuity, it too does not necessarily always have to be new. Rather, it provides a way for the origins of very familiar methodologies to be reconfigured within what is a less-customary concern with the performativity of methodologies. Theories and methods are not inconsequential to the what-happens-next but are 'simultaneously a technology of practice and an intervention in the world' (Whatmore 2006, 601). What focuses interest here is that methodologies need not only be concerned with how the social world can be investigated, but how they may also be designed for capture and for care, that is, how they may be attentive to how the social world may be engaged.

This paper thus returns to, and re-turns, situated knowledge in respect of debates that are challenging the repertoire within which situatedness has been conventionally understood. These challenges include a re-ordering of the hierarchy of socio-material relationships in ways which dislodge the human from its apex; a refocusing of agency within practices, including methodological practices, rather than discourses; a returning to the politics of knowledge rather than that of identity; and a retooling of understandings of relationality and change. In detailing this return, we propose the value(s) of an ecological epistemology to acknowledge these challenges; by this we mean an epistemology that can acknowledge the methodological necessity of articulating the dynamic inter-relationships between living things and their multiple milieus (Grosz 2008).

We want to stress that an ecological epistemology does not presume neutrality of point of view, nor does it presume the givenness of the nature–culture distinction: it is political and carries with it the imperative for moral and principled judgement; indeed, it does so in specific ways. On the one hand 'not all "ecological" situations are equal, especially when they include members of the human species among their protagonists' (Stengers 2010, 32). But equally importantly from the viewpoint of epistemology, an ecological articulation can be recognised as a practice that 'corresponds to the wager that the difference between the living and the non-living can become an object of practices instead of definitions' (Stengers 2000, 88). This emphasis on practice is one we will return to later in the paper, but for now we want to suggest that such an approach represents a renewal of vital praxis where the altered grounds of debate create challenges because of their potential for an ongoing multiplication of frames of reference for understanding the difference within and between living and non-living forces. In doing so, they allow us to reconfigure the notion of situatedness in terms of an ecological approach that is inter- maybe even trans-disciplinary and co-evolutionary, in which knowing and being are mutually implicated (Barad 2007). To illustrate how this might be so, let us give an example of the agency of worms in making relations of situatedness.

Border agencies: dreaming with worms

According to Bennett, Darwin spent many hours watching worms (Bennett 2010). He noted how worms bring matter to the surface, as their digestive processes enable refined layers of leaf mould to be deposited on the surface around their burrows as castings. Indeed Bennett suggests that Darwin believed that in these mundane activities worms make history – or we would say, make grounds, because they provide the ecological conditions that 'make possible "seedlings of all kinds", which makes possible an earth hospitable to humans, which makes possible the cultural artifacts, rituals, plans, and endeavours of human history' (Bennett 2010, 95–96). Bennett finds another example of this ground-breaking practice in a study of worms examined by Bruno Latour. What garners Latour's attention, and that of the scientists with whom he is working, is the presence of trees of a type that are typical of the savanna in a rainforest. In asking what caused this apparent incursion across the border between the rainforest and the savanna, Bennett notes that it was eventually concluded that, for some unknown reason, sufficient quantities of worms had gathered at the border of the rainforest and had produced enough aluminum to change the silica of the savanna soil to make it more hospitable to rainforest trees. The soil beneath these trees 'in' the rainforest was of the type found in the savanna rather than the rainforest. This problematic phenomenon was, in fact, an extension of the rainforest rather than an incursion of the savanna. In short, for Bennett worms provide an opportunity to think about the work or methodologies of borders and bordering, including the border of human others as well as that of rainforest savanna, and what situatedness might look like in these dynamic, more-and-other-than-human scenarios.

For Bennett and for us, they force us to acknowledge that situatedness should not solely, and should never simply, take account of a range of differences, identities or intersectionalities between human actors whose agency, whilst recognised as unevenly distributed, is often homogenised. Rather, situatedness has to be understood in terms of co-fabrication where different kinds of materialities intra-act (Barad 2007). And this intra-action must be understood in relation to the drawing of lines or borders, the politics of taking sides (inside or outside, this side or that), and the dynamics of partial, asymmetric connections across and between lines, figure and ground. This is the work of bordering that we suggest is what is at issue in an ecological epistemology. The radical potential of such a view comes from the 'implosion of boundaries between subject and object, or between the material and the semiotic, that puts borders in a constructive and transformative tension' (Timeto 2011, 161). Such potential is made visible for us in an exploration of the significance of borders in the use of fractals, figures and patterns in understanding situatedness in an ecological epistemology.

Re-turning to situatedness

In feminist studies of the gendered politics of knowledge in the fields of education, literature, science and the arts, the concept of 'the knower' was put forward to acknowledge that social location is integral to how we know, to who is affirmed and respected as knowing well (and by implication who is not) and, in consequence, to the kind of knowledge that is produced (Hughes 2013). Feminists observed how science was historically largely a sphere of male employment and masculine ways of knowing and pointed out that science produces knowledge that has largely excluded, neglected and disadvantaged women. In doing so, feminists problematised the concept of objectivity by showing that the parade of detachment and disinterestedness at its heart was a form of masculinity that reinforced the male subject as a warrantable and advantaged knower. Objectivity, as it is normatively understood and practiced within science, was re-described as the 'God Trick' (Haraway 1988), the occupation and exercise of a position of masculine privilege and omniscient knowing. In the analysis of such a position, feminist Marxist standpoint came to the fore and re-interpreted Marxist theory in gender terms.

As feminist history testifies, standpoint itself was soon attacked as excluding the range of issues of difference that must account for class, race, sexuality, age, ability and so forth. One response was an additive response, 'adding' in the dimensions of class, race and so on. More latterly, the notion of intersectionality has been elaborated to address more complex kinds of multiplicity than could be addressed by 'counting to three', since as Haraway observes (1990) there are significant limits to 'adding' on race or class. However, while the project of intersectionality (Crenshaw 1989, 1991) aims to disrupt simple additive or cumulative approaches to identity (i.e. race + gender + sexuality + class = complex identity), and to problematise social processes of categorisation through strategic deployments of marginalised subjects' experiences, intersectional projects often replicate precisely the approaches that they critique. And as Nash (2008) notes, a clearly defined methodology for intersectionality is still lacking.

So we return to Haraway's (1988) work as a founding moment in which the concept of situatedness was articulated. In this we re-enact, as Barad (2007, 71) has indicated, a diffractive approach that is concerned with 'reading insights through one another in attending to and responding to the details and specificities of relations of difference and how they matter'. For Haraway, situatedness always had to be a mobile, recursively de- and re-constructive project in which the standpoints of the subjugated offered not the only, or even necessarily the best, but a better vantage point for knowing and for living (Campbell 2004). As she says, 'We need the power of modern critical theories of how meanings and bodies get made, not in order to deny meanings and bodies but in order to build meanings and bodies that have a chance for life' (580). The deconstructive elements of Haraway's epistemology recognise that knowledge is always only ever partial (another term to which we will return): 'There is no single feminist standpoint because our maps require too many dimensions for that metaphor to ground our visions' (590). Nonetheless, Haraway herself did not *reject* standpoint, in part because it provided a bulwark against the apparent relativism that seemed to be associated with situatedness. Rather, she proposed that the 'standpoints of the subjugated ... are preferred because in principle they are least likely to allow denial of the critical and interpretive core of all knowledge' (584). Standpoint in Haraway's view is thus not about coming from a particular place, but of being situated in relations of multiplicity, or perhaps better, standpoint is the being in and of relations of situatedness. It is also about position*ing* – which is always a dynamic relation, and not a fixed place or identity that can all too easily solidify into an essence rather than persist as a process – and as such is able to provide the grounds of reflexive practice.

As Code (2006, 119) remarks, 'the mobile positioning that Haraway advocates is neither careless nor antirealist ... It is about *negotiating* empiricism'. Such negotiation recognises how values are integral to science and how it is necessary to develop an ethics of mattering (Barad 2007) and a reflexive-diffractive consciousness of the partial locations of multiplicity. The emphasis on negotiation enables feminism critically to deconstruct long-held notions that the only valid knowledges are those practiced by way of a disengaged transcendence. But equally importantly it also provides a reconstructive element:

> In contrast to the god-trick of claiming to see the whole world while remaining distanced from it, subjugated and critical knowledges work from their situatedness to produce partial perspectives on the world. They see the world from specific locations, embodied and particular, and never innocent; siting is intimately involved in sighting. (Rose 1997, 308)

One important element of our return to Haraway is thus to refocus attention on the generative significance of relations for her understanding of situatedness, to the connections as well as the divisions she draws between both the human and non-human, and to the relations between objects and their environments.

Situatedness as ecological practice

Configuration, Suchman (2012, 50) tells us, is 'at once reiterating the separate existence of the elements assembled, and drawing the boundaries of new artefacts. It alerts us to attend to the histories and encounters through which things are figured into meaningful existence.' What, then, are the separate elements, histories and encounters of debate that *we* are separating out and pulling together, and diffractively drawing into conditions of relatedness, to create the emergence of a *return*? They include scholarship in specific fields, old and new, including anthropology, sociology, education, geography, literature, queer studies, media and communication, computing and information theory. Cross-cutting interdisciplinary vectors include the neo-vitalism of Deleuzian ontology with its attention to the forces of life as multiplicities and becomings (Braidotti 2006; Coleman 2011; Fraser, Kember, and Lury 2006; Grosz 2008, 2011; Manning 2013); the discussion of partial connections, fractals and the dividual offered by Marilyn Strathern (1991); and the critiques of representationalism (Clough and Halley 2007; Whatmore 2006) that have developed from an 'awareness of representation as a dynamic and generative process where environment, rather than reality, only constrains representation instead of determining its outcomes' (Timeto 2011, 154).

But this changing landscape also includes a broader engagement within feminism with science and technology studies. Here, of particular importance has been the work of feminist scholars such as Lucy Suchman (1987/2007), who explores the inter-relationship of co-ordinated plans of action and situatedness; Anne-Marie Mol (2003) and her much acclaimed account of the multiplicity of bodies, practicing bodies and health care; Susan Leigh Star (Star and Grieseman 1987), whose work includes the study of travelling objects that acquire coherence across different epistemological communities; and Katie King (2012) who explores the implications of networked entanglements of writing technologies for who can know and what can be known. Their writing inspires us to look anew at what has 'become naturalised over time' and how things can be 'figured together differently' (Suchman 2012, 49 passim). In all of their work, knowledge is not outside or other than the objects of that knowledge, but is rather one element among others. And it is ecological thinking and practice, so we suggest, that best acknowledges this insight insofar as it 'co-implicates nature, culture and knowledge into a complex and interdependent whole' (Robbert 2011, 1). In doing so, it leads to an understanding of knowledge as 'event' and contributes to diagnosing 'the "new immanent modes of existence" our modern practices may be capable of' (Fraser 2010; Stengers 2010, 10). As Bell (2012, 113) explicates, 'the ecological perspective reminds us that any entity exists multiply in ways that may not be initially apparent, for entities' entangled and dependent existences mean that none is fully defined by its entanglement in any one particular assemblage'.

To develop our understanding of what might be involved we draw on the work of Isabelle Stengers (2000, 2010). For Stengers, ecology is 'the science of multiplicities, disparate causalities, and unintentional creations of meaning', and

> The field of ecological questions is one where the consequences of the meanings we create, the judgments we produce and to which we assign the status of 'fact', concerning what is primary and what is secondary, must be addressed immediately, whether those consequences are intentional or unforeseen. (2010, 34–35)

Importantly for an ecological epistemology, Stengers challenges bifurcations in knowledge such as those related to nature–culture, fact–value, object–subject and vitalism –mechanism but simultaneously warns against mistaking moments of relations of coming together as consensus rather than symbiosis. Her work indicates that an ecological epistemology should be concerned with the productive processes of 'reciprocal capture' which, though they carry risk, give 'primacy to heterogeneity, to a "grasping together", actualizing traits belonging both to the environment and to machinic functions which did not pre-exist as such, independently of the event of their inter-capture' (Stengers 2000, 89).

For Stengers, these processes of reciprocal capture or grasping together require us to 'dream along with' other disciplines in constructive, rather than deconstructive or destructive, practices. The aim of such interdisciplinary practice is for disciplines to 'propose other ways of dreaming, other ways of addressing themselves to what they do, and therefore other ways of addressing others. Or equally, other ways of presenting themselves, both to themselves and to others' (Stengers 2000, 86). Importantly though, an ecological epistemology must necessarily be process oriented and focus on how things change rather than how things are. It requires a non-essentialist understanding of the identity of things, in which it is relations between an entity and its environments that are constitutive of what something is and what it can be. It is perhaps not surprising, then, that Code (2006, 21) describes ecological thinking as *naturalising* 'feminist epistemology's guiding question – 'whose knowledge are we talking about?'

In what follows we pursue the question of what an ecological epistemology might offer to the understanding of situatedness further by suggesting that the practices of reciprocal capture or grasping together can include not only the Baradian notion of 'cut', but also 'contrast', the 'knot' and the 'figure', all of which, we propose, are captured in a concern with patterning, or an understanding of situatedness in relations of bordering or boundary-making. For us, attention to pattern provides an important way of locating situatedness within the moments of difference between gathering/grasping together and dispersal/letting go; it draws attention both to repetition and difference, to entanglement and to partial relations between figure and ground, entity and environment. In doing so it provides a way to move from a social to an ecological epistemology.

Patterning: cuts, knots, contrasts, fractals and figures

In what follows we ask: if we are to practice knowing in an expanded universe of becomings, if we are always in the middle – part of what we study, not above or beyond what we observe, if we are not on the way to some kind of synthesis or final conclusion, if knowledge is one practice among others, how are we to make a start or come to an end? If the concept of situatedness within ecological epistemologies is to do more than reinforce fixed locatedness, if it is also to be *practised*, how will knowledge that makes a difference emerge?

Our answer to this question is to suggest a re-turn to situatedness, not as a position or an identity, but as emergent in the diverse processes of differentiation, the patterns of movement, that constitute the moving surface or ground of figures of knowledge. Haraway has provided one response to this through her suggestion of thinking diffractively; for her, diffraction is a form of patterning through which we can generate alternative ways of thinking. It is what occurs when a wave encounters an obstacle, whether that is waves hitting a rock or through experiments with light through single- and double-split experiments. For Haraway,

> Diffraction does not produce "the same" displaced, as reflection and refraction do. Diffraction is a mapping of interference, not of replication, reflection or reproduction. A diffraction pattern does not map where differences appear, but rather maps where the effects of difference appear. (1992, 300)

Indeed, as Barad (2007, 36) notes diffraction patterns are 'not merely about differences, and certainly not differences in any absolute sense, but about the entangled nature of differences that matter'.

For us, patterns are a way of recognising such differences. Furthermore, as Araujo (2007, 16 passim) notes, pattern

> meanders through the interstices of various disciplines, refusing to be stabilised into a fixed practice or fully grasped by an established field of knowledge ... [It] cannot be easily confined into a single discipline ... always exceeds the architectural in some capacity ... is intrinsically connective, rather than contained, bridging between architecture and fashion, fashion and mathematics, mathematics and textile design, textile design and biology, biology and architecture and so on.

Stenner (2012) provides the example of the patterns that starlings made as he watched them swooping and dispersing amongst the fallen West Pier in Brighton and Hove. He notes 'The starlings fascinate me because they seem to 'pulse' between order and chaos. By playing the *difference* between gathering and dispersal, pattern can add a little order to chaos and a little chaos to order' (137, emphasis in original).

Mathematical approaches to pattern point to a dialectic between number and figuration (in the sense in which Suchman and before her Haraway imply); as Araujo (2007, 11–12) notes:

> On the one hand, it looks at pattern as a visible indication of a hidden logic. In this case, emphasis is given to the way pattern works, and to how its perceptible processes might prove useful to elucidate natural enigmas. On the other hand, mathematics employs pattern as a neutralizing backdrop that allows for the exceptional to stand out, so that by establishing it as the ordinary, one is also capable of discerning the extraordinary – that which works against it. It is interesting to notice that the visual structure of pattern, invariably constituted of a play between figure and ground, reflects the two models upon which its employment in mathematics is based. In the first instance (as a visible indication of a hidden logic), pattern operates as figure, located as the foreground. In the second instance (when it is employed as a milieu for mapping the exceptional), pattern recedes to the background.

Yet pattern provokes more than the visual senses. Patterns are textured and provide texture; they acknowledge the sensory importance and complex knottings of the semiotic materiality of knowledge practices. Manning (2013, 165 passim), for example, claims that patterns are the 'ineffable more than of experience'; they are 'modes of attunement' that 'populate expression at the edge of intelligibility' while Jeffries (2012) describes how one of the strengths of thinking with patterns is their oscillating effect. We can see this where energy creates the harmonic motion of, say, waves on a beach. Patterns of movement can also create oscillations or alternations in mood such that they can provoke 'our bodies into a visceral response rather than a purely visual grasping of form alone' (Jeffries 2012, 130).

But given such an abstract understanding of pattern how are we suggesting that such patterns inform our understanding of situatedness – how might we practice the ontological-epistemological-ethical work of patterning? One answer to this question is provided by Barad's influential concept of the 'cut'. In her use of this term, Barad, like Stengers, is concerned to overcome binary categories, and to emphasise the entanglement of matter (including language as matter) via the notion of intra-action:

> A specific intra-action (involving a specific material configuration of the 'apparatus of observation') enacts an agential cut (in contrast to the Cartesian cut – an inherent distinction – between subject and object) effecting a separation between 'subject' and 'object'.

That is, the agential cut enacts a local resolution within the phenomenon of the inherent ontological indeterminacy. (Barad 2003, 815)

Crucially, Barad (2003, 815 passim) emphasises that 'relata do not preexist relations; rather, relata-within-phenomena emerge through specific intra-actions' such that 'intra-actions enact agential separability – the local condition of exteriority-within-phenomena. The notion of agential separability is of fundamental importance, for in the absence of a classical ontological condition of exteriority between observer and observed it provides the condition for' the possibility of situated knowing as a practice that can make a difference.

For Barad (2003, 815) 'the agential cut enacts a local causal structure among "components" of a phenomenon in the marking of the "measuring agencies" ("effect") by the "measured object" ("cause")'. In making this argument, Barad does not presume that the cut delineates a part as distinct from a whole or cuts a part out from a whole but rather that the cut makes a connection: as Strathern (1991) observes, there are no parts and wholes, but only partial connections. Indeed for Barad, the act of cutting splices things together as well as apart and cuts are never once and for all but continual and continuing:

> Cuts cut 'things' together and apart. Cuts are not enacted from the outside, nor are they ever enacted once and for all. (Barad 2007, 179)

Manning (2013) puts forward an alternative, perhaps complementary, term to cut: contrast. In providing a powerful articulation of the importance of pattern, Manning observes that, for Whitehead, a pattern is a field of force, a manner rather than a matter: 'The manner of a pattern is the individual essence of the pattern. But no individual essence is realizable apart from some of its potentialities of relationship, that is, apart from its relational essence' (Whitehead 1978, 115, quoted in Manning 2013, 165).

At an analytic level, we regularly seek patterns in data as a way of recognising the becoming of matter. In doing so, we look to understand the manner of pattern in terms of orderliness, consistency and repetition. Intersectionality may provide one such example of patterning though, so we suggest, it suffers a loss of dynamism and intra-action insofar as it presumes the fixity of the relations between figure and ground. Manning's account of contrast in Whitehead is a way of avoiding precisely the fixity of this relation: contrast fields pattern, she says, 'spurring the actualization of matter through a process of subtraction'. Importantly, however, she also argues that 'The "realization" of pattern does not *replace* the pattern: contrast subtracts from the resonant field of patterning even as it holds the resonance of the pattern in quasi-appearance' (2013, 165). And of course, this is also what is captured in Strathern's (1991) use of the notion of the fractal (as a pattern): in the patterning movements of a fractal, a thing is not so much an intersection of relations as it is a figure of mutually transformative relations, each element/ relation of which it is composed being itself a relation.

And alongside cuts, contrasts and fractals we return to figures, as Haraway employs them, and to the patterning of movements, to the borders between figure and ground that do not simply separate but also connect, do not isolate a figure from the ground but put that figure into multiple relationships with a ground that is itself neither fixed nor flat. From a classical sociological perspective, Elias (1982) describes figuration as the networks of interdependencies that individuals form, and argues that lives are lived within social figurations that are dynamic as connections and relationships become more or less important and more or less active. He draws a parallel with dancing: people come together momentarily but dance within structured patterns that are relatively independent in terms of time and space of those who are dancing (Stenner 2012). Yet while Haraway also speaks of an ontological choreography she has a rather different understanding of the epistemological status of the figure.

For Haraway, to practice figuration as a knowledge practice is to 'somehow collect up and give back the sense of the possibility of fulfillment, the possibility of damnation, or the possibility of a collective inclusion in figures larger than that to which they explicitly refer' (Haraway 2000). Describing herself as 'a person cursed and blessed with a sacramental consciousness and the indelible mark of having grown up Irish-Catholic in the United States', Haraway puts forward an understanding of the figure as an image, a sign that is the thing in itself: in her work the figures of the cyborg, or the OncoMouse, are a way of acknowledging an 'implosion of sign and substance, a literalness of metaphor, the materiality of trope, the tropic quality of materiality' (Haraway 2000). For Haraway, figures are a way to articulate the patterning of movement insofar as they both connect and communicate: 'Figurations are performative images that can be inhabited. Verbal or visual figurations can be condensed maps of contestable worlds' (Haraway 1997, 17).

As part of an ecological epistemology then, cuts, knots, contrasts, fractals and figures are ways to map patterns of movement such that the multiple relations between figure and ground, object and subject become visible as matters of concern. Strathern, once again, provides a powerful way to understand what is at issue here. In her discussion of the figure—ground relationship she suggests that it should not be seen in terms of part —whole – as implied by the notion of a figure being cut out of the ground, but rather as two dimensions or as two perspectives: figure as another ground and ground as another figure: 'Since each is seen as an invariant in relation to the other, the dimensions are not constituted in any totalizing way' (1991, 113) – they are partial connections. And it is finally here, in the consideration of the partial connections, the cuts and the contrasts between figure and ground, entity and milieu, text and content, that we re-turn to situatedness, which we now propose, as a co-invention that, fractally, recursively, opens onto other co-inventions. This is an understanding of situatedness, not as a position or an identity, but as emergent in the diverse processes of differentiation, the patterns of movement, that constitute the moving surface or ground of figures of knowledge.

Facts and values

There remains of course one further set of questions. For Barad and for Stengers, as for Haraway, the question of the ethics of how to configure the patterns in such relations is of vital importance. Barad, for example, is at pains to make it clear that the cut is an ethical act in the delineation of how knowledge is bounded and performed of which we are a part:

> We are responsible for the cuts that we help enact not because we do the choosing (neither do we escape responsibility because 'we' are 'chosen' by them) but because we are an agential part of the material becoming of the universe. Cuts are agentially enacted not by willful individuals but by the larger material arrangement of which 'we' are a 'part'. The cuts that we participate in enacting matter. (Barad 2007, 178)

In this regard, as Bell points out, we must cut well; 'Given the potentially infinite number of relevant elements in an intra-acting materially enacted world, the inexhaustible plethora of "entangled genealogies" (Barad 2007), the event of a new conception, fact or correlation has to be one that, by definition, makes a demonstrable difference. The limit is precisely indifference. In other words, the advice to one who wishes to tell an entangled genealogy is not so much to represent accurately as it is to "cut well", which is to say *provocatively* or perhaps "generatively", inviting the concern of others' (Bell 2012, 117).

As we have noted, in the re-turn that we are outlining here, there is a common concern with diffraction rather than reflection. Barad, for example, notes,

> a diffractive methodology is a critical practice for making a difference in the world. It is a commitment to understanding which differences matter, how they matter and for whom. It is a critical practice of engagement, not a distance-learning practice of reflecting from afar (2007, 90)

while, as Haraway (2008, 83) notes, Stengers argues that to create new knowledges,

> Decisions must take place somehow in the presence of those who will take the consequences. To get "in the presence of" demands work, speculative invention and ontological risks. No-one knows how to do that in advance of coming together in composition.

And here too we suggest that an ecological rather than social epistemology has something to offer since it requires us to return to fact–value dichotomies in an expanded set of habitats.

As Stengers notes 'Only humans on Earth act "in the name of values" and contrast them with "facts". But, and this holds true for humans as well as non-humans, the *creation of value* cannot function in this register of opposition' (37; see also Fraser 2010). In challenging such binaries, Stengers is drawing our attention to the problematic nature of bifurcated epistemological models. Bifurcation as splits, oppositions, divergence, branches and divisions of knowledge lends itself, by way of contra-distinction, to an assumption of understanding as points of consensus, of moments of convergence. Stengers explicitly warns against mistaking such convergence as consensus or synthesis (or facts). She notes: 'Ecology doesn't provide any examples of such submission. It doesn't understand consensus but, at most, symbiosis, in which every protagonist is interested in the success of the other for its own reasons' (Stengers 2010, 35). She refers to this process as one of symbiotic agreement that is 'an event, the production of new, immanent modes of existence and not the recognition of a more powerful interest before which divergent particular interests would have to bow down. Nor is it the consequence of a harmonization that would transcend the egoism of those interests' (35). Such a description is, we suggest, not inappropriate as a way to describe the workings of, for example, inter- or multi-disciplinarity, a multiple situatedness in which disciplines enter into relations with each other, maybe even co-operating with one another, but are nonetheless neither themselves necessarily transformed nor subsumed within some consensual synthesis.

Alongside symbiotic agreement, Stengers also describes, as mentioned above, a process of 'reciprocal capture'. This can be spoken of 'whenever a dual process of identity construction is produced: regardless of the manner, and usually in ways that are completely different, identities that coinvent one another each integrate a reference to the other for their own benefit' (36). Reciprocal capture is a transversal concept that shifts attention away from rights and legitimacy (of, say, methodology, paradigm, concept) and 'emphasizes the event, an "It works!" that belongs to the register of creation' (42). And this is where there is a re-turn to practice rather than discourse. As Savransky (2012), drawing on Stengers, argues, the moment of reciprocal capture may be

tied to ethical creativity in terms of practices of care, producing 'new modes of existence and thus adding something to the world in a way that is more democratic, and
more ethical, than the modern, all too modern, social scientific knowledge practice'.
This is, cannot be other than, a move from '"affirming productivity" to "actually producing" – from ideas to practices', to a process of co-invention.

Conclusion

Our paper is concerned to re-turn the grounds of debate that seek to illuminate what
situatedness might mean when we encompass the material-semiotics of a more-and-
other-than-human world. We have indicated how, since Haraway's use of situatedness,
there has been a growing recognition of the significance of recognising that humans are
of, not solely living in relation *to*, a 'vibrant' and textured material world, a world that
can be independent of human concern, that may, indeed, have its own concerns.

In responding to this challenge we have articulated the notion of an ecological epistemology and put forward a number of practices, associated with patterning, that seek to
de-privilege the weight given to reflexive accounts of identity in the production of situated knowledge. In contrast to such accounts, we think the term ecology is helpful
insofar as it enables us to acknowledge the ongoing and dynamic interrelation of processes and objects, beings and things, figures and grounds. Indeed, we think it affords
the possibility of opening up a mode of investigation that addresses the potential – of
what might be as well as what is – in any situation or relation of situatedness. This is
because it focuses attention on the way in which mutually adaptive (but not necessarily
symmetrical) bordering relations between elements in the ecology may unfold 'hidden'
dimensions in processes of contrast and comparison. Whether and how this potential is
made visible is what is at stake in processes of figuring out, of configuration, or grasping together that are able to open up the possibility of collective inclusion beyond the
representational demands of identity.

Our aim has been to emphasise the co-connections – or articulations – between
practices and being in the production of knowledge. Following Haraway, we use articulation in a double sense, that is, as in the sense of articulated vehicles where the focus is
on joining up and connecting, as well as in the linguistic sense of enunciation and communication. Articulation is a practice that is concerned with how connections can make
an entity of two different elements. Such a linkage is contingent rather than absolute or
irrevocably determined. Articulation, then, is a political practice for grasping things
together, of overcoming dichotomies and 'irreconcilable subjects and objects associated in turn with separated social and natural worlds (Stenner 2012, 145 passim)
and, we would add, always with the possibilities of reciprocal capture. However, importantly, it is also a device for being demanding about how technologies of knowing/
being are deployed in practice and being similarly demanding of raising questions
about alternative figurations.

Such an articulated approach requires research in gender and education to more fully
'dream along with' other disciplines as a form of respectful engagement and to become
more intra-disciplinary in approach. This may well be through greater attention to
working with or drawing upon the work of other disciplines. That this is attendant with
dangers of co-option has been well noted (McNeil 2010) but engaging in this way
enables the ongoing interrogation of how the politics of boundary-making sustains divisions and hierarchies and has the potential to more fully understand which practices
matter. More singularly, it requires attention to how the human is of the world in ways

that include the materiality of bodies and things and how this extends our accountability and responsibility for developing understandings of the differences that matter (Barad 2007).

Note

1. We use this cumbersome phrase to acknowledge both the technical and natural heterogeneities of the world so as to acknowledge aspects of what is sometimes called more-than-human and sometimes non-human.

References

Araujo, A. 2007. "Introduction: A Pattern Constellation." *Haecceity* 3 (1): 9–22. Accessed February 2, 2013. http://sydney.edu.au/sup/journals/haecceity/pdfs/3/intro_3_1/pdf

Barad, K. 2003. "Posthumanist Performativity: Toward an Understanding of How Matter Comes to Matter." *SIGNS: Journal of Women in Culture and Society* 28 (30): 801–829.

Barad, K. 2007. *Meeting the Universe Half-Way: Quantum Physics and the Entanglement of Matter and Meaning*. Durham, NC: Duke University Press.

Bell, V. 2012. "Declining Performativity: Butler, Whitehead and Ecologies of Concern." *Theory, Culture and Society* 29 (2): 107–123.

Bennett, J. 2010. *Vibrant Matter: A Political Ecology of Things*. Durham, NC: Duke University Press.

Braidotti, R. 2006. *Transpositions: On Nomadic Ethics*. Cambridge: Polity.

Campbell, K. 2004. "The Promise of Feminist Reflexivities: Developing Donna Haraway's Project for Feminist Science Studies." *Hypatia* 19 (1): 162–182.

Clough, P., and J. Halley, eds. 2007. *The Affective Turn: Theorizing the Social*. Durham, NC: Duke University Press.

Code, L. 2006. *Ecological Thinking: The Politics of Epistemic Location*. Oxford: Oxford University Press.

Coleman, R. 2011. *The Becoming of Bodies: Girls, Images, Experience*. Manchester: Manchester University Press.

Crenshaw, K. 1989. *Demarginalizing the Intersection of Race and Sex: A Black Feminist Critique of Antidiscrimination Doctrine, Feminist Theory, and Antiracist Politics*, University of Chicago Legal Forum, 139. Accessed November 10, 2012. http://faculty.law.miami.edu/zfenton/documents/Crenshaw–DemarginalizingIntersection.pdf

Crenshaw, K. 1991. "Mapping the Margins: Intersectionality, Identity Politics, and Violence against Women of Color." *Stanford Law Review* 43 (6): 1241–1299.

Elias, N. 1982. *The Civilizing Process: State Formation and Civilization*. Oxford: Basil Blackwell.

Fraser, M. 2010. "Facts, Ethics and Event." In *Deleuzian Intersections: Science, Technology and Anthropology*, edited by C. B. Jensen and K. Roedie, 52–82. Oxford: Berghahn Books.

Fraser, M., S. Kember, and C. Lury, eds. 2006. *Inventive Life: Approaches to the New Vitalism*. London: Sage.

Grosz, E. 2008. *Chaos, Territory, Art: Deleuze and the Framing of Earth*. New York: Columbia University Press.

Grosz, E. 2011. *Becoming Undone: Darwinian Reflections on Life, Politics and Art*. Durham, NC: Duke University Press.

Haraway, D. 1988. "Situated Knowledges: The Science Question in Feminism and the Privilege of Partial Perspective." *Feminist Studies* 14 (3): 575–599.

Haraway, D. 1990. *Simians, Cyborgs and Women: The Reinvention of Nature*. New York: Routledge.

Haraway, D. 1992. "The Promises of Monsters: A Regenerative Politics for Inappropriate/d Others." In *Cultural Studies*, edited by L. Grossberg, C. Nelson, and P. Treichler, 295–337. New York: Routledge.

Haraway, D. 1997. Modest_Witness@Second_Millennium. FemaleMan© _Meets_OncoMouset: Feminism and Technoscience. New York: Routledge.

Haraway, D. 2000. *Birth of the Kennel. A Lecture by Donna Haraway*. August. Accessed February 1, 2013. http://www.egs.edu/faculty/donna-haraway/articles/birth-of-the-kennel/

Haraway, D. 2008. *When Species Meet*. Minneapolis: University of Minnesota Press.

Harding, S. 1993. "Rethinking Standpoint Epistemology: 'What is Strong Objectivity?'" In *Feminist Epistemologies*, edited by Linda Alcoff and Elizabeth Potter, 49–82. New York: Routledge.

Harstock, N. 1983. "The Feminist Standpoint: Developing the Ground for a Specifically Feminist Historical Materialism." In *Feminism and Methodology*, edited by S. Harding, 157–180. Bloomington: Indiana University Press.

Hekman, S. 1997. "Truth and Method: Feminist Standpoint Theory Revisited." *SIGNS: Journal of Women in Culture and Society* 22 (2): 341–365.

Hill Collins, Patricia. 1986. "Learning from the Outsider Within: The Sociological Significance of Black Feminist Thought." *Social Problems* 33 (6): S14–S32.

Hughes, C., ed. 2013. *Researching Gender*. London: Sage.

Jeffries, J. 2012. "Pattern, Patterning." In *Inventive Methods: The Happening of the Social*, edited by C. Lury and N. Wakeford, 125–135. London: Routledge.

King, K. 2012. *Networked Reenactments: Stories Transdisciplinary Stories Tell*. Durham, NC: Duke University Press.

Lury, C., and N. Wakeford, eds. 2012. *Inventive Methods: The Happening of the Social*. London: Routledge.

Manning, E. 2013. *Always More than One: Individuation's Dance*. Durham, NC: Duke University Press.

McNeil, M. 2010. "Post-Millennial Feminist Theory: Encounters with Humanism, Materialism, Critique, Nature, Biology and Darwin." *Journal for Cultural Research* 14 (4): 427–437.

Mol, A.-M. 2003. *The Body Multiple: Ontology in Medical Practice*. Durham, NC: Duke University Press.

Nash, J. 2008. "Re-Thinking Intersectionality." *Feminist Review* 89: 1–15.

Robbert, A. 2011. "Nature, Media and Knowledge: A Transdiciplinary Study of the Nature and Impact of Ecological Research in Science, Culture and Philosophy." Unpublished MA, San Francisco: California Institute of Integral Studies. Accessed January 7, 2013. file:/// Users/warwick/Desktop/Robbert,%20Adam%202011%20Nature,%20media,%20and% 20knowledge:%20A%20transdisciplinary%20study%20of%20the%20nature%20and% 20impact%20of%20ecological%20resea.webarchive

Rose, G. 1997. "Situating Knowledges: Positionality, Reflexivities and Other Tactics." *Human Geography* 21 (3): 305–320.

Savransky, M. 2012. "Capturing the Social Sciences: An Experiment in Political Epistemology." Paper presented at the London conference in critical thought. Accessed January 13, 2013. http://criticallegalthinking.com/2012/08/01/capturing-the-social-sciences-an-experiment-in-political-epistemology/

Smith, D. 1997. "From the Margins: Women's Standpoint as a Method of Inquiry in the Social Sciences." *Gender, Technology and Development* 1 (1): 113–134.

Stanley, L., and S. Wise. 1993. Breaking Out Again, Feminst Ontology and Epistemology. London: Routledge.

Star, S., and J. Grieseman. 1987. "Institutional Ecology, 'Translations' and Boundary Objects: Amateurs and Professionals in Berkeley's Museum of Vertebrate Zoology, 1907–39." *Social Studies of Science* 19 (3): 387–420.

Stengers, I. 2000. "God's Heart and the Stuff of Life." Pli 9: 86–118. Accessed January 17, 2013. http://web.warwick.ac.uk/philosophy/pli_journal/pdfs/stengers_pli_9.pdf

Stengers, I. 2010. *Cosmopolitics 1*. Minneapolis: University of Minnesota Press.

Stenner, P. 2012. "Pattern." In *Inventive Methods: The Happening of the Social*, edited by C. Lury and N. Wakeford, 136–146. London: Routledge.

Strathern, M. 1991. *Partial Connections*. London: Rowan and Littlefield.

Suchman, L. 1987/2007. *Plans and Situated Actions: The Problem of Human-Machine Communication*. Cambridge: Cambridge University Press.

Suchman, L. 2012. "Configuration." In *Inventive Methods: The Happening of the Social*, edited by C. Lury and N. Wakeford, 48–60. London: Routledge.

Timeto, F. 2011. "Diffracting the Rays of Technoscience: A Situated Critique of Representation." *Poiesis Prax* 8 (2–3): 151–167.

Whitehead, A. 1978. *Process and Reality*. New York: Free Press.

Whatmore, S. 2006. "Materialist Returns: Practising Cultural Geography in and for a More-Than-Human World." *Cultural Geography* 13 (4): 600–609.

Index

Note: 'N' after a page number indicates a note.

Printed in Australia
Ingram Content Group Australia Pty Ltd
AUHW011901241024
401774AU00007B/425

9 781138 391529